The Prison Officer

The Prison Officer

Second edition

Alison Liebling, David Price and Guy Shefer

WILLAN PUBLISHING

PRISON SERVICE JOURNAL

Published by

Willan Publishing
2 Park Square
Milton Park
Abingdon
Oxon
OX14 4RN

Published simultaneously in the USA and Canada by

Willan Publishing
270 Madison Avenue
New York
NY 10016

First published 2011

ISBN   978-1-84392-269-8 paperback
       978-1-84392-270-4 hardback

British Library Cataloguing-in-Publication Data

A catalogue record for this book is available from the British Library

Project managed by Deer Park Productions, Tavistock, Devon
Typeset by GCS, Leighton Buzzard, Bedfordshire
Printed and bound by T.J. International, Padstow, Cornwall

Contents

List of figures and tables   *ix*
List of abbreviations   *xi*
Preface to the second edition   *xiii*
Foreword   *xv*

1   Introduction: prison officers at their best   1
    Introduction   1
    From the modern to the late-modern officer   3
    The rationale for the book   5
    Introducing appreciative inquiry   6
    Notes   12

2   Who is the prison officer?   14
    How many prison officers are there?   15
    Female prison officers   16
    Ethnic origin of prison officers   18
    Age of prison officers   19
    Recruitment, turnover rates and length of service of
        prison officers   20
    Employment conditions: pay and hours   22
    Staffing levels and prisoner : officer ratios   29
    Prison officer views   32
    Conclusion   39
    Notes   40

3   **Understanding prison officers and their role**   42
    A typical day for a prison officer   46
    Role model prison officers   48
    Role model officers at Whitemoor prison   51
    Wing differences and adjudications   57
    Conclusion   60
    Notes   61

4   **The complexities of the role**   63
    Prison officers: stress and assault   63
    Assaults   67
    The role of female staff in male prisons   72
    Exploring diversity: role differences in England and abroad 76
    The role of personal officers   77
    Conclusion: the role of the modern prison officer   78
    Notes   81

5   **Staff–prisoner relationships: the heart of prison work** 83
    Striving for 'right relationships'   87
    Officer and prisoner views of each other   95
    The significance of staff–prisoner relationships   99
    What did prisoners consider important in relationships
        with officers?   104
    The importance of fairness   105
    The granting and receiving of respect   108
    Boundaries, relationships and corruption   111
    Limits to relationships   114
    The overuse of power   115
    Conclusion   119
    Notes   119

6   **The centrality of discretion in the work of prison officers** 121
    Prison officers and the 'defects of total power'   126
    Gresham Sykes and the late-modern prison officer   128
    The 'un-exercise' of power   131
    The power base of prison officers   134
    Police discretion   136
    Prison officers and prison rules   137
    Prison officers and the use of discretion   140
    Prison work as peacemaking   146
    Daily penal practices and the trained application of reason 147
    Notes   180

7	**Prison officer culture and unionisation**	**153**
	Introduction	153
	Studies of police culture	155
	Culture and the effects of prison work	158
	Prison officer culture	160
	The value of prison work	165
	Prison officer unionisation	169
	The origins of the Prison Officers' Association	171
	'The Role of the Modern Prison Officer'	174
	Recent developments	176
	Conclusions	181
	Notes	183
8	**The prison officer in a modern bureaucracy**	**185**
	Introduction	185
	The structure of the Prison Service in 2010	186
	Management change in the Prison Service	189
	The move to modernisation and managerialism	190
	The Lygo Report and Next Steps	193
	Officers' thinking about management	196
	Thinking theoretically about managerialism	199
	What are the implications of managerialism for the prison officer?	199
	Notes	202
9	**Conclusions**	**204**
	Conclusion: the prison officer in the twenty-first century	206
	Notes	209
	Appendix: The Prison Staff Quality of Life Survey	210
	References	218
	Index	*230*

List of figures and tables

Figures

2.1 Officer grades and other employees of the Prison
     Service (2006)   17
2.2 Female representation in officer grades 2000–6   17
2.3 Prison officers by age   20
2.4 Prison officers by length of service   21
2.5 Length of service: male and female officers   22
2.6 Average gross annual pay: male prison officers against
     other occupations, 2005   24
2.7 Average gross annual pay: female prison officers
     against other occupations, 2005   25
2.8 Average weekly hours (without overtime): male prison
     officers against other occupations, 2005   26
2.9 Average weekly hours (without overtime): female
     prison officers against other occupations, 2005   27
2.10 Average gross weekly earnings: male prison officers,
     1990–2005   28
2.11 Number of prisoners to each prison officer, June 2006 31
2.12 Number of prisoners to each officer, eight prisons,
     June 2006   31
2.13 Percentage of female prison officers, Prison
     Service establishments, June 2006   32
2.14 Percentage of female prison officers, eight prisons,
     June 2006   33

2.15   Mean scores for peer and senior management dimensions
       of the SQL staff survey in two prisons (discipline
       staff only)   36
2.16   Mean scores for prison-orientation dimensions of the
       SQL staff survey in two prisons (discipline staff only)   37
3.1   Prison officer job description   43
3.2   Adjudications arising from paragraphs of Rule 47
       broken (percentage) (HMP Whitemoor July 1997 –
       February 1998)   59
4.1   Assaults on staff per hundred of the prisoner
       population, 1996   68
5.1   The significant role of prison officers   101
5.2   The dynamics of the officer–prisoner relationship   113
6.1   The 'right place' for prison officers   140
8.1   NOMS Vision and Values, 2008   195

Tables

2.1   Employees of the Prison Service, June 2006   16
2.2   Ethnic background of unified prison staff and
       prisoners, 2006   18
2.3   Pay comparisons of prison officers in the private and
       public sectors, 2005   23
3.1   Role model characteristics of prison officers   49
3.2   Factors common to 'role model' prison officers   52
3.3   Gilbert's 'work style descriptors'   54
3.4   Proven adjudications at Whitemoor by location of
       incident (July 1997 to February 1998)   58
4.1   Symptoms of stress   65
4.2   Assaults on prison officers, 2008   69
4.3   Prison assaults summary statistics (England and Wales)   70
5.1   The best officers   105

List of abbreviations

ACA   Audit and Corporate Assurance (formerly Standards Audit Unit)

ACA	Audit and Corporate Assurance (formerly Standards Audit Unit)
ACA	American Correctional Association
ACCT	Assessment, Care in Custody, and Treatment
ACPS	Advisory Council on the Penal System
AI	Appreciative Inquiry
ASHE	Annual Survey of Hours and Earnings
BME	Black and Minority Ethnic
CRC	Control Review Committee
CSH	Contracted Supplementary Hours
DCMF	Design, Construction, Management and Financing
DOM	Director of Offender Management
DSPD	Dangerous and Severely Personality Disordered
DST	Dedicated Search Team
HMCIP	Her Majesty's Chief Inspector of Prisons
HMP	Her Majesty's Prison
IEP	Incentives and Earned Privileges
IRC	Immigration Removal Centre
IT	Information Technology
JIRPA	Joint Industrial Relations Procedural Agreement
KPI	Key Performance Indicator
KPT	Key Performance Target
LBB	Locks, Bolts and Bars
MDT	Mandatory Drug Testing
MQPL	Measuring the Quality of Prison Life
NAB	NOMS Agency Board

NEMC	NOMS Executive Management Committee
NOMS	National Offender Management Service
OSG	Operational Support Grade
OSR	Operational Staffing Requirement
PO	Principal Officer/Prison Officer
POA	Prison Officers' Association
PRB	Pay Review Body
PSA	Public Service Agreement
PSO	Prison Service Order
PSU	Prison Service Union
SCWS	Staff Care and Welfare Service
SIR	Security Information Report
SMT	Senior Management Team
SO	Senior Officer
SOS	Significant Others Scale
SOTP	Sex Offender Treatment Programme
SQL	Staff Quality of Prison Life
SSU	Special Security Unit
TOIL	Time Off In Lieu
TUC	Trades Union Congress
USP	United States Prison
VERSE	Voluntary Early Retirement and Severance Programme
VP	Vulnerable Prisoner
VPU	Vulnerable Prisoner Unit
YOI	Young Offender Institution

Preface to the second edition

We were delighted that a second edition of *The Prison Officer* was requested by the Prison Service, as the first edition had been popular enough to sell out. Returning to the text and to conversations with officers and others about their role made it clear that considerable changes had occurred since we completed the first edition in 2000. New research has emerged and private sector competition has become more significant in forcing changes to (or, in new speak, 'modernising') the working practices of prison officers. Substantial revisions to this edition were made during 2007 and 2008. Revisits to Whitemoor and interviews with individual officers were carried out during the course of and following this process. A repeat of the 'original Whitemoor study' was requested (we shall consider the results from that study in a separate publication, to follow). Considerably more has been learned about the work of prison officers since the first edition was published in several research projects conducted by members of the Cambridge Institute of Criminology's Prisons Research Centre and others. We incorporate some of the key findings of that research in this edition and have updated the references and further reading accordingly. It took longer than it should have done to make these changes. The pressures of an active research life and continuing changes and uncertainties about the prison officer added to our many other reasons to procrastinate.

We wish to thank those officers, governors, other senior managers and academic colleagues who have assisted us for their enthusiasm, encouragement and help throughout the preparation of this edition. Particular thanks are due to Brendan Christie, Steve Rodford, Colin

Moses, Phil Wheatley, Mike Phair, Peter Siddons, Matt Tilt, John Podmore, Hazel Roberts, Haf Davies and Ken Everett. Thanks are also due to Ann Phillips, for administrative assistance, and to a group of prison officers at Acacia prison in Western Australia who, during the course of another project entirely, showed so much interest in our discussions about their role that they provided the stimulation needed to finally get on with the new edition. It is important to us that our work on prison life leads us to such energetic and responsive participants.

As we finally go to print, we are aware that life for prison officers is about to change again. This book has inadvertently become a baseline for what must be a completely new study, for some future occasion.

Alison Liebling
David Price
Guy Shefer

Cambridge 2010

Foreword

By the former Director General of the Prison Service

This is a genuinely thought-provoking book which provides a detailed examination and analysis of the Prison Officer's crucial role in a successful Prison Service. It draws on all the available research evidence but particularly on the recent work done by researchers from the Cambridge Institute of Criminology. They have used extensive access to prisons to understand how our prisons work and what 'good' Prison Officer work looks like. As I read the book, I could not resist applying the analysis and the new insights it provides to my many years working in prisons and found it helped me make better sense of my experience. I expect that many others will have the same reaction. It is undoubtedly right that good Prison Officer work is highly skilled, involves complex judgements at speed and under pressure and requires excellent inter-personal skills. As a result, order is strengthened, peace restored and feelings of fairness and decency reinforced. Good relationships between staff and prisoners also help to motivate prisoners to succeed, give up crime and tackle those issues that are holding them back. In short, the right sort of relationships between Prison Officers and prisoners lie at the heart of all things that successful prisons should be aiming to do.

The evidence the book provides will be of real interest to anyone who wants to understand how prisons work and how they might be made to work better. Tight funding and strongly expressed politically and public concerns about prisons will continue to be realities that prison staff, their managers and prisoners will have to recognise and deal with. The book is a helpful reminder of the centrality of right relationships and good Prison Officer work in any decent, humane and effective Prison Service.

Phil Wheatley
Former Director General, HM Prison Service
November 2010

Chapter 1

Introduction: prison officers at their best

What makes a good officer? ... I don't know. It must be a pretty hard balance because I mean you've got to try and develop your interpersonal relationships with others so that you can control an environment without resorting to violence every minute of the day. And you've got to be aware of security requirements as well. I think ... you need somebody who's very comfortable with themselves so that they feel secure enough ... I'm sure a lot of it comes with experience and time in the job and ... you know, learning from past errors and so forth, but I think you need people with brains ... I don't think it's just a matter of being able to turn up here ... I think there's a lot more to it. (Prisoner, in Liebling *et al.* 1997)

It is in fact remarkable how little serious attention has been paid to prison officers in the quite extensive literature on prison life. It is almost as though they were, like the postman in GK Chesterton's celebrated detective story, so commonplace and routine a feature of the scene as to be invisible. Yet their role is of critical importance. (Hawkins 1976: 85)

Introduction

This book arose out of several pieces of commissioned research and some lively discussions with senior managers, prison staff and prisoners about 'the role of the prison officer' over a number of years. Some of our recent research has looked, in particular, at prison officers 'at their best' and we intend to draw on that material here. We were invited to produce a single, accessible volume in which some helpful thinking about the modern prison officer could be made available to those working in prisons, others looking for an introductory survey of the literature, and students. It is, we hope, an informative, readable and appropriately sympathetic analysis of the often neglected or stereotyped prison officer and a helpful guide to further reflection and reading.[1]

Prison officers are in no sense 'mere turnkeys' in the modern prison, despite the centrality of security to their daily work. It is still the case that working in security departments carries kudos, that dedicated search teams can develop unhealthy cultures, and that some segregation units are dangerous places. But prison work has become varied, testing and specialised. So much of the work of prison staff is taken for granted or regarded as common sense, and yet we would argue, as others have, that the special abilities of prison officers are much more than this. Prison officer work is, even within the prison, 'low visibility' work. The only people who see all their daily practices and who know their working personalities well are prisoners. The arguably primary *peacekeeping* role played by staff and achieved through talk has been largely overlooked both in the literature and in training (contrast Bittner 1967; Sykes and Brent 1983; McKenzie and Gallagher 1989; Chan 1997 for a discussion of this aspect of policing). Prison officers may *underuse* their power more often (and to better effect) than they overuse it. These issues of the use of power and discretion, the art of peacekeeping and the centrality of talk to their work – albeit critical to our understanding of prison life and of the role of prison staff – have rarely been addressed.[2]

Few clear ideas exist about what sort of role the prison officer occupies, about whether this role is changing, what the best of prison officer work looks like, what training should deliver and what key skills, characteristics or, in modern terminology, competencies this training should build on and develop. Is it possible to offer a 'clear and viable vision of what being a prison officer means' (Hay and Sparks 1991)? We attempt this in Chapters 3 and 4. Our book is essentially about exploring the role of the prison officer in an 'appreciative' way, and in a way which draws on observed features of their work.[3] We draw on available theoretical ideas from the prisons and the policing literature where this is helpful. We show that prison officers have undervalued skills, and that the interactive and decision-making aspects of their work are highly significant aspects of the officer's role.

From the modern to the late-modern officer

Few detailed narratives exist of prison work. Some studies have explored what prison officers think but very few have considered, sociologically, what prison officers do. There has been one detailed account of the role of *The English Prison Officer since 1850*, published by J. E. Thomas in 1972. Thomas argued that prison officers were structurally embedded in a major conflict of role, and that this conflict or confusion – between security and rehabilitation – formed the substance of much of the history of prison work. He argued that, as the penal system declared increasingly reformative goals, prison officers were excluded from their implementation:

> In spite of assertions that the officer has been, and is associated with, these goals ... his role has always been to control, and ... his success or failure as an officer is measured against his ability to do that. In fact, his opportunities to take on work which is not solely custodial have been narrowed in the past ninety years. (Thomas 1972: xiv)

Thomas felt that the paramilitary (uniformed and hierarchical or pyramid-like) and 'crisis-controlling' structure of staff organisation inevitably resulted in a top-down occupation where training was limited, discretion was minimal and tasks were clearly prescribed. In this kind of organisation, discipline and custody were primary and were naturally embodied in the chief officer.[4] Prestigious specialist work was offered to others appointed for the purpose or became the preserve of non-uniformed governor grades, increasingly regarded as the moral guardians of their charges. The 'golden age of prison reform' (1930s–1970s) left officers to one side, to be castigated as the obstructive, anti-reformist opposers of 'progress' (Thomas 1972: 152–80). There were important exceptions (for example, the 'Norwich system'; Emery 1970) but, in general, officers' attempts to become more professionally involved in welfare were unsuccessful. Officers watched discipline decline, and became caught up in an alienating position, on the one hand 'protesting about the ill-effects of reformation', on the other 'demanding that they be involved in it' (Thomas 1972: 206). This ambivalence towards 'progressive' work, the tension between this and traditional prison work (and the organisation of it), and a preference for the custodial and control tasks, characterised the prison officer:

> The English prison service from 1877 to 1965, in which most of the features of the officer's role were established, had a clear task. It was a small service, tightly knit and organised in a para-military structure. Since there was clarity of task there was clarity of role. As a result the Commissioners knew what kind of officers they were looking for ... The Gladstone Committee began that process of organisational confusion which, even at a distance of seventy years, culminated in the Mountbatten Report. These years saw the increasing alienation of the prison officer from the aims of the organisation, aims which he found confusing, and in some cases, repugnant. A very important factor in this alienation was the drawing together of the Commissioners and governor grades, and the prisoners ... The variation of the governor's role to that of a reformer, led the officers to believe that they were now second in importance to the prisoners. (Thomas 1972: 218)

Thomas described his work as 'a study of alienation' (1972: 220). We hope to consider his argument in the light of our (arguably less pessimistic) exploration of the modern prison officer's role. We consider his account further in Chapter 5, and we draw our conclusions in Chapter 9. We are not setting out to update Thomas' painstaking history but offer, here, a live account of prison work and ways of understanding the role of the prison officer in the late-modern context.[5] We have argued elsewhere that prison officers are in some ways the 'invisible ghosts' of penality (after Jefferson and Grimshaw 1984; Liebling 2000). Prison staff are often either neglected or negatively stereotyped in the existing literature (Gilbert 1997). Critics craft their accounts as though the 'ideal' function of the prison is clear and the actual role of staff falls short of this ideal (e.g. Morris and Morris 1963; Cohen and Taylor 1972; however, see also Thomas 1972; Jacobs 1977; Sparks *et al.* 1996). This is a position we try to avoid, and we might argue that some aspects of the conflict between 'custody' and 'care' may be slightly less troublesome than they have been in the past.[6]

The rationale for the book

This book arose originally out of an evaluation of the Incentives and Earned Privileges (IEP) policy, introduced in 1995 (Liebling *et al*. 1997), and more directly out of a Prison Service-commissioned literature review on prison officers completed in January 1998 (Price and Liebling 1998), and a detailed study of prison staff at work in one maximum security establishment (Liebling and Price 1999). This work has been developed in subsequent research we have carried out at Wandsworth, Belmarsh and Manchester, and in 'quality of life' surveys conducted elsewhere. The IEP research demonstrated that prison officers resorted to formal and administrative means of sanction of prisoner misbehaviour more frequently when their relationships with prisoners on a wing were distant or difficult. This resort to formal sanctions resulted in withdrawal of consent by prisoners and other modes of resistance. Good staff–prisoner relationships, on the other hand, facilitated more informal and in most respects legitimate methods of 'policing' but the maintenance of these good relationships resulted in some departures from formal procedures. It was in order to explore these (largely quantitative) findings about different ways of operating further that we carried out a detailed scrutiny of staff–prisoner relationships and prison officer behaviour in a single 'case study' maximum security prison. We were, as a result of interest shown in the previous studies, able to carry out the research in an unusually exploratory way. This nine-month study required extended periods of observation and reflection, the generation of trust between ourselves and prison staff, and a willingness on the part of staff to talk openly about their work and to carry out tasks in the usual way, once they got used to a research presence in the prison. In this project, we clarified our research questions as we progressed, forming and re-forming our methodological agenda as we began to understand this complex aspect of prison life more fully. What started out as a study of staff–prisoner relationships grew into a study of the use of discretion and the broader nature of prison officer work. We have remained intrigued (and often impressed) by the work of prison officers ever since.

Unusually, but very usefully, we were granted unlimited access to all areas of this prison (Whitemoor) over the nine month period. We used mainly qualitative (but some quantitative) methods, including an 'appreciative inquiry' approach (see below and Liebling *et al*. 1999). We used observation, 'reserved participation', a search for

5

'role model' staff and some 'shadowing' exercises of officers through their shifts, and we collected institutional data (such as adjudication details). In this introductory chapter we describe our appreciative inquiry approach and explore the concept of peacekeeping as it relates to prison officers and their work.

Introducing appreciative inquiry

Appreciative inquiry (AI) is an approach to organisations which is based on strengths rather than weaknesses, and on visions of what is possible rather than what is not possible (Elliott 1999; see also Liebling *et al.* 1999). It identifies achievements and 'best memories' and, through this technique, locates 'where the energy is' in an organisation. Its practice involves using an 'appreciative protocol' or short list of generative questions, posed as though in an extended conversation, about the best aspects of prison officer work. It was through AI that we were able to discover new and valuable ways of looking at the work of prison officers. The method is based on interviews, conducted almost as conversations, which deliberately seek best experiences, accomplishments and peak moments in organisations (see Elliott 1999). Unlike traditional social science research which tends to focus on problems and difficulties, AI tries to allow accounts of good practice to emerge and aims to understand what makes best practice possible. What are the conditions under which we each perform at our best?

Using this technique at Whitemoor (and subsequently in other prisons), we learned that 'life at its best' for prison staff was quiet, 'a day going by with no trouble', when there is a feeling of teamwork ('when we all pull together') and of support, mainly from immediate colleagues but also from senior management. Lack of tension and confrontation made 'a good day'. This did not mean a day without work, but a day without major incidents. Challenges could be enjoyable, as staff enjoyed solving problems and making decisions. Taking part, being fully involved and being expected to 'deliver' made the job agreeable ('if you do something right, you feel good when you've done it right, and I enjoy being able to do that'), but staff all began their account of the best of their work with the *absence of trouble*. This 'vision of the best kind of day' was very strongly shared by officers. When we first heard these accounts, we wondered whether staff were describing their successful days negatively – as *simply* the 'absence of trouble' – or as a mundane concern for routine administration. But we realised that this is precisely the conceptual problem we wish to identify in this book. Resolving and avoiding conflict, avoiding the use of force and under-enforcing some of the rules were not omissions but were acts requiring skill, foresight, diplomacy and humour:

> You couldn't really say what an ideal day is, because an ideal day is no trouble. So any day with no trouble is an ideal day. I mean, you'll get the inmates come up to the gate ranting and raving, but if it's dealt with without any violence then that's an ideal day, simple as that really. (Officer)

> The best day ... um, I suppose it would be the day [describes an incident] – it went very smoothly, there were no injuries, no unnecessary force or anything like that, it was very professional. (Officer)

This was often despite difficulties with routine administration – staff smoothed over bumps, tied loose ends together through informal means and solved endless problems in a normal working day. Senior managers recognised the demands of this type of work for officers and the difficulties of fully accepting the authority of their role, not retreating from it. Officers described what we have called 'peacekeeping' (they did not use this term themselves, but we recognised it from the policing literature) as a key part of the best of their work. Their positive efforts to negotiate peace – to *achieve* 'quiet' – tend to be overlooked and undervalued:

> A successful day is one where you open up in the morning with 120 inmates, and at the end of the day you've got the same 120 inmates and the routines have run well, there's been no need for confrontation and staff and inmates are quite happy. Inmates aren't happy being in prison, but if at the end of the day, they can say 'they've treated us fair, they haven't stitched us up, we've had our meals, had our exercise, had our association, done our work but there's been nothing that I've wanted to have a go about to someone' – then that's got to have been a successful day – and it hasn't sent staff stress levels peaking. And I can go home and not have to think that I need half an hour to sit down and get the jail out of my system before I can sit and talk to my wife and children. (Officer)

There is an important gap here in the literature, in research, in training and in prison officers' self-conscious grasp of what it is that makes their job highly skilled. The movement from tension to 'peace' is not described:

> I remember one in particular, one Monday on here that stands out, I'll never forget it as long as I live. It was just so frustrating, I was nearly in tears I was that angry. Things were going wrong and I was losing control of them, and it was my job to make sure that these things did not go wrong and eventually things came together but I had to work very hard to do it. (Senior officer)

The 'very hard work' involved in re-establishing order, in retaining or restoring relationships and in keeping communication flowing is absent from most accounts of prison officer work. This general lack of consideration of the nature of prison officer work was identified by Hay and Sparks in a 1991 article in the *Prison Service Journal*:

> Like a footballer who can score a wonderful goal but not really describe how he did it, prison officers sometimes exercise social skills of great refinement and complexity without dwelling upon or articulating what they are doing. (Hay and Sparks 1991: 3)

It is significant that prison staff[7] (and others)[8] take for granted, or regard as 'common sense', their negotiation or 'peacemaking' skills. Solving situations and defusing tension were definite talents or 'competencies' which were deployed often. Successful interventions in potentially conflictual situations signalled this kind of competence and professionalism:

> *Can you give me an example of a time when you felt that you really got it right between you and a prisoner(s)?* (Interviewer)

> I feel that I am quite good if a con has been gobbing [shouting] to talk him down and get rid of it. Which I have done a few times. (Officer)

This kind of activity involved judgement, experience and sensitivity to the specific context of the wing. Being a good prison officer involved being good at not using force but still getting things done; it meant being capable of using legitimate authority and being in control without resorting to the full extent of their powers. It meant establishing relationships and investing those relationships with real aspects of one's personality. This routine part of prison officers' work was highly valued among officers – but was not often seen (or perceived as seen) by those who managed and rewarded them. Their best moments in the job ('the best day you remember as a prison officer') often involved promotion, recognition and reward – some specific acknowledgement that they were 'good at the job'. But 'good days' were defined by the atmosphere of the prison: 'when things turn out right', all the bits flow smoothly ('if we're asking for movements [to other parts of the prison] we're getting it, or if we're not, we're getting a reason why not'); when communication was good. There were two types of 'good' days:

When do you most enjoy coming to work here … a day when you went home and thought, 'Woah, really good day today'? (Interviewer)

That's difficult, because you can have good days, which are good, and you can also have bad days which are good. (Officer)

Is there any difference in what's good about them? (Interviewer)

Yeah. A good good day, if you wish, could be a day where you come on in the morning and everything seems to go right from half past seven, everyone turns up for work, prisoners are happy, they all go to work, all the feeding goes properly, nothing goes wrong – everything runs smoothly, and you feel at the end of the day, great, everything's gone well. I've had no prisoners shouting at me, threatening me, all the staff have been good, they've done their jobs, all the prisoners have done their jobs, everyone's got what they want, and you feel good about it. I can go home of a night, or you go for a pint afterwards with a few lads and you think yeah, no problems. And then you can have a bad day which can also turn out good. If you have an incident, albeit a fairly major one, and the reason it turns out good is because you know what you've done and you know what your staff have done, they've done professionally and to the best of their abilities. For example, a cell fire that we had four or five weeks ago – all the staff knew what they had to do, I knew what decisions I had to make, the orders I gave to the staff they carried out without question, the orders I gave to the prisoners they carried out without question, there was no arguing, no what ifs?, buts, can I have this?, nothing, everybody did everything correctly and it all fitted together like a jigsaw should. It worked perfectly. Although it was a real horrible day, and people went home smelling of smoke and there was water everywhere and prisoners were upset and staff were totally shattered, it was a good day. Because although it didn't go 'right', because when things did go pear-shaped, everybody did things as they should have done, when they should have done, and how they should have done, and it turned out great. (Officer)

So, we learned from this exercise how enthusiastically staff respond to unconditional positive regard; we learned how quick they are to trust uncritical observers of their work; how ready they are to communicate, to explain and to be generous; how little is needed to stimulate their cooperation and interest. Staff described their ideal working environment as rather like the conditions of an appreciative inquiry: they are seen, heard, respected, rewarded; they feel safe, supported and nurtured. Some initial defensiveness gives way to an open, honest and deeply felt sense of the complexity and significance of their work. The first lesson of the appreciative inquiry exercise was that staff have a clear and positive vision of their working environment and of their own role in prison life. This vision is relatively easily tapped and articulated – despite expectations held, to some extent by ourselves and certainly by others – that staff are (as a group, if not individually) fixed in a position of cynicism and negativity.

They articulated a sense of uncertainty about the 'modern' way of being a prison officer, although they were clear about the need for balance between care and control. They understood, at a 'deep' level, the concepts of respect, boundaries and honesty, and they saw these things as crucial to the successful performance of their work. Yet exactly how 'respect' and 'boundaries' were practised by officers differed. They are committed to a view of their job which requires all problems to be resolved through relationships and open communication where at all possible. They also believe that their own position has to be moulded around their own personalities – that their personality characteristics should shape the job of being a prison officer. This can work very well, and constitutes a kind of integrity which is fundamental to successful prison officer work. Staff are aware of the tensions between consistency and personality; they are constantly picking their way through this minefield. Prisoners and staff have highly refined 'bullshit detector' skills. They know how difficult and dangerous human behaviour can be. Inevitably, individual differences result in variety among staff: this variety is seen by most as highly valuable. Staff also recognised that different approaches may be required towards individual prisoners. Complex assessments and adjustments develop over time, so staff work out what works with different individuals. Staff needed continuity for this very valuable 'relationship negotiating' dimension of their work, and they derived satisfaction from 'getting it right' with a wide range of prisoners (especially difficult ones).

The second lesson we learned from our appreciative inquiry exercise was that staff are highly motivated towards and derive considerable satisfaction from 'getting relationships right'. They are proud when they manage to 'create a pleasant atmosphere on the spur'. Relationship building behaviour establishes credit, which officers expect to draw on successfully at difficult or testing times, and often can do so.

We try to look systematically, in the next chapter, at what is known about prison staff. Who are they? What do they do? How much are they paid and what hours do they work compared to their police colleagues and other occupational groups? What does their world look like? In subsequent chapters, we try to describe their work, in particular the best of it, and we ask, what are their 'wishes for the prison'? In Chapter 3 we consider the role of the prison officer and the various conflicts inherent in the job. We look at formal job descriptions, at empirical research exploring their work and at what officers have to say about their role. We look briefly in Chapter 4 at the diversity of roles played by prison staff working in different types of establishment. We also draw on what we know of prison work in other jurisdictions. How does the role vary both within and between establishments? We look in Chapter 5 at the famously central role played by staff–prisoner relationships in the (particularly) British tradition of prison work. Why are relationships so important? What do they achieve, and how are they established, deployed, controlled? Chapter 6 explores the conditions of prison work – how much power do officers actually hold? Once we acknowledge that there are defects in the structures of 'total power' often assumed to be embodied by the prison officer, we consider what the implications are of this more complex position. Prison officers are both powerful and in some ways vulnerable, and they depend on their verbal and personal skills (or 'verbal judo'[9]) to make their role effective. We consider the use of discretion by prison staff and compare this to the much more widely recognised use of discretion in policing. Why is there so little discussion of discretion in prison work when the task of 'policing the prison' has so many similarities with the policing of any community? Chapter 7 explores the question of prison officer culture. Is there an identifiable 'culture' or set of cultures which characterise the working personality or occupational style of prison staff? If so, what shapes it and what functions does it serve? We look in this chapter at the role of the Prison Officers' Association and the part it plays in modern penal practice. In Chapter 8, we consider the rapidly changing context in which prison officers work. What are the implications for prison staff of the modern, managerialist world of which they are part, and how far does this world impact on the prison as a workplace? We draw our conclusions in Chapter 9, suggesting that the role of the prison officer is arguably the most important in the prison.

Notes

1 For the enthusiast, we have marked recommended further readings in the References section with an asterisk. We hope that not only for officers undergoing training but also for experienced staff, there might be helpful material here for discussion.

2 Some US studies have explored the use of discretion; see, for example, Gilbert (1997). A recent English study by Crawley provides useful further exploration of 'the social world of the English prison officer' (Crawley 2001, 2004). Other recent studies of prison officers include work by Helen Arnold (2005, 2008) and Sarah Tait (2008a, 2008b, 2008c).

3 The term 'appreciative' refers to a specific methodological approach (see later, and Liebling, assisted by Arnold 2004: ch. 4). It does not mean that critical judgement is suspended. See also Elliott (1999).

4 Chief officers were the head of the officer grades but were abolished when Fresh Start unified the officer and governor grades in 1987 (see further Chapter 8).

5 We use the term 'late-modern' advisedly, to distinguish the contemporary period from the period generally regarded as 'modern' (the 1850s–1970s). Late modernity has many continuities with the modernising (enlightenment) project, but is characterised by a rapidly changing social context: a new insecurity of employment; the use of information technology; the generalisation of expectations and fears brought about by mass media; the 'de-subordination' of lower-class and minority groups; the questioning of authority and traditional values; the erosion of 'localised trust' (see Giddens 1990); and the rise of managerialism. These developments have altered the frameworks in which penal practices are

conducted, as we show in Chapter 8 (see Bottoms 1995; Taylor 1999; Garland and Sparks 2000; Pratt 2000).

6 Thomas argues that the way to identify an organisation's primary task is to identify the 'manifest disaster criterion'. Escape remains the key disaster for a prison. But arguably, and partly as a result of the new terminology of the 'failing prison', other regime-related matters increasingly form part of this disaster threshold, and one recent Director General identified increasing suicide rates as a major and unacceptable attribute of a prison in trouble. Certainly during the mid to late 1990s (partly due to technological and professional advances) the risk of disturbance or riot declined in its significance to the senior managers of the English prison. As population pressures increased during the second half of the 2000s, risk of disorder re-emerged as a central concern. Another indication of 'the priority of an organisational task' is the allocation of resources.

7 In this account, when we use the term prison staff, we are referring to uniformed officers. We have not included any separate study of prisoner custody officers in private prisons for the purposes of this book. We are aware, however, that important similarities of role exist. Ongoing research comparing practices in public and private sector corrections will address this theme more directly (see, for example, McLean and Liebling 2008).

8 Line managers, critics of the prison, those who shape policy, and so on.

9 We have to thank our Slovenian friend and criminologist, Gorazd Mesko, for this term, used by prison officers in Slovenia to describe their work.

Chapter 2

Who is the prison officer?

> No one worries about the staff. (Prison officer, cited in Liebling 1992: 118)

According to Hay and Sparks (1991), there is a distinct lack of information in theoretical and policy-oriented writing about what it is that prison officers do, both in terms of the tasks they are asked to carry out and the methods they use to achieve these tasks. Although in recent years some studies of prison staff working life have been conducted (Crawley 2004; Arnold 2005; Arnold *et al.* 2007; Bennett *et al.* 2008), prisoners still get far more attention from researchers than prison officers. The academic literature does not tend to concern itself empirically with the demographic profile of the people who become prison officers, and in the media, on television or in films, prison officers are often referred to as 'guards' or 'warders', stereotypically painted in unforgiving and unsympathetic colours. Such typifications fail to capture the people behind this uniform.

It can be difficult to find material about prison officers in published form and even more difficult to find material about officers working in the private sector. Much of the more recent data on which this chapter is based was requested directly from the Prison Service and will refer to prison officers working in the public sector unless otherwise stated. Based on this data and a few other sources (particularly Prison Service Pay Review Body 2005 and 2006) we will report in the following sections of this chapter on the number of prison officers and their share in the overall Prison Service workforce, their gender distribution, ethnicity, their age and length of service, their payment, the ratios of prisoners to officer in each prison and the views they hold about their quality of working life based on recent staff surveys.

How many prison officers are there?

Over 49,000 people work for the Prison Service from governors to operational support grades, medical officers to chaplains, and psychologists to administrative civil servants. The largest group by far within this total is made up of prison officers. As Table 2.1 shows, in June 2006, there were 19,529 officers, 3,961 senior officers, 1,276 principal officers and 1,442 managers (previously known as governor grades). Interestingly, while the increase in officer grades in the last six years has been minor at 2 per cent overall, the manager workforce has increased by 37 per cent compared to its size in 2000.[1]

As Figure 2.1 shows, prison officers represent 40 per cent of the total employees of the Prison Service. Within the unified staff, prison officers represent 75 per cent of the total, principal officers and senior officers represent 20 per cent and the manager grades represent 5 per cent.

So, who are prison officers? What do we know about them?

Writing in 1987, Vivien Stern portrayed prison officers in the following way:

> ... a close-knit group of mainly family men – looking to each other for social life and support, feeling misunderstood, unappreciated and looking at life with a semi-humorous, semi-bitter, cynical pessimism – a group where breaking ranks in any way is very difficult, because the bonds are strong professionally, socially and culturally. The attitudes of women prison officers ... are remarkably similar in tone and ethos.

Stern was writing two decades ago. Does this picture reflect prison officers in the twenty-first century? The nature of imprisonment has changed greatly in the intervening years, so what changes have taken place to the profile of the late-modern prison officer? A basic summary of the facts would tell us that most are male, white and aged between 35 and 45. Around one in five are female. Fewer come from a minority ethnic background. The rest of this chapter explores these figures in more detail.

15

Table 2.1 Employees of the Prison Service, June 2006

Grade	Number	Increase compared to 2000
Unified (Total)	**26,208**	4%
Officer grades	**24,766**	2%
Prison officer	19,529	2%
Senior officer	3,961	4%
Principal officer	1,276	2%
Manager grades	**1,442**	37%
Senior manager A	38	
Senior manager B	50	
Senior manager C	59	
Senior manager D	148	
Governor 5	1	
Manager E	462	
Manager F	597	
Manager G	87	
Non-unified	**22,880**	25%
OSG (Operational Support Grade)	7,436	
Admin	7,657	
Chaplaincy	314	
Healthcare	1,077	
Psychology	973	
Others	5,423	
Total employees of the Prison Service	**49,088**	13%

Female prison officers

As Figure 2.2 shows, 22 per cent of prison officers are female (4,345 in total). The proportion of female prison officers has risen sharply in recent years (in 2000 only 17 per cent were female). The female percentage is slightly lower as the grades advance: 19 per cent of senior officers are female and only 14 per cent of principal officers are female. However, this proportion has risen even more sharply in recent years. In 2000 only 9 per cent of senior officers and 8 per cent of principal officers were female so their representation has more or less doubled in six years. This increase stems from the high proportion of new entrant prison officers who are female. Between

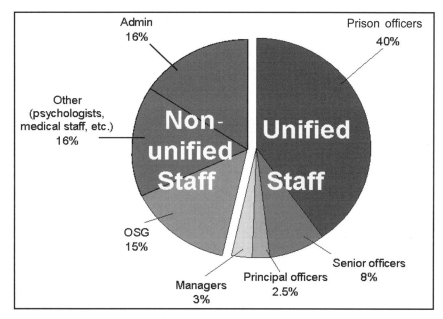

Figure 2.1 Officer grades and other employees of the Prison Service (2006)
(NB: All figures are approximate due to rounding-up)

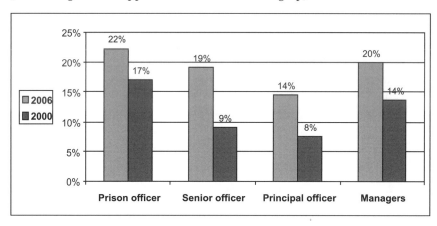

Figure 2.2 Female representation in officer grades 2000–6
(NB: All figures are approximate due to rounding-up)

1 April 2005 and 31 March 2006, for example, 31 per cent of newly recruited prison officers were female (Prison Service 2006).

With regard to female representation within manager grades there are differences between junior managers and senior mangers. Senior managers have the highest female representation: 25 per cent of senior managers are female. The number is slightly lower, however, among manager grades E and F, where only 20 per cent of prison managers are female. Manager grade G, who predominantly work in works departments, are almost exclusively male with only 1 female out of 89 managers.

Female officers and managers more often work in female prisons. This means that despite the 22 per cent total of female officers, in any individual prison the proportion is likely to be influenced by the type of prisoners held (see below).

Ethnic origin of prison officers

Table 2.2 shows the ethnic origin of unified staff, together with similar figures for the England and Wales prison population.

It is clear that ethnic minority groups are under-represented within the unified ranks in comparison with the prison population. At the beginning of the decade the Home Office set targets for the Prison Service to reach in their employment of ethnic minority staff, with non-white employment required to rise in the Prison Service to 7 per cent by 2009. In 2005–6 8.2 per cent of newly recruited officers were BME and the overall number of ethnic minority staff (not only unified) working in the Prison Service was 5.7 per cent, slightly less than the annual target for 2005–6 which was 6 per cent. As Table 2.2 shows, however, within the unified staff, who have the highest level of contact with the prisoners, the representation is lower, at only 4.5 per cent. This is higher than it was several years ago. In 2000 2.9 per cent of unified staff were BME. However, it is important to note that the number of BME prisoners has increased more significantly in that period. In 1999 18.2 per cent of prisoners were non-white while in

Table 2.2 Ethnic background of unified prison staff and prisoners, 2006

	White		Black & minority ethnic (BME)		No data	
	No.	%	No.	%	No.	%
Unified prison staff	23,881	91.1	1,201	4.5	1,126	4.2
Prison population	50,588	73	18,082	26.1	550	0.7

Source: Prison Service (2006).

2006, as Table 2.2 shows, this number increased to 26.1 (more than one in four).

The under-representation of minorities within the officer ranks stands in contrast to the situation in the United States. In the Federal Bureau of Prisons, fewer than two-thirds of staff (in this case, all employees) are white; 21 per cent are African-American and a further 11 per cent are Hispanic.[2] It is difficult to make direct comparisons because of the different respective racial make-up of both the general and the prison populations of England and Wales and the US (more than 70 per cent of prisoners in federal prisons in the US are either Hispanic, Afro-American, Native American or Asian), but it is clear that ethnic minority groups constitute a far greater presence within all kinds of prison employment in the latter. In a recent prison survey of more than 4,860 prisoners, ethnic minorities, especially Black and Asian prisoners, reported low evaluations of quality of life survey items concerning the quality of processing race complaints and the fairness of their treatment in comparison with the White majority (Cheliotis and Liebling 2006). This is an issue that has important implications.

Age of prison officers

Figure 2.3 shows the age distribution of prison officers (not including principal and senior officers) in 2006. Over 40 per cent of officers are aged between 36 and 45 and the rest are distributed symmetrically between the oldest and youngest age groups. More than half (51 per cent) are over 40.

These numbers represent a moderate ageing process. While in the year 2000 more than 55 per cent of officers were under 40, in 2006 less than 49 per cent of officers were under 40. This ageing process has been taking place since the mid-1990s. In the early 1990s the trend was in the opposite direction. Following the recruitment needs ensuing from changes made to working hours by Fresh Start (see Chapter 8) at the end of the 1980s and the voluntary early retirement and severance programme (VERSE) introduced a few years later, the age profile of prison officers lowered considerably. However, the officers recruited after Fresh Start are now maturing and are moving from the 20–30 age group into the 36–45 group. This ageing process may have benefits. There is some suggestion in the literature that older officers may have more favourable attitudes towards prisoners, are less punitive and are less custody oriented (Klofas and Toch

19

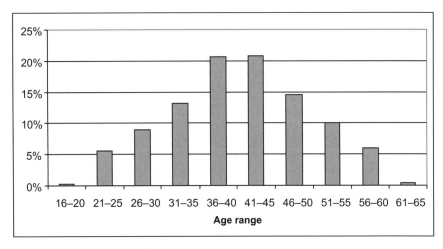

Figure 2.3 Prison officers by age

1982; Klofas 1986; Jurik 1985; see Farkas 1999 for a summary). Prison officers working in the private sector are younger than in the Prison Service. More than 60 per cent are under 40 and more than 30 per cent are under 30.[3]

Recruitment, turnover rates and length of service of prison officers

Between 1 April 2005 and 31 March 2006, 1,259 new prison officers were recruited to the Prison Service.[4] This number is equivalent to about 6 per cent of the total workforce of prison officers. However, the overall growth in the number of prison officers in 2005 was only 1 per cent and this is the outcome of a 5 per cent turnover rate among prison officers during 2005.[5] Three per cent of prison officers resigned and another 2 per cent were dismissed during this year.[6] According to the Prison Service Pay Review Body (2005) this is a relatively low turnover rate in comparison to the national labour turnover rate which, on average, is between 15 and 20 per cent. It is particularly low in comparison to the turnover rate of the officers in private prisons which is, on average, 30 per cent. This high rate consisted of a 27 per cent resignation rate (nine times higher than in the Prison Service) and 3 per cent dismissal rate.

How experienced are prison officers? Figure 2.4 shows that over 55 per cent of officers have been in the Service for ten years or less,

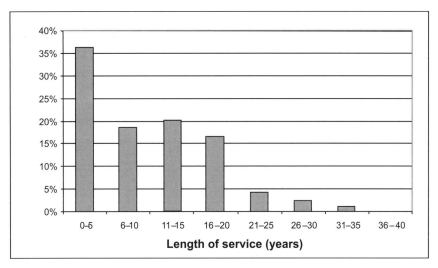

Figure 2.4 Prison officers by length of service

and 36 per cent (more than one in three) of officers have five years or less experience. A substantial proportion (25 per cent), however, have been working for the Prison Service (as officers) for more than 15 years.

These numbers do not include senior officers and principal officers. When they are included the picture is somewhat different. Only 49 per cent of all officer grades have been working in the service for ten years or less and only 30 per cent have been in the Service for five years or less.

Figure 2.5 illustrates the different lengths of service for male and female prison officers and shows the distinct time-advantage held by male prison officers. Seventy-nine per cent of female prison officers have less than ten years of experience compared to just 48 per cent of male officers.

The average length of service of officers working in the private sector is much shorter. According to the Prison Pay Review Body (2005) almost 80 per cent of officers in private prisons have been working in prison for less than five years and over 40 per cent have been working in private prisons for less than a year. Part of the explanation for this difference is the high turnover rate in private prisons, but it is also the outcome of the fact that many of the private prisons are relatively new.

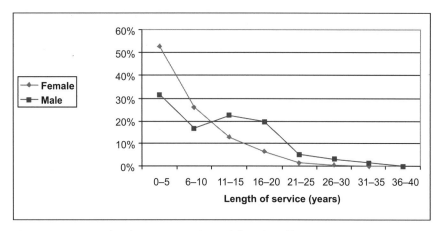

Figure 2.5 Length of service: male and female officers

Employment conditions: pay and hours

Whatever other rewards the job of a prison officer might bring, financial remuneration is important in any career. What kind of salary can a prison officer expect – and how does it compare to other similar occupations?

In the public sector the minimum gross annual basic wage (which is also the entry wage) for a prison officer (at the time of writing this chapter) is £17,319 with a maximum of £25,490 (however, see further below). There are two long-service increments for standard grade officers, taking the maximum salary to £25,918 and £26,433 respectively, and also a local pay allowance of between £2,600 and £4,000 depending on location. There are a few more per-hour allowances for specific roles or assignments such as dog handling or physical education, on-call allowance and bed-watch payments. Governors also have discretion to invite staff to volunteer to contract to work regular extended hours (which are known as CSH – contracted supplementary hours) up to a maximum of nine hours a week. The Prison Service pays for such hours at a flat rate. Senior officers earn a gross annual basic pay of £28,202 and are also entitled to the same local pay allowance.[7]

As Table 2.3 shows, the private sector salaries are significantly lower than the public sector salaries. The entry level salary is 11 per cent lower in the private sector, and the gap increases to a 41 per cent difference when comparing the average basic pay.[8] Officers in

Table 2.3 Pay comparisons of prison officers in the private and public sectors, 2005

Sector	Entry level salary	Average basic pay	Percentage difference
Public	17,319	23,629	11
Private	15,636*	16,762**	41

* Average starting basic pay in the private sector normalised to a 39-hour week. This includes officers working in private detention centres.

** Average basic pay in private sector normalised to a 39-hour week. This includes officers working in private detention centres.

Source: Prison Service Pay Review Body (2005) (http://www.ome.uk.com).

private prisons also enjoy fewer benefits (pension, holidays, sickness entitlements, etc.) compared to public sector officers and the Prison Service Pay Review Body (2005) found that when these benefits are valued the advantage of the public sector over the private sector with regard to junior prison officers increases to 65 per cent. These differences may reduce over time as more generous pay awards are made in the private sector.

The increase in the size of the gap between the entry-level salaries and the average basic pay in the private and public sectors can be attributed to the fact that prison officers in the public sector have much greater opportunities for pay progression based on the length of their service than in the private sector. In addition there are many more newly recruited, inexperienced officers in private prisons. In the Prison Service nearly 40 per cent of officers are on the highest long-service point and over half are on the normal scale maximum (normally reached after nine years) or on one of the long-service points. By contrast 55 per cent of private sector staff are at levels equivalent to OSG, officer and senior officer levels have less than two years service and only 20 per cent have more than five years.[9]

Figures 2.6 and 2.7 show a comparison of the annual gross pay of male and female prison officers with the annual gross pay of other occupations. The data in both figures is taken from the Annual Survey of Hours and Earnings (ASHE) – an annual government publication of earnings. The ASHE surveys around one per cent of employees in all occupations, using information provided by employers. The data in this section come from the 2005 report.[10] What these two figures show is that while the average annual gross pay of the male prison officers is higher than the average annual gross pay of the female

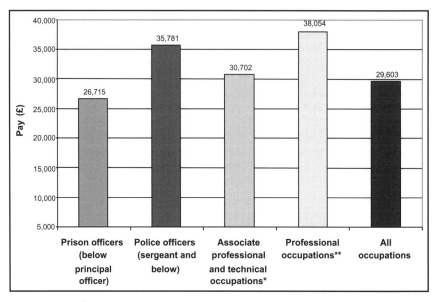

* Associate professional and technical occupations is the category which both prison officers and police officers belong to in this survey. Other occupations in this category include fire services officers, technicians in science and engineering, building inspectors, nurses and other paramedical workers, youth and community workers and other social welfare associate professionals.

** Professional occupations include scientists, engineers, IT people, higher education teachers, etc.

Figure 2.6 Average gross annual pay: male prison officers against other occupations, 2005

prison officers, female prison officers are better placed than the male in comparison with other occupations.

As can be seen from Figure 2.6, the average *gross* annual pay of male prison officers (in this case prison officers and senior officers) is £26,715. This is slightly higher than the highest *basic* pay for prison officers which, as we noted above, is £25,490. This could be explained by the fact that the survey also included senior officers and it may also indicate that the local and specific allowances and the contracted supplementary hours (CSH) have a significant impact on the gross annual average salary of prison officers.

Even with the allowances, however, the salary of male prison officers compares unfavourably with police officers (those at sergeant or lower rank), who can expect to receive gross annual pay of £35,781.

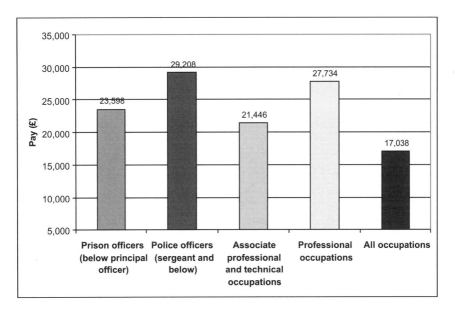

Figure 2.7 Average gross annual pay: female prison officers against other occupations, 2005

It should be noted that police officers are well above the general average annual payment of the occupations which are included in the category 'Associate professional and technical occupations'. Unlike police officers, the annual pay of male prison officers is lower than the average annual payment of this category. The salary of male prison officers is also lower than the average annual pay of all occupations and is far below the average salary for professional occupations.

Although a female prison officer is paid the same salary as a male prison officer in the same grade and length of service, a comparison of Figure 2.7 with Figure 2.6 shows that the gross annual payment of female officers (£23,598) is more than £3,000 lower than the payment of their male counterparts.

There are two possible explanations for this. First, these are figures for both officers and senior officers, and only 19 per cent of senior officers are female. Secondly, levels of pay partly reflect length of service and female prison officers have a shorter average length of service. Female prison officers, however, are much better placed than their male colleagues when compared with other occupations (but not with respect to police officers). Their salary is well above the average of all occupations; it is above the average of the category 'Associate professional and technical occupations' and it is not far behind the category 'Professional occupations'. This reflects the poorer position of females within most occupations and the fact that female prison officers are working significantly more hours each week than the average working hours of female employees in other occupations (as Figure 2.9 shows).

The ASHE provides details of weekly working hours of male and female prison officers. Figures 2.8 and 2.9 show these for male and female prison officers respectively.

It can be seen that there are no significant differences between the weekly working hours of male and female prison officers. Furthermore, Figures 2.8 and 2.9 show that both male prison officers and female prison officers are working more hours than in most other occupations.

All new prison officers recruited on or after 1 October 2009 are subject to new terms and conditions based on a 37-hour working week with the option to work up to 41 hours and five weeks' annual leave on entry, rising to six after ten years' service. There will be two tiers of prison officer, distinguishing between the variety of roles within this grade, and two corresponding pay bands, depending on

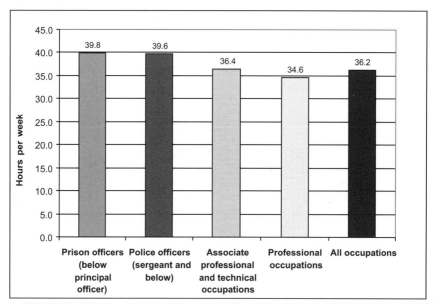

Figure 2.8 Average weekly hours (without overtime): male prison officers against other occupations, 2005

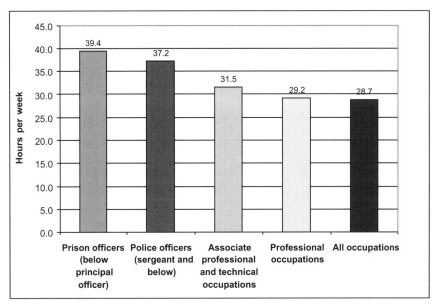

Figure 2.9 Average weekly hours (without overtime): female prison officers against other occupations, 2005

the role undertaken – a higher pay band for prison officer 1 roles and a lower pay band for prison officer 2 roles. All new prison officers start employment as prison officer 2. Prison officer 1 roles apply to a smaller number of roles 'which call for a distinct set of skills, knowledge and supplementary training': Prison Officer – PEI; Prison Officer – Instructor (Qualified); Prison Officer – Offender Supervisor; Prison Officer – Interventions; and Healthcare Officer. At the time of going to press, the revised appointment salary for new prison officer 2s was £17,187 for new appointments (composed of £14,690 base pay plus £2,497 for unsocial hours working); £18,135 for operational support grades moving on conversion to a prison officer 2 role (composed of £15,500 base pay plus £2,635 for unsocial hours working). Eligible new officers can commit to work one to four 'additional committed hours' per week as a variation to their contract.

Police officers also have the availability of extra pay through overtime. With regard to prison officers, as mentioned above, governors have discretion to invite staff to volunteer to contract to work regular extended hours up to a maximum of nine hours a week. In the year ended 30 June 2005 staff at more than half the prisons worked additional hours in this way.[11] The Prison Service pays for such hours at a flat rate. Beyond these arrangements staff do not normally earn extra pay for working overtime, instead receiving time off in lieu (commonly known as 'TOIL') when it is available. According to the Prison Service Pay Review Body (2006), for establishments where data were available at the end of June 2005, there were 10 hours per officer of TOIL outstanding. The data also indicated that, between the end of December 2004 and the end of June 2005, the amount of TOIL outstanding increased by 5 per cent. This is partly the outcome of lowering staffing levels, a development to which we will refer in the next section.

Figure 2.10 shows a comparison of average weekly earnings of male prison officers,[12] police officers and all occupations over the last 15 years.[13]

It can be seen that prison officers are placed less favourably today than in the past both in comparison to police officers and to other occupations. In 1990 male prison officers earned almost the same as male police officers and slightly more than the overall average of all occupations. In 1999 prison officers' salary became slightly lower than the average of all other occupations and the gap between police officers and prison officers increased as police officers earned 28 per cent more than prison officers. The small gap between the salary of

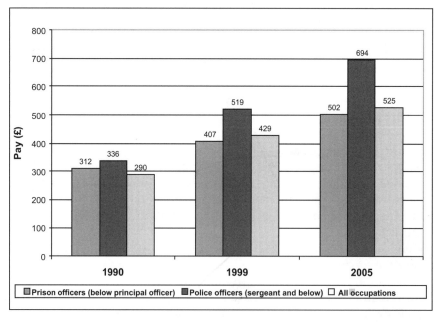

Figure 2.10 Average gross weekly earnings: male prison officers 1990–2005

prison officers and all occupations (in favour of the latter) did not change much between 1999 and 2005. However, the gap between prison officers and police officers continued to increase and in 2005 male police officers earned 38 per cent more than male prison officers.[14] A partial explanation for this change could be found in the changing age profile of prison officers (that is, younger and less experienced officers earn less) but some of the shift should be related to changing pay and conditions in a new streamlined, efficient and competitive prison environment.

It is inevitable that people rate their conditions of employment against others and the most common comparison is with regard to salary. Although arguably doing a similar type of job and working as many hours, prison officers earn significantly less than police officers. Male prison officers also earn less than other associate professionals and less than the average of all occupations even though they work more hours than most other occupations.

Staffing levels and prisoner : officer ratios

When comparing the overall number of prisoners to officers in the public sector, the ratio, as of June 2006, is around 2.8 prisoners per officer. This ratio does not tell us much about the specific ratio of prisoners to officers in each prison since prison officers are not evenly distributed around prison establishments. Prisons are of very different sizes, and they have different security levels and purposes (and physical designs), each of which affect the required staffing level. It is still interesting to note, however, that in comparison to 1990 the overall ratio of prisoners to officers in the Prison Service has significantly increased, which means that the staffing levels are lower today then they were in 1990 (i.e. there are fewer officers for each prisoner). In 1990 there were about 2.3 prisoners per officer[15] but since then, the number of prisoners in the public prisons has increased by more than 40 per cent while the number of officers has increased by 20 per cent. Prior to 1990, for almost four decades the trend was the opposite: staffing levels increased from a level of 6 prisoners per officer in the early 1950s to the above level of 2.3 prisoners per officer in 1990.[16]

All these figures represent only the public sector. The numbers of prison officers working in private prisons are not published on a regular basis. However, a written report by the Secretary of State to the House of Commons in June 2004 (House of Commons

2003–4) shows that staffing levels in the private sector are lower (i.e. there are fewer officers per prisoner in the private sector). This is particularly true for category B prisons which, according to this report, had 3.97 prisoners per officer in comparison to 2.78 prisoners per officer in the public sector (i.e. 1.2 prisoners more per officer in private prisons). The gap was much narrower in category C prisons where there were 3.63 prisoners per officer in private prisons and 3.58 prisoners per officer in public prisons. With juveniles, however, the trend has changed and private prisons have more staff than public prisons – 1.61 prisoners per officer in private prisons and 1.78 prisoners in public prisons (House of Commons 2003–4).

Returning to the public sector, the number of prison officers that should work in each prison, or the Operational Staffing Requirement (OSR), is decided by the Prison Service. According to the Prison Service Pay Review Body (2006), at 30 June 2005 there was a deficit of 735 or 2.9 per cent of officers and managers compared with the OSR at establishments across England and Wales. After taking account of additional staffing available through the use of the contracted supplementary hours (CSH) scheme, the deficit fell to 271 or 1.1 per cent of the OSR which according to the Prison Service Pay Review Body (2006) is within tolerance. The highest deficit of 3.2 per cent is in the South West area while the best staffing levels exist in Yorkshire and Humberside where staffing levels are 1.5 per cent above the OSR.

Figure 2.11 shows the prisoner : officer ratio for all public prisons in England and Wales. As shown, there is a substantial difference between the prison with the highest prisoner : officer ratio (Sudbury, a male open prison, with 8.4 prisoners per officer) to that with the lowest ratio (Whitemoor, a high security prison, with 0.9 prisoners per officer).

Figure 2.12 shows the same information for eight establishments that have been chosen to represent each main type of prison – male high security, male local, male category B, male category C, male open, young offender institution, female open and female closed. The figure shows that it is closed prisons with higher security ratings and young offenders institutions that have the higher prison officer : prisoner ratios. This means that in addition to the higher levels of physical security at the high security establishments, there are also higher numbers of prison officers relative to prisoners. Young prisoners are considered to be relatively volatile and harder to control than adults. This, and the need for high level regime prisons, explain the high staffing levels in young offenders institutions.

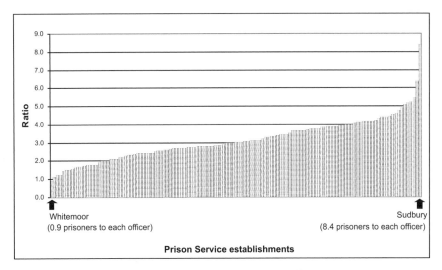

Figure 2.11 Number of prisoners to each prison officer, June 2006

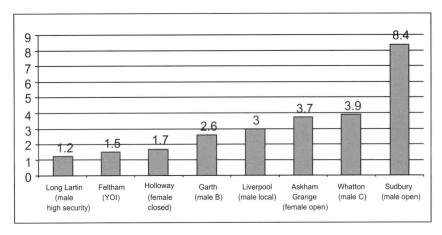

Figure 2.12 Number of prisoners to each officer, eight prisons, June 2006

The proportion of female officers also varies according to establishment type, as Figure 2.13 below shows. There are many more female officers in female establishments. It is difficult to establish why some male establishments have more female officers than others. There may be some relationship between numbers of female staff and the location or age of establishments (newer prisons may have more female officers than older prisons, which could be a function of local recruitment by establishments).

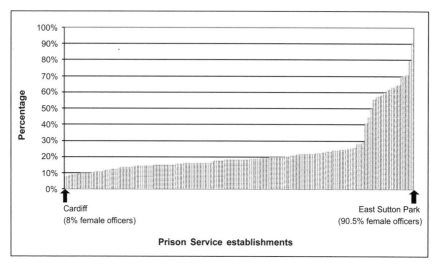

Figure 2.13 Percentage of female prison officers, Prison Service establishments, June 2006

Figure 2.14 shows the percentage of female officers in the same eight prisons used previously to indicate varying officer : prisoner ratios. There is no link between the security level of an establishment and the number of female officers *per se*, and the figure shows the significant difference between female representation in female establishments compared to male prisons.

Prison officer views

So far this chapter has concentrated on detailed statistical information about prison officers, describing them in terms of their pay and related characteristics. We turn now to more social matters. What sort of people are prison officers, and what views do they hold about working in prison?

In 1982, the Office of Population and Surveys conducted a large survey of prison staff. They concluded:

Socially, they are a remarkably homogenous group of people. The great majority are middle-aged family men. The majority also have military backgrounds though by no means all of these were recruited directly from the armed services. They have the kind of educational and occupational history usually

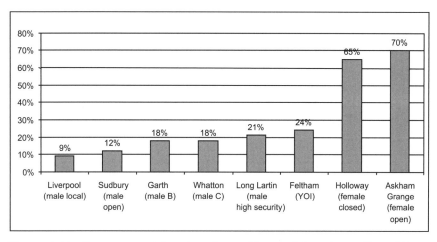

Figure 2.14 Percentage of female prison officers, eight prisons, June 2006

associated with manual workers … They have, however, few other characteristics that would place them as members of the working-class community … They work exceedingly long hours in a disciplined environment in a way that brings them together as a distinct community. This is particularly true of those serving in Dispersal and Closed Training Prisons. (Marsh *et al.* 1985: 97)

There have been major changes since the early 1980s in the demographic profile of prison officers and in the numbers of hours that prison officers work, as this chapter has shown. The hours are not as 'exceedingly long' since the ending of overtime with Fresh Start at the end of the 1980s and female representation in the ranks has grown. Within the officer group, there are fewer direct recruits from the armed services and there is now a mandatory fitness requirement for prison officers. (However, the requirement that new prison officers must hold five GCSE passes, introduced in 1998, was rescinded because there were too few candidates who met this criterion). The highly prized job security, (which 'nearly everyone thinks … is excellent': Marsh *et al.* 1985: 98), has suffered somewhat (or is at least perceived to have suffered) in the light of privatisation, market testing and early retirement initiatives. This latter point will be taken up in Chapter 8 of this book.

The next prison staff survey was conducted more than a decade later by the Prison Service (Prison Service 1994). Only one question appeared in both surveys and concerned how satisfied Prison Service staff were with their current job. In 1982, 77 per cent of prison officers stated that they were satisfied; in 1994, this figure had slipped to 60 per cent (of all prison staff surveyed).

In recent years the Prison Service has conducted an annual National Staff Survey via the Internet. The 2005 survey included 62 items which covered 10 dimensions related to different areas of staff working life. The survey was aimed at all staff in all prisons and headquarters groups. A total of 18,704 staff members participated in it, so it could be assumed that the evidence from the survey provides a good basic general picture about staff views with regard to different aspects of their working life. The survey suffers, however, from a low response rate of 31 per cent, which could be the result of unsatisfactory arrangements with regard to keeping the confidentiality of the questionnaire data. The authors of the Prison Service Pay Review Body (2006: 14) were concerned by this low response rate and called for the improvement of this aspect of the survey in the future.

According to the survey, 71 per cent of staff were satisfied with the job they were doing, and this score is consistent with earlier versions of the survey in previous years. Sixty-six per cent of staff were proud to work for the Prison Service and 69 per cent generally felt safe in their working environment. Staff were relatively satisfied with line managers. Seventy-five per cent thought their line managers were supportive if there was a problem and other items regarding line managers attracted similar scores. Staff were less happy, however, with senior management teams. Forty-four per cent of staff thought that their senior management team provided effective leadership and 50 per cent thought that the senior management team were sufficiently visible in the organisation. Staff were also less happy about the quality of communication and the level of their involvement in, and influence on, decision-making. Only 41 per cent were happy about the level of communication in their prison and only 37 per cent felt they had an opportunity to contribute their views before changes were made which affected their job. Some form of harassment, discrimination or bullying was reported by 29 per cent of staff over the last 12 months (in 2005).

A new staff survey that has recently been conducted is the SQL (Staff Quality of Prison Life) survey. This survey was developed by the Prisons Research Centre at Cambridge University at the request of the Prison Service following the use of several earlier versions in specific research projects (see Gadd *et al.* 2007; Tait *et al.* in progress). During the development stage it was administered in six prisons with an overall sample of 666 respondents. The survey was administered primarily in full staff meetings and the response rate was above 95 per cent. The survey was administered among all staff but we will report here only the results for the unified grades which include prison officers, senior officers and principal officers. The final version of this questionnaire has 129 items grouped into 17 dimensions.[17] The survey includes a qualitative section where staff members are asked to write down what the three most satisfying aspects of their jobs are, and what the three most stressful aspects are. In addition to the 129 items where staff are asked to circle whether they agree or disagree with each statement, staff are also asked to assess their quality of life and level of stress on a 1–10 scale (where 10 represents high quality of life and low stress respectively). The mean scores of these items, with regard to overall quality of life, ranged from 7.6 in the prison where staff reported the highest quality of life, to 5.4 in the prison where staff reported the lowest quality of life. As for the level of stress (again on a scale of 1–10), here the range of mean scores was narrower – 5.6 in the prison where the level of perceived stress was the lowest to 6.3 in the prison where the level of perceived stress was highest.

Although the survey was administered at this stage in very different types of prisons, there are some major trends which appear in most of them. Figures 2.15 and 2.16 present the scores of selected dimensions from two prisons that participated in the development stage of the survey – a high performing prison which had many high dimension scores and a second prison with lower dimension scores. Figures 2.15 and 2.16 show that although the scores of almost all dimensions are higher in 'prison A' than in 'prison B' the overall trends in both of them are similar (and these trends were quite similar in all six prisons). The scores are on a scale of 1 to 5 where 1 indicates a very low (negative) score, 5 a very high (positive) score and 3 is the neutral mark (in practice, however, the range of scores was between 1.7 and 4.2 so scores of above 3.5 could be considered as relatively high-positive).[18]

Figure 2.15 presents the scores of the four 'working circles' dimensions (the relationship of staff with and perception of their peers, their line managers, their senior managers and the Prison Service) in those two prisons. Each of these dimensions include items like, 'I trust the senior managers' (or 'my colleagues' or 'my line manager', etc.) or 'I am valued by the senior managers (or 'my colleagues/ my line managers', etc.). It can be seen that the closer the working circle, the higher the score. Officers were highly positive about their relationships with their peers. This dimension consistently produced

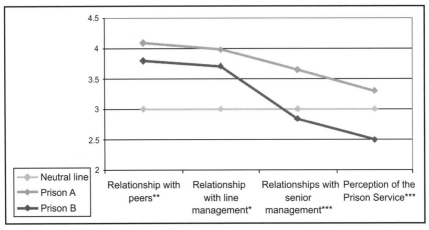

*   Significant difference p < 0.05
**   Significant difference p < 0.01
*** Significant difference p < 0.001

Figure 2.15 Mean scores for peer and senior management dimensions of the SQL staff survey in two prisons (discipline staff only)

very high scores across establishments indicating a strong sense of camaraderie and cohesiveness among prison officers. These positive perceptions extended to a large degree to the dimensions covering staff relationships with their line managers, which also produced relatively high scores in most prisons. Officers were less happy with their senior management teams, and the dimension 'Perception of the Prison Service' attracted the lowest scores of these four dimensions.

Lack of trust towards senior managers and the Prison Service has a long tradition among prison staff and is arguably inherent in staff culture. It is often transmitted together with other 'working personality' characteristics in new entrant training courses (Arnold *et al.* 2007). Indeed, in five out of six prisons where staff were asked to report what the most stressful aspects of the job were, the most frequent source of stress was 'management' or issues that directly related to management. However, as shown in Figure 2.15, the scores for the senior management dimensions varied considerably between prisons. While in some prisons (as in prison B) they were low, in others (as in prison A) they were relatively high (above 3.5). The prisons where the senior management dimensions had attracted high scores were also the prisons which had the most highly scoring dimensions. Statistical analysis showed that in four prisons the scores for this dimension

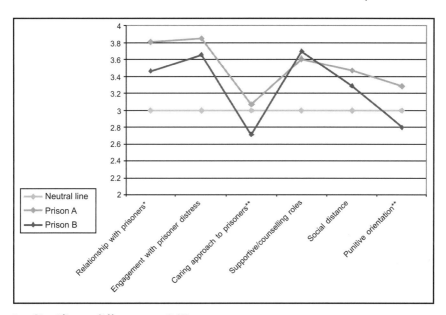

* Significant difference p<0.05
** Significant difference p<0.01
*** Significant difference p<0.001

Figure 2.16 Mean scores for prison-orientation dimensions of the SQL staff survey in two prisons (discipline staff only)

were strongly correlated to the item in which staff assessed their overall quality of life.[19] These results might imply that the senior managers have a significant impact (more than other variables) on the quality of life for staff. They can make a (positive) difference to staff working practices, rather than remaining the obvious traditional target for the frustration and dissatisfaction of staff from various aspects of their job. The survey does not provide an answer to the question of what makes a good (or poor) senior management team, but some hints might be found in the main complaints officers raised against their senior managers (and the Prison Service), particularly in the prisons where the scores on these dimensions were relatively low. There were two main arguments staff raised. One had to do with different aspects of managerialism. In four out of six prisons, one of the two most frequent sources of stress was the heavy workload. Staff also complained about the amount of paperwork, about low staffing levels and about constant changes in policies. Staff were particularly cynical about the culture of performance measurement

– only 12 per cent of officers (in three prisons where this item was included in the survey) had confidence in the system of performance measurement used in their prison. These issues are service-wide, however, and individual senior management teams have little power to offset increasing pressures on staff in the name of performance.

In addition to issues related to managerialism, staff complained about lack of recognition and support, and lack of interest in staff well-being – only 26 per cent agreed that the 'success they achieve in their working day is recognised and rewarded' and 44 per cent agreed that 'praise for my work and achievement is rarely given'.

Prison officers often argue that prison authorities are only interested in the well-being of prisoners and not in the well-being of staff. It is hard to decide whether this argument reflects primarily dissatisfaction with what they perceive as the lack of interest of prison authorities in staff well-being or some rather punitive views which resent any improvement in the living conditions of prisoners. Figure 2.16 presents the scores of dimensions concerning staff views and perceptions of their relationship with prisoners and their views towards rehabilitation and social distance from prisoners (based on the professional orientation dimensions developed by Klofas and Toch 1982).

As Figure 2.16 shows, the dimension 'Relationship with prisoners' had relatively high scores which suggests that most officers perceive their relationships with the prisoners to be good.[20] Seventy per cent of staff thought they had good relationships with prisoners, and 77 per cent of staff reported that they try to build trust with prisoners. Staff saw their involvement in rehabilitation and supporting prisoners as a highly important and essential part of their job. The dimensions 'Supportive/counselling roles' and 'Engagement with prisoner distress' had high scores across establishments. In four out of six prisons the second most frequent source of job satisfaction was 'helping prisoners' or 'making a difference' (the first source of job satisfaction in all prisons was 'working with colleagues'). Eighty-nine per cent of staff thought that supporting prisoners was part of their job, and 71 per cent thought officers should be involved in rehabilitation programmes. While staff felt trusted by the prisoners they were much more cautious about trusting prisoners back. Seventy-eight per cent of discipline staff agreed or highly agreed with the statement 'you can't ever completely trust a prisoner'. This has much to do with security and control. Many staff members associate trusting prisoners with the risk of conditioning or escape. Fifty-five per cent of officers thought that their prison was too comfortable for prisoners and this score might explain the relatively low score of the dimension 'Caring approach to prisoners'. The fact that scores on the dimension 'punitive orientation' varies significantly between prisons suggests that officer culture is not uniform and that important differences between prisons can be found (see further, Arnold *et al.* 2007; Tait 2008b).

In 2006, then, we found that prison staff were generally satisfied with and committed to their work. They felt safe in their working environment and they had a clear understanding of their role. Staff did not tend to believe that their prison had a good image in their local area, particularly in some parts of the country.

The problems that staff find in living with their public image is something that has characterised prison work for a long period. Almost 30 years ago, Colvin conducted his study of staff at Manchester Strangeways prison, and found a number of officers who felt they had the image of 'bullies', 'brutes', 'sadists' or 'thugs':

> Although the officers seem able to live with their public image, and although they may be able to displace much of its impact, their situation is hardly fertile ground for the construction of a stable and favourable conception of self. (Colvin 1977: 137)

Crawley, in her recent study of prison officers' work, found similar perceptions. Some prison officers she interviewed felt that they were treated by outsiders as if their contact with the prison contaminated them. According to Crawley prison officers (and their partners) were not always happy to tell other people they worked for the Prison Service. Most officers are aware that 'as an occupational group they are perceived in a negative light by the general public. Moreover negative media reporting and dramatic (often fictional) representations have done little to dismantle the stereotype' (Crawley 2004: 244).

Conclusion

This chapter has given a brief account of the available data on who prison officers are. We have looked mainly at gender, ethnic background, age and experience, and their conditions of employment. It has also explored some of their views and opinions. The profile of staff is important in understanding 'what goes on in prison'. It is also important to recognise the changing profile of prison officers and to consider some of the implications of this.

With this background accomplished, it is possible to move on to what it is that prison officers do in their daily work: the tasks they perform, the skills they use to perform such tasks, and the words they use to describe them. Prison work requires specific skills and modes of behaviour that are valuable and ought to be prized. The ability to cajole a wing full of prisoners behind their cell doors each night is an activity that requires highly developed expertise ('verbal judo' in another language). The way in which prison officers work is explored in detail in the following chapters. Why is it that being a successful prison officer requires such complex skills and techniques – why is prison work difficult, when officers appear to have almost total power over the prisoners they manage?

Notes

1 This has partly to do with the fact that the definitions of the manager grades were recently modified and they now include prison staff members who were not previously counted as manager (or governor) grades.
2 Information from the Federal Bureau of Prisons website, at http://www.bop.gov.
3 Source: Prison Service Pay Review Body (2005) (http://www.ome.uk.com).
4 Source: Prison Service (2006).
5 Source: Prison Service Pay Review Body (2006) (http://www.ome.uk.com).
6 Source: Prison Service Pay Review Body (2005) (http://www.ome.uk.com).
7 Source: Prison Service Pay Review Body (2006) (http://www.ome.uk.com).
8 Source: Prison Service Pay Review Body (2005) (http://www.ome.uk.com).
9 Source: Prison Service Pay Review Body (2005) (http://www.ome.uk.com).
10 http://www.statistics.gov.uk. The ASHE report does not specify whether the sample included officers from the private sector or only the public sector. However, since private prisons constitute less than 10 per cent of all prisons in England and Wales, their impact on the findings are marginal.
11 Source: Prison Service Pay Review Body (2005).
12 ASHE figures for female prison officers only go back to 1996 and for female police officers only go back to 1999.
13 Source: ASHE (2005) and Office for National Statistics: New Earnings Survey 1999 and 1990.
14 Thirty-four per cent more when the comparison is between the gross annual pay.
15 Source: Prison Service (1990: 42).
16 Source: Prison Service (1990: 42).
17 Original dimensions for the SQL questionnaire: Treatment by senior management; Attitudes towards senior management; Perception of Prison

Service; Relationship with peers; Relationship with line management; Treatment by Senior Officers (SOs) and Principal Officers (POs); Commitment; Safety/control/security; Recognition and personal efficacy; Involvement in prison; Involvement in work; Stress; Relationships with prisoners; Professional support; Social distance; Authority maintenance; View on punishment and control. See Appendix.

18 The score system derives from the 5-point Likert format of each of the items of the questionnaire. The dimension score is the mean score of all the items which make up the dimension.

19 In all four prisons, Pearsons r > 0.6 (strength of correlation).

20 This can sometimes be misleading, see further Liebling *et al.* (2005).

Chapter 3

Understanding prison officers and their role

Staff were gatekeepers, agents of criminal justice, peacemakers, instruments of change and deliverers and interpreters of policy. (Liebling and Price 1999: 86)

I think the straightforward answer to what the prison officer does on the wing ... is that he operates the routine and the regime as decided by the governor ... So you get the core prison officers who are the ones who can do the routine. They unlock, they lock-up, they can do the routines. That's the absolute base level that prison officers can do to get the money. But that's not sufficient. It's about the other bits – it's about interacting with prisoners, having the proper relationship with them, it's helping them with their problems, dealing with their short-term needs and wants and their long-term needs and wants. (Senior manager)

What is the role of the modern prison officer? Arguably the primary role of a prison officer is the maintenance of safe custody (Thomas 1972). But there is clearly more to the officer's role than this. A good place to start is with the official definition of the prison officer's job – Figure 3.1 shows the information available on the Prison Service website for applicants interested in joining the Prison Service. This is a concise summary of the tasks facing a prison officer.

It is clear from the job description that prison work can be complex and challenging. Some of the broad objectives are apparently contradictory, prisoners are often found in highly charged emotional

Prison officers work in different types of prisons — open (low security), female, high security, juveniles, young offenders and remand centres. They help ensure the security and safety of prisoners.

What prison officers do

- help offenders deal with being in prison and help them to address their offending behaviour

- supervise prisoners' activities

- aid in rehabilitating and training offenders, giving prisoners advice, support and counselling via a Personal Officer scheme

- deal with any disruptions to the regime, maintaining control and order and helping to create a safe and secure environment

- receive and process new prisoners into prisons, assessing their needs and identifying possible self-harm issues

- search prisoners, accommodation blocks, vehicles, grounds and visitors into prisons.

Key skills for prison officers

- interest in dealing with social problems

- ability to react quickly and effectively under pressure, i.e. in incidents, acts of disorder

- sensitivity to others' problems and issues

- good communication skills

- an ability to get on with people from different social backgrounds

- initiative, good leadership and people management skills

- an ability to defuse conflict in a professional and sensitive manner.

Source: Prison Service website.

Figure 3.1 Prison officer job description

states and a single 'ill-considered word or action' can sometimes precipitate violence or tragedy. It is plain enough that the prison is a 'strange and demanding environment' (see the Prison Service website for further details).

Despite the apparently simple daily tasks of a prison officer ('you will unlock prisoners, deal with any requests they may have, make sure they are where they should be and doing what they should be doing') it is the relationships an officer establishes with prisoners that hold the key to being a successful prison officer. These should be 'honest', but officers also need to know how to cajole, negotiate, persuade – 'you will require good listening, assertive, influencing, negotiating and verbal communication skills'. Further, these relationships have to be seen within other dimensions of this complex job: maintaining security, providing care, performing routines efficiently, balancing sometimes contradictory goals, and so on.

There is little in this formal definition about the rewards of the job of prison officer, other than the implicit suggestion that making a positive contribution to the care of those in custody might be rewarding in itself. We get an idea of the kind of personality that might be involved: someone that has 'strength of character, a balanced and mature approach to life, plenty of patience, understanding and common sense' – here, it is already possible to see why many prison officers compare their role to that of a parent.

However, the outline does not say much about how a prison officer might be expected to go about these many difficult tasks, nor does it provide any basic detail about the structure of a typical prison day, the working environment or their colleagues, for example.

Much sociological literature suffers from the same deficit – a lack of attention to the work and responsibilities of the prison officer. Some empirical studies have been carried out, many of these in the US (for example, Jacobs 1977, 1978; Johnson 1977; Johnson and Price 1981; Lombardo 1981; Toch and Klofas 1982; Klofas 1986; Marquart 1986), some in Australia (for example Williams 1983; Williams and Soutar 1984) and some in the UK (Morris and Morris 1963; Emery 1970). Many of these studies are now dated, in particular in their depiction of the nature of prison work, although there are useful insights which remain of interest (such as the finding that officers share a liberal socio-political perspective on the causes of crime and may have a 'greater commitment to rehabilitation than the academic penologists and prison administrators' (Jacobs 1978: 193). Some significant recent work conducted in the UK (Biggam and Power 1997; Liebling and Price 1999; Arnold 2008; Shefer and Liebling 2008), Australia (Rynne, personal communication) and the US (Gilbert 1997) suggest that officers may define their role differently, some preferring a mainly custodial interpretation, others having a 'treatment' orientation. These basic orientations are linked to staff perceptions of prisoners, their attitudes towards non-custodial staff and the type of rewards they seek in their work (Williams 1983). The need for clarity may encourage officers to adhere to a disciplinary or rule orientation, to treat all prisoners alike and to develop individual and collective psychological defences in the form of negative stereotypes over time (Williams 1983: 53–4). Officers in the modern prison deliver (and help to deliver) professional treatment and development programmes for sex offenders, violent offenders, drug users and others, and arguably have developed a strengthened 'treatment intervention' role over recent years. Research has shown that officers who have a favourable or human services orientation towards prisoners have a more satisfying occupational experience (Whitehead *et al.* 1987).

Despite the research mentioned above, we would argue that prison staff have been generally neglected in the academic literature. Writing in 1991, Hay and Sparks (1991: 1) wondered whether 'the role of the prison officer [had] become so poorly defined, or alternatively so contradictory, as to make it unusually hard for anyone to occupy it satisfactorily'. Hay and Sparks felt that policy documents and official pronouncements on the role of the prison officer – like the job description above – said little about what officers should do on a daily working basis. Prison officers 'have not been well served by those above them whose job it is … to provide them with a clear and consistent sense of identity and purpose' (Hay and Sparks 1991: 3). Within what guiding principles should officers work? How should they describe what they do?

The role of the prison officer is a difficult one to explain accurately. Most of the work is 'low visibility' and staff work to overall goals that may be in conflict with each other. How individual prison officers reconcile these problems in individual situations encountered during a typical working day is one of the main subjects of this book (see especially Chapter 6 on the use of discretion).

First, this chapter provides a basic description of prison officer work. We illustrate a typical day for a prison officer, using research we conducted as a template. There are over 140 public and private sector prison establishments in England and Wales, and each one operates slightly differently. As a result, the routine outlined below is a composite picture; it contains some of what we have seen of how officers might spend their time and a sense of the different roles that can be assumed by an officer. The chapter then goes on to define the role of the prison officer from the ground, using research that explored with prison officers and prisoners what qualities were considered important in being a 'role model' prison officer (Liebling and Price 1999; see also Arnold 2008).

A typical day for a prison officer

We focus here on the landing officer: arguably the key role in any prison. What might a day look like to an observer?

The amount and type of physical interaction between an officer and a prisoner varies depending on the designated role of the officer and the individual prisoner.[1] Landing officers unlock a landing in the morning and, generally, remain on the wing or spur while breakfast is served, controlling the flow of prisoners collecting their meals. Interaction might occur about the order in which the spurs are to receive breakfast, or a question or comment about some other aspect of the prison routine might come from a prisoner.[2] When most prisoners are off the spur at work (with officers sometimes needed to chivvy one or two along or to check why a prisoner is not going to work that day), landing officers are normally placed on the required daily task of checking locks, bolts and bars (LBBs) or another spur-based task (searching, for example). Teamed up with another officer, they move round a spur one landing at a time checking each cell and all communal areas. Within the wing, this is usually the quietest period of the unlocked day – both prisoners and officers are working at set tasks. Officers on LBBs speak to prisoners, perhaps asking them to step out of their cells if they are 'banged up' (not at work) – this is often a quick and relatively formal interaction, although some officers might banter and talk with prisoners (particularly those they get on with well) more than others. The prisoner might request to fetch some hot water or to hand in an application (written request) before he is locked up again. LBBs are often carried on during the afternoon work period. Thus the role of the landing officer is one of maintaining security and control, and in carrying out both relating effectively to prisoners.

The afternoon activity (work, training or education) period is more relaxed – much of the set work of the day is done both by prisoners and officers. On occasions, officers and prisoners might be observed leaning over the railings together chatting, often about prison issues but more general conversation might develop: the progress someone is making on education, a family issue, a crime, the news, a football match. When prisoners return from their activities – in the morning or the afternoon – the wing becomes much busier, and interaction between officers and prisoners is more varied and frequent. Longer and deeper conversations are normally reserved for an office or a quieter period of the day. The progression of prisoners to get their lunch or dinner often produces rapid bursts of talk – good humoured insults are traded – but prisoners are usually too anxious to get their meal and start eating to talk for longer than a few minutes.

Evening association tends to be seen as 'prisoner time'. Some officers play pool or table tennis with prisoners or chat, but other officers are either busy and unable to talk or prefer to leave prisoners alone unless they wish to approach an officer. This does not stop the occasional casual remark or round of banter, however. Prisoners approach officers – particularly officers they know well – at any time, often to talk about any (prison-related) issue: a problem with a visit, a request for an application form, a query over private cash or a part of a procedure or the regime. Conversations are generally cooperative and civil. All-out arguments are rare – raised voices and emotions are more common among prisoners, with officers more frequently taking on the 'peacemaking' role.

There are occasions where there is a more formal opportunity for officers and prisoners to talk to each other about subjects other than prison – in sentence planning or personal officer interviews, for example – but general conversation about subjects other than prison is relatively rare. In part, this may be due to staff fears about 'conditioning' and 'boundaries' but it also reflects each side's knowledge of the reason for any relationship in the first place – often an instrumental one ('they need us, and we need their cooperation').

Staff shifts are an important factor in the physical structuring of their relationships with prisoners. Prison officers are contracted to work an average 39-hour week (meal breaks not included) and most work every other weekend. Because prisons operate 24 hours a day, a complex pattern of shifts determines the deployment of staff. This inevitably means that in the course of several weeks prisoners see a number of different officers. With time used for training, holidays and sickness (which can be high among officers), officers work on average 31.2 'effective' hours each week, scheduled in shifts covering the 24-hour period. The structural constraint of this lack of continuity is an important factor in the development and endurance of relationships. Events constantly 'happen' that affect a wing's operation (e.g. tensions between prisoners, staffing and management changes or disagreements, and general 'events' – a fire, an alarm, a successful parole result, a fight, a cell change, or even – as we once witnessed – a bird flying on to the wing where a staff member who was afraid of birds worked). Each event can bond, sever, strain, generate laughter or lead to a different atmosphere on the wing. Officers who come back on duty having been off for a week sometimes find it difficult to catch up on all the small and subtle but important changes that have occurred. Similarly, prisoners often express frustration that they have not been able to see their personal officer for an extended period because of shift patterns and leave. In local prisons where the turnover of prisoners is particularly high, a change in the mix of prisoners can have a profound effect on the wing.

In one day, an officer can be a supervisor, custodian, disciplinarian, peacekeeper, administrator, observer, manager, facilitator, mentor, provider, classifier and diplomat. Different situations require slightly different blends, and different types of establishments or populations may demand a slightly different mix. Versatility and flexibility are key requirements.

Role model prison officers

The above sketch gives a brief idea of the many tasks in which officers are engaged during a typical day, from turning down a request, to giving unwelcome news, to assisting a prisoner with their sentence plan, to rub down searching or strip searching.[3] It illustrates the centrality of relationships to prison life. At every point of the day, the relationships an officer has established with prisoners are called upon: to unlock prisoners successfully without rancour, to cajole stragglers along to work, to make sure that the visits policy is explained clearly to dispel anxiety in a prisoner who is missing his or her family. Even in seemingly 'technical' matters – for example, censoring letters (an officer can draw upon their knowledge of a wing and the prisoner in reading letters) or in completing the locks, bolts and bars (checking around a prisoner's cell – their home – in a way that does not disturb or upset them) – relationships matter.

These relationships are mediated through the officer's own personality. What kinds of personal skills are required to be a successful prison officer? Is it possible to identify a 'role model' officer? A study in Denmark (Kriminalforsorgens Uddannelsescenter, 1994) addressed those questions. The team of researchers asked prison officers and their managers to identify the qualities that the ideal prison officer might have. They asked staff to nominate an individual who they thought operated effectively, handled conflict situations well and set a good example for other staff. The researchers then interviewed these nominated officers about their working styles, attributes and thoughts about their work. They were then able to produce a long profile of the skills that an ideal prison officer should possess. A selection of these qualities is listed in Table 3.1.

Table 3.1 Role model characteristics of prison officers

---

1 Physical characteristics
- good physical condition
- satisfactory strength to respond to hard working conditions
- ability to act with reasonable self-confidence and personal authority
- verbal skills

2 Mental capacity
- ability to think
- able to hold many things in mind at the same time

3 You should have the ability to:
(i) Learn:
- have the ability and need to learn new things
- be receptive to new ideas and alternative solutions
- understand consequences and connections in what oneself and others do
- come up with ideas and proposals and be able to see them through
- view and assess complex situations and deal with them

(ii) Watch:
- be alert and aware of yourself through observations and information
- be able to see, understand, evaluate and account for a situation without distortion
- be able to overview several activities at the same time without confusion
- be able to 'control' own attitudes and prejudices when people act in ways that disturb or annoy you, and to keep these people in order

(iii) Make decisions:
- use new information, understand it, form your own opinions and make your decision
- be loyal to decisions already made
- be flexible and able to change opinion when the circumstances change

(iv) Solve problems:
- be able to mentally prepare information to solve problems
- try to reach solutions which will be understood and accepted
- relate to others in a way that brings opinions from them
- be satisfied with half-solutions when the perfect solution is impossible

(v) Do administrative tasks:
- handle 'paperwork' exactly and quickly
- be organised
- understand and accept the necessity of routine work

Table 3.1 continues over

Table 3.1 continued

---

4 You should be able to:
- interact with others
- bear difficult emotions
- seek to understand other people's thoughts and emotions
- be sensitive in personal interaction
- be interested in one's environment as much as in oneself
- stand out as trustworthy
- live with the fact that from time to time it is hard to see the overall context
- live with the negative societal picture of the prison officer and imprisonment
- have a sense of humour
- lead others and create respect around oneself without becoming aggressive
- have self-confidence and self-esteem
- handle conflict situations
- communicate ideas clearly and easily and influence others
- express oneself in a clear and obvious way that is right for the person and the situation
- give clear signals that cannot be misinterpreted by the other person, and make sure that the receiver understands the signals
- acquire verbal and non-verbal signals from different individuals and groups with varied cultural characteristics
- build trust by one's actions
- possess self-confidence
- acquire positive energy outside the institution
- be professional enough to act 'sensibly' under pressure from colleagues and prisoners
- live with and strengthen relationships with others
- stand alone without support when the situation demands
- say 'no' when the situation demands
- be reliable, trustworthy and responsible for the tasks given to you
- be flexible enough to handle more than one duty and long irregular working hours
- understand different people's attitudes and behaviour and be able to express the reasons for their attitude and behaviour
- keep going, even if there is no pressure on you to do so.

Source: Kriminalforsorgens Uddannelsescenter (1994).

What is evident from this profile is that many of the attributes required to be a 'role model' prison officer are in tension. If we look at the section titled 'Make decisions', for example, two attributes follow one another: be loyal to decisions already made; and be flexible and able to change opinion when the circumstances change. 'Solutions' requires the officer to be satisfied (and, implicitly, be able to recognise this point) with 'half-solutions' to problems but other attributes require the right solution to be sought. The profile is an aspirational one – no one person can be all of these things. If these are the attributes of the 'perfect' prison officer, can such an officer exist?

Role model officers at Whitemoor prison

We were intrigued by the Danish study and used it in our study of staff–prisoner relationships at Whitemoor. We asked prison officers, their managers and prisoners which prison officers they admired most and why. One general conclusion was that a mix of officers was necessary:

> You need the friendly and the fair; you need the very strict; you need the very easy. You need all of them. *Porridge* is the closest that outside people understand. You need your McKays and your Barracloughs, as well as everybody in-between. If we were all exactly the same, the job wouldn't tick, would it? (Officer)

> You need professional skills – leadership, decision-making, problem-solving skills, good communications skills; and the correct personal qualities – integrity, energy, enthusiasm, taking personal responsibility ... but you need a blend. You don't want too many people with the same quality in one area. I don't think that there is a perfect officer. It's all about how you get individuals generally using common sense working with other people, being reasonable to their colleagues as many people of one type. (Senior manager)

Importantly, we found that slightly different 'role model' officers, and reasons for the choices of these officers, were given for different locations within the prison and by different groups. For example, managers were more likely to cite factors such as reliable attendance, enthusiasm and smartness; officers looked for reliability and willingness to do jobs when asked, the ability to 'keep a calm head' and the ability to resolve conflict. Prisoners preferred officers who were 'down to earth' and not 'petty'. However, throughout these different areas and the many different viewpoints, there was a common 'core' of desirable characteristics that were relevant in all locations and that were identified by senior managers, prison officer colleagues and prisoners alike (see Table 3.2). Good officers had verbal skills of persuasion, could use authority appropriately, had human relations skills and leadership abilities and could use straight talk or honesty. They had the ability to maintain boundaries – all boundaries – with different departments, between management and staff, and with prisoners. They had personal strength or 'moral courage' and a sense of purpose. They needed patience, empathy, courage and a professional orientation.

Table 3.2 Factors common to 'role model' prison officers

- Having known and consistent boundaries. It did not matter so much precisely where these boundaries were, provided they were effectively communicated to prisoners and consistently policed.
- A quality for which we were unable to find a better term than 'moral fibre' – confidence, integrity, honesty, strength or conviction, good judgement (flexibility).
- An awareness of the effects of their own power.
- An understanding of the painfulness of prison.
- A 'professional orientation'.
- An optimistic – but realistic – outlook: the capacity to maintain hope in difficult circumstances.

The 'professional orientation' is usefully described by Gilbert, who uses work descriptors or typologies first used by Muir in relation to the police (Gilbert 1997; Muir 1977). Gilbert argues that studies of prison officers have not typically recognised the 'rich diversity of work behaviours' displayed by staff, and he supports our view that those characterisations which do exist tend to consist mainly of negative stereotypes (Gilbert 1997; see also Liebling *et al.* 1999). He developed a typology which characterises prison officers' working styles as 'professionals',[4] 'reciprocators', 'enforcers' and 'avoiders'. These working styles – into which we could place many officers we have encountered during fieldwork – provide a useful conceptual scheme for understanding the professional role described to us by prisoners and staff.[5] The nature and the extent of discretionary power used by prison officers differs, Gilbert argues, in these four broad ways:

- *The professional* – is open and non-defensive, makes exceptions when warranted, prefers to gain cooperation and compliance through communication, but is willing to use coercive power or force as a last resort.

- *The reciprocator* – wants to help people, assists them in resolving their problems, prefers clinical or social work strategies, may be inconsistent when making exceptions, prefers to 'go along to get along' and tends not to use coercive authority or physical force even when it is justifiable.

- *The enforcer* – practises rigid, 'by the book' aggressive enforcement, actively seeks out violations, rarely makes exceptions, has little empathy for others, takes unreasonable risks to personal safety, sees most things as either good or bad, and is quick to use threats, verbal coercion and physical force.

- *The avoider* – minimises offender contact, often does not 'see' an offence, avoids confrontation and coercion, views interpersonal aspects of the job as not part of the job, often backs down from confrontation and blames others.

What is interesting about Gilbert's typology is its usefulness in linking the variations we have witnessed with 'what should be' in most of our respondents' views. We would not always agree with Gilbert's normative judgements and his work is based on US examples. But this account is intended to provide empirical descriptions and some of the conceptual tools required to think about the work of prison officers. We hope to assist in this way with the more difficult normative task. What should officers be like? There is overlap between some of the categories – for example, some of the 'role model' staff identified at Whitemoor could be described as a combination of the 'professional' and 'enforcer' types. This version of the 'professional' officer may be the desired type in this sort of setting. Gilbert provides a detailed list of what he calls (after Muir 1977) 'work style descriptors' (see Table 3.3).

The best officers we saw were discerning, committed and unafraid to use force. They were neither over-eager to resort to force, nor reluctant. They were confident, physically fit (usually) and had a fairly clear sense of their broader purpose. They did not bear grudges (see Wilson 2000) and were enthusiastic, despite setbacks.

According to each particular wing of the prison, these role model characteristics changed a little, to adapt to the different circumstances and 'working way' of each area. Whitemoor (a high security or dispersal prison[6]) had four wings. At the time of our original research, A and B wings housed vulnerable prisoners (VPs); C and D wings were mainstream dispersal wings. There were subtle but important differences within each 'pair' of wings. In addition to the common

Table 3.3 Gilbert's 'work style descriptors'

The professional
- Develops the housing unit (wing)
- Takes educated risks
- Provides prisoners advice on rules and regulations
- Increases pressure over time to change behaviour
- Uses the 'write-up' (adjudication) as a last resort
- Tries to preserve the dignity of prisoners through the use of non-demeaning behaviours and attitudes
- Views offenders as not much different from self
- Empathises with the human condition of prisoners
- Allows for exceptions in own and others' behaviour
- Uses coercion and force judiciously
- Calm and easy-going
- Articulate and open
- Focuses on ensuring due process and decency in security and control tasks
- Views most other officers as being enforcer-oriented

The reciprocator
- Allows prisoner leaders to keep the wing quiet – a mutual accommodation
- Uses clinical/social work strategies to help prisoners 'worthy' of assistance
- Rationalises situations
- Attempts to educate, cure or solve the prisoner's problems
- Low tolerance for rejection of offered assistance
- Easily frustrated
- Often does not use coercion when it should be used
- Inconsistent job performance
- Irrational behaviour by prisoners stymies the officer
- Often displays a superior attitude towards others
- Highly articulate

The enforcer
- Aggressive rule enforcement
- Issues many 'tickets' (places many on report)
- Actively seeks violations
- Frequently uses force or excessive force
- Tends to view treatment functions as what 'others' do with/for prisoners
- Strict security and control orientation, limits service delivery duties
- Little or no empathy for the human condition of prisoners
- Prisoners often submit grievances over this officer's behaviour

- Rigid, rule-bound, makes few exceptions even when appropriate
- Maintains a dualistic view of human nature (good/bad, officer/prisoner, strong/weak)
- Dislikes management
- Postures for effect – Crazy/brave 'John Wayne' behaviours, takes unnecessary risks
- Views other officers as 'soft'/'weak' if not like him/her
- Views officers like him/her as being the majority of officers

The avoider
- Often leaves situations as quickly as possible
- Tends to view human communications with prisoners as not being part of security and control
- Uses the mechanical aspects of security and control to reduce contact with prisoners
- Often among the last to arrive at an emergency scene
- Likely to select isolated/prisoner-free positions
- Plays the 'phoney' tough and frequently backs down
- Tends to blame others for avoidance behaviours or inadequacies
- Structures the work to avoid observing infractions and use of coercion
- Avoids confrontations and interactions with prisoners

Source: Gilbert (1997).

'role model' characteristics above, prisoners and staff in the different wings put emphasis on different characteristics of their most admired officers. While the function of many of these and the specialist wings at Whitemoor has changed, as is so often the case in prisons, we draw on this account to illustrate a typical range of wing functions and styles.[7]

On *A Wing*, a vulnerable prisoner wing which housed the Sex Offender Treatment Programme (SOTP: an intensive offending behaviour programme), role model officers were often those engaged in SOTP work. These officers 'stood out' and were perceived by prisoners as caring and working hard for them. A Wing role models were patient with prisoners, knew their prisoners and were not afraid of interacting with them; they were comfortable in close relationships with prisoners, but were aware of their boundaries and unafraid to enforce the rules where necessary. Officers had a paternalistic-therapeutic orientation towards prisoners – they recognised their problems and were willing to help. They had a sense of humour with prisoners and colleagues, although this was generally not the quick-fire banter often found on C and D Wings, the main dispersal wings.

For *B Wing*, a VP wing without the explicit focus on the SOTP, role model officers were also listeners; they too could recognise that some of their prisoners had problems and difficulties – although such problems were less likely to be as explicitly offence-oriented as on A Wing. It was important that officers did not judge prisoners or cast moral aspersions on their offences. Good staff were aware of their power and of the difficulties of exercising it properly on a VP wing.[8] Role model staff appreciated respectful treatment from prisoners, but were prepared to forgive transgressions, up to a point. Rather than the 'close' and often personal relationships found on A Wing, officers on B Wing had 'working' relationships, which at their best were 'understanding' and 'helpful'.

Role model officers on *C Wing*, a dispersal wing, were efficient and competent. They expected to work hard, but they also expected some cooperation from prisoners. They would permit the expression of some of the frustrations of prison life, but had clear boundaries that were effectively communicated to prisoners. Their 'line' was a stricter one than on D Wing (see below). They would use their discretion, but within clear parameters. They were also individually (and, to some extent, as a team) consistent over time. They worked well with other staff and with some common sense of purpose, linked to maintaining 'a tight ship' and clear boundaries on the wing. There were fairly formal relationships with prisoners, but this was informed by a close knowledge of individuals on the wing. One area of the wing, known as 'blue spur', was the 'incentive spur', where prisoners on the enhanced level of the IEP scheme could apply to be placed as a reward for their good behaviour. On this spur, the general C Wing formality was broken and the relationship became one of 'shared' investment in a small community.

On *D Wing*, the other traditional dispersal wing, role model staff were confident but had a more relaxed and interactive style than their colleagues on C Wing. They were prepared to respect the agency (individuality) of prisoners (perhaps a little too much in the eyes of some of their colleagues and managers) and to joke and banter with them, but could be absolutely firm when this was needed. They were willing to take on extra duties when requested by colleagues and would tackle tasks without prompting. There was less commonality of working styles between officers on the wing compared to C Wing, but there was good teamwork and a strong sense of attachment to the wing. Relationships between staff and prisoners were very good humoured and traded on mutual insults – but there was clearly respect on both sides for the abilities and ways of the other. The 'peace' was kept on D Wing, paradoxically, through a lot of noise and a lot of talk. D Wing had a lot of ex-SSU staff[9] who were also keen gym attendees. There was no doubt that strong, articulate, challenging prisoners respected strong, street-wise and confident staff.[10]

This is not to say that every good officer on each wing matched their role model characteristics; indeed, it could have been the case that no officer was a perfect representation of the desired role model. A broad mix of officer styles, skills and attributes was considered vital to the efficient running of a wing.

We observed that in general, officers from A and B Wings (the VP wings) were nominated less often, or less quickly, as role models than officers from the ordinary dispersal wings. In particular, senior managers mentioned officers from C and D Wings and we sometimes had to prompt them specifically about the VP wings to elicit mention of officers from that part of the prison. Once asked, officers came easily to mind. This 'invisibility' seemed linked to a common perception that somehow work on VP wings was 'easier' than the 'real prison work' found on ordinary dispersal wings. This was not our experience, as both halves of the prison seemed to us to bring special difficulties and to require special skills. C and D Wings were more visible and seemed to require and receive more senior management attention, with prisoners arriving and departing more frequently, often to the segregation unit.

Wing differences and adjudications

All adjudications at Whitemoor over an eight-month period were analysed in order to explore possible differences between the wings empirically.[11] Adjudications are not a simple measure of either prisoner behaviour or officer style, but they are an interesting starting point for exploring possible differences in both. Wings which accommodate prisoners who are part of an intensive offending behaviour programme (like SOTP) are less likely to contravene the rules because of the sort of prisoners they are as well as because the relationships they are required to establish with staff are different. The nature of offending behaviour courses may encourage a more 'consultative' or 'conciliatory' approach by prisoners. Other factors, such as the number of formal complaints, formal applications, the length of time prisoners have served and the overarching vulnerability sex offender prisoners may feel could further qualify statistical adjudication differences. However, knowing all this (and, to some extent, controlling for some of these variables), the results of our study showed clear differences which seemed to be related to some of the observations made above. The number of proven adjudications were low on A Wing (a VP wing), but much higher on D Wing (a dispersal wing), and highest of all within the segregation unit, as Table 3.4 shows. An incident leading to an adjudication occurred approximately every ten days on A Wing, but every two and a half days on D Wing. They were almost daily occurrences in the segregation unit. Although the segregation unit had a population of around 25 prisoners – compared to well over 100 on the wings – it contributed well over a third of all adjudications at the prison.[12]

Table 3.4 Proven adjudications at Whitemoor by location of incident (July 1997 to February 1998)

A Wing	B Wing	C Wing	D Wing	Seg.	Other*	Total
24 5.1%	58 12.3%	72 15.3%	99 21.0%	178 37.7%	41 8.7%	472 100%

*'Other' comprises all areas of the prison other than the wings and the segregation unit, for example healthcare, visits and the workshops.

The total number of adjudications on C Wing (a mainstream dispersal wing, but the less lively of the two) was influenced by the fact that one spur held 'enhanced' prisoners only: of all adjudications from C Wing that were traceable back to a specific location, only one occurred on this spur, with 15 each occurring on the other two spurs over this period. There were also differences between the wings on the types of offences (or rather, those for which prisoners were most commonly placed on report). Four offences arose most often:

- *paragraph 9(a)* – possession of an unauthorised item (17 per cent);
- *paragraph 17* – threatening, abusive or insulting words or behaviour (17 per cent);
- *paragraph 19* – disobeying a lawful order (26 per cent);
- *paragraph 20* – failing to comply with any rule or regulation (16 per cent).[13]

Together, offences against these paragraphs made up over three-quarters of all disciplinary offences at the prison. Paragraph 1 – used if a prisoner committed any assault – contributed a small but significant proportion to the total number of adjudications (6.8 per cent).

Figure 3.2 shows offences against these four main paragraphs according to the amount they contributed to the total number of proven adjudications on each wing. Paragraph 17 (threatening, abusive or insulting words or behaviour) made up 33 per cent of A Wing's total adjudications (though this was only eight offences of a total of 24). Paragraph 9(a) (possession of an unauthorised item) contributed almost the same amount to D Wing's total (though this amounted to over 30 separate incidents). Two interesting trends can be seen in Figure 3.2.

• The contribution offences against paragraph 17 (using threatening, abusive or insulting words or behaviour) made to each wing's total declines from A Wing to D Wing.

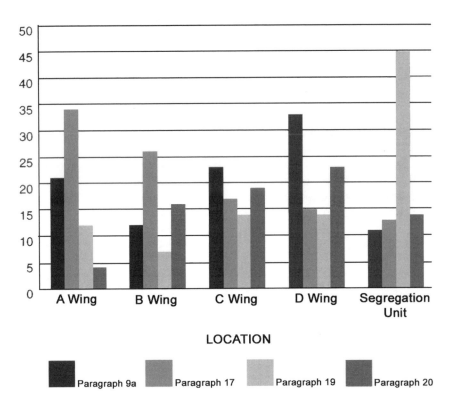

LOCATION

Paragraph 9a   Paragraph 17   Paragraph 19   Paragraph 20

Figure 3.2 Adjudication arising from paragraphs of Rule 47 broken (percentage) (HMP Whitemoor, July 1997–February 1998)

- Conversely, the total contribution of offences against paragraph 20 (failing to conform with any rule or regulation) went up from A Wing to D Wing.

Both prisoner behaviour and officer responses to prisoner behaviour differed according to location and population. Our observations (and the rest of the data) led us to conclude that officers on the VP wings were more inclined to sanction small resistances (see also Sparks *et al.* 1996), and that prisoners on vulnerable prisoner units tended to confine their misbehaviour to verbal complaints. Prisoners on D Wing were 'allowed' a certain amount of 'resistant language', but were sanctioned instead for more serious breaches of the rules, including trade.

Incidents that led to proven adjudications also differed according to the day of the week, with incidents rising in number from a low on Sunday to a high on Wednesday and then declining again towards the end of the week. Again, this pattern could be linked to routine features of prison life, such as pay day, and an arguably more relaxed atmosphere at the weekend (see also Sparks *et al.* 1996).

Conclusion

This outline of different role model staff in just one prison and the extent of variation between wings illustrate the wide range of roles that prison officers can adopt, but tries to demonstrate the common 'core' characteristics of the best staff as identified by prisoners and their officer colleagues. We found that many officers gravitated to a particular wing or section of the prison whose working style suited their own personality. This point demonstrates the need for officers to 'be themselves' as far as possible – to invest the role of the prison officer with their own personality and characteristics. The prison may be a highly artificial environment, but values of truth, honesty and integrity were vital. Officers were certain that you could not be effective if you were not yourself. There was an important need to be 'professional', but this professional orientation was best achieved through working with the grain of your own personality.

One of the most significant themes to arise from our own research was the question of role and whether this was clear. What was 'being a prison officer' at Whitemoor about? Did the prison have a clear purpose and direction? The answer differed slightly from officer to officer. All were convinced of the need to maintain security, and the need to keep order on the wing (a version of Dunbar's term 'dynamic security', Dunbar 1985). The emphasis given to helping prisoners tackle their offending behaviour was greater for some officers than for others. Some officers, for example, were keen to stress the importance of helping prisoners to maintain family contacts. What this meant was that each officer had their own 'bigger picture' consisting of a view about the role of imprisonment, the role of their own prison, the role of their particular wing and, therefore, their own role as a prison officer. This individualisation of some of the most important questions in a prison was in some ways unfortunate and detracted from the otherwise impressive work being carried out. We look at role diversity in the next chapter. Some diversity of role is inevitable and desirable, particularly given the diverse nature of the prison population and the need to have a wide range of officers bringing different strengths to the job. There are limits to this need for diversity when it comes to overall purpose. One of the main conclusions of our research at Whitemoor – and we have heard this plea from prison staff elsewhere – was that it might have been an outstanding establishment if its own best work had been channelled in a more consistent and recognised direction. This is a point we return to in Chapter 6.

Notes

1 For example, a censor usually saw a large number of prisoners for very short, relatively formal periods at his (or her) office door during the morning. (Censors are allowed to open both the incoming and outgoing mail of any prisoner, except for legal correspondence. All correspondence to and from prisoners held in units housing any Category A prisoners, and to and from any prisoners on the E list, must be read 'as a matter of routine' (Security Manual, 36.14). All letters to and from prisoners in closed prisons must also be examined for illicit enclosures.) A cleaning officer had more sustained contact with a smaller number of prisoners throughout the day, from morning and afternoon labour to the serving of breakfast, lunch and dinner. The 'default' job of the prison officer – the landing officer – brought with it numerous occasions on which he or she might interact with a prisoner, adding up to at least ten or fifteen minutes of conversation with certain prisoners each day.

2 With breakfast served, the landing officer gravitated towards the 2's gate (the gate onto the second landing) and the centre officer to check prisoners' names off as they moved to work or education. Again, comments and interaction were generally limited at such a time – a

'morning' or equivalent as the prisoners passed through. There was much more interaction between prisoners – particularly on some wings – than between prisoners and officers.

3 The searching of a prisoner's body and clothing for unauthorised articles including concealed drugs or weapons.

4 Gilbert uses the term 'professional' here as a categorisation. As employees, he refers to prison staff as 'paraprofessionals', that is they are not professionals in the 'classic' sense of the term but they do apply a 'specific body of knowledge and skill' in their work (see Gilbert 1997: 50).

5 Other similar 'prototypes' appear in the literature, for example Ben-David and Silfen's 'punitive', 'custodial', 'patronage', 'therapist' and 'integrative' (see Ben-David and Silfen 1994).

6 Dispersal prisons contain a high proportion of category A (maximum security) prisoners.

7 For a more recent account of wing differences and characteristics at Whitemoor, see Drake (2008).

8 Sparks *et al.* (1996) found that some prison officers in the Vulnerable Prisoner Unit (VPU) at Albany were unaware of their own power and used it carelessly, often offending prisoners who felt that they in turn were powerless to say anything in their defence.

9 Special Security Unit – a unit within Whitemoor which housed exceptional risk category A prisoners, those deemed most dangerous to the public and most at risk of escape. Following the escape of six prisoners from the Unit in 1994, the regime followed was very strict, with a minimal use of discretion among officers. The Unit also encouraged officers to work closely as a team and appeared to inspire a great deal of confidence in the officers who worked there. The management of the Unit at the time of our research is discussed further in Chapter 5.

10 The role of D Wing is now very different. See later.

11 An adjudication is a formal hearing following a charge of misbehaviour or rule breaking by prisoners.

12 A substantial number of these adjudications were straightforward – one prisoner was placed on report 17 times over the period (a far greater individual total than any other prisoner over this period) simply for refusing to return to normal location.

13 These reference numbers refer to the pre-1999 Prison Rule 47 paragraph numbering.

Chapter 4

The complexities of the role

This chapter explores some specific factors affecting prison work – in particular, the role of stress and the vulnerability of officers to assault. We explore some of the diversities of role, some international differences, the introduction of female staff into male prisons (no research exists as far as we are aware to date on the deployment of male officers in female prisons). We end with a return to officers 'at their best' and their 'wishes for the prison'. Our conclusions draw together the experiences we have had with prison staff at many establishments over recent years, and in particular our forays into appreciative inquiry at Wandsworth, Belmarsh, Manchester, Holme House and Risley.

Prison officers: stress and assault

While the academic literature has traditionally neglected questions of role and working practice, there are many academic studies on two particular factors that impinge on the officer's job: the first of these is *stress*, and the second is the risk of *assault*. The majority of these studies are American in origin and they are primarily quantitative in technique. It is important to bear in mind the differences between prison work in England and Wales and that in the United States, but the stress literature does produce some common findings. The most important of these is that prison officers seem to suffer from high levels of stress, partly due to the environment in which they work and partly due to role conflict. However, because of methodological problems with many of the studies of stress and the dated nature of some, the following conclusion probably remains valid:

> [I]t is probably safe to say, based on the available research, that corrections work is stressful, although the extent to which stress is present is certainly not clear. Further, it is by no means established that corrections work is more stressful than other occupational fields such as heavy construction, nursing, secretarial work, and even waiting tables. (Huckabee 1992: 481)

Importantly, most studies on stress in prison work locate the source of that stress in 'role conflict' (see Wilson 2000 for a review). This refers to the difficulties officers face in reconciling the two main aims of their work, of 'custody' and 'care'. On the one hand, officers are charged with the maintenance of security and control; on the other, they are asked to help prisoners, befriend them and encourage them to deal with their offending behaviour. Officers can frequently be unsure which aspect of their role should take precedence in any situation. Thus, when Cheek and Miller (1983) asked officers to outline the most stressful aspects of their job, officers pointed to matters such as a lack of clear guidelines for job performance and conflicting orders (as well as poor communication and a lack of management support). Studies by Long et al. (1986), Stohr et al. (1994), Lasky et al. (1986) and Triplett et al. (1996) support these findings. When officers are caught between the risk of prisoner suicide on the one hand and the risk of escape on the other, which takes precedence and how do they decide? Or is this an artificial dilemma? We argue later that some of the historical role conflict experienced by officers seems to have declined. What behaviours required to prevent escapes conflict with behaviours required to prevent suicide? Vigilance and 'knowing your prisoners' are relevant in both situations. More sophisticated and recent research finds less conflict between the security and 'human services' dimensions of prison officer work (see, for example, Hemmens and Stohr 2000) and there is considerable evidence to support the basic compatibility between 'security' and other tasks (the 'dynamic security' model favoured by Dunbar 1985), provided the security function is not overwhelming. This potential compatibility between 'the two faces of the correctional role' (ibid.) is confirmed by our own research and by other studies.

A project by Cox et al. (1997) examined work-related stress in three English prisons. The findings support the view that organisational problems may be more stressful to the prison officer than the interaction with prisoners (or rather that organisational problems may be the underlying cause behind some of the stresses of prisoner interaction in failing to provide officers with a solution to problems of 'role conflict'). This project looked at establishments with relatively similar security levels but different populations: a large local prison with well over 1,000 prisoners; a category B male prison of around 400 prisoners; and a closed YOI with a population of about 800. Table 4.1 shows the level of self-report of non-specific symptoms of general malaise (for example, feelings of being worn out or tense and anxious). All three prison groups reported higher levels than the UK norm; however, the three groups were also consistently below a sample of local government manual workers.

The main areas of dissatisfaction for officers in the three prisons were the lack of management recognition of their work, problems with support from headquarters, and finding time for additional tasks.

In two research projects carried out by one of the present authors, prison officers reported high levels of stress, depression, poor physical health and a sense of isolation.[1] Ninety-five per cent of over two hundred staff interviewed reported that in their view, prison officers suffered from unreasonable levels of stress in the job:

> They do. I've one off at the moment. A good lad, must have about fifteen years' service in; he's seen it all, done it all. A fortnight ago he was good as gold on the landings, yet he's suddenly gone off with anxiety. He's been in touch with the governor; he just can't face coming in at the moment, the pressures have got to him. So you do get it. Different people might go home and start drinking; there's all sorts of ways. (Principal officer)

Table 4.1 Symptoms of stress

Group	Male Local	Male B	Male YOI	UK norm	Professional/ admin staff	Local govt manual workers
Symptoms of being 'worn-out'	16.3	18.1	17.2	15.9	17.5	20.5
Symptoms of being 'tense and anxious'	6.2	8.1	8.9	9.9	8.7	10.5

Source: Cox *et al.* (1997).

Almost two-thirds of the staff thought that the main cause of staff stress was 'the nature of the job'. Some of the officers identified operational problems as being central to the levels of stress they experienced 'just trying to get the job done'.

> My job? Well, it depends what job you're on ... dealing with a thousand and one requests: private cash, visits, legal aid and all that. Between food and water, there are all these things to do. (Prison officer)

Almost half of the officers interviewed knew an officer who had committed suicide. A further 10 per cent knew officers who had attempted suicide. Others knew officers who had contemplated suicide, and one or two talked at length to the researchers about their own thoughts of suicide. Two officers related their own suicide attempts:

> I know two that's actually done it, and three or four what's either been unsuccessful or who've contemplated it. One, young lad, was domestic. One was partly work related. You never know, had they been in a manual job they may have been able to cope with their difficulties better than being in a stress job. I realised that after being off for two months myself. When I got rid of it all and thought, you can see why people get fed up. You don't realise it until you've been away from it for a long time. (Prison officer)

Officers talked about feeling isolated and unsupported at these times. Staff care teams exist in all prisons and there is a national Staff Care and Welfare Service (SCWS), which deals with problems relating to transfers, physical illness, stress, conditions of service, debt, disciplinary matters and career matters (including medical retirements). SCWS also carries out critical incident debriefs (47 arranged in 2006–7) and refers staff to external counselling (151 in 2006–7). Staff sometimes express reluctance to use these services, either for cultural reasons (it is not considered acceptable to show weakness and ask for help) or because they are regarded as 'in-house' services and staff have concerns about the consequences of appearing weak (see, further, Crawley 2001).

In recent years, an additional source of stress to many staff has been the privatisation and market testing of prisons. The threat of regularly 'market testing' some prisons, of the possibility of job loss or of changing employer, and the use of the existence of private sector prisons as a management 'tool' (see James *et al.* 1997: 102) have all had (and continue to have) significant repercussions upon prison officers and on establishments (see, for example, Liebling *et al.* 2001; Elliott *et al.* 2001). The performance culture both enhances the standard of prison officer work and raises the stakes. There are, of course, stresses for managers facing staffing (that is, detailing) difficulties caused by shortages of staff, high staff turnover, high numbers of inexperienced staff and (perhaps more controversially) the effects of frequent sickness absence. If prison officers have received little academic attention, their managers have received less.[2]

Research carried out by Wright and colleagues in the US has shown that autonomy (having some control over the work process) and participation in decision-making led to greater job satisfaction, fewer stress symptoms, greater organisational identification and commitment, lower turnover among prison officers and greater efficacy in working with prisoners (Wright *et al.* 1997; also Stohr *et al.* 1994). They argue that research is needed to establish whether more discretion and freedom in decision-making among correctional staff has organisational benefits (such as lower assault rates) or organisational risks (higher assault rates).

Assaults

Figure 4.1 shows the rate of assault on an officer or other staff member at selected groups of prisons for 1996 (the last year that Prison Disciplinary Statistics were published separately). The figure is for the number of assaults on staff for which a guilty verdict was given at an adjudication hearing and is shown per hundred of the prisoner population (so, for example, in local prisons there were 5.6 assaults on officers or staff members per hundred of the prisoner population for which prisoners were found guilty at an adjudication). It is not strictly possible to read the figure as an indication of the risk of assault for staff working in each kind of prison. First, not all assaults may be reported, and the reporting rate may be higher in some prisons than in others (in tightly managed dispersals, for example). Second, officer : prisoner ratios differ from prison to prison (as we saw in Chapter 2), so there may be more staff around to be assaulted in some establishments. Third, the definition of what constitutes an 'assault' may be different within different prisons or according to different officers. However, the figure does give a broad idea as to the varying

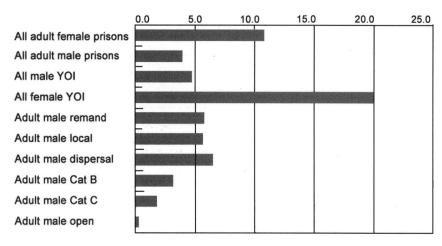

Source: Home Office (1997).

Figure 4.1 Assaults on prison staff per hundred of the prisoner population, 1996

levels of assault rate in the different kinds of prison. Table 4.2 gives more recent figures for serious assaults on staff by prison type and per member of staff (2006–7). What is perhaps surprising (but also consistent) is the high assault rate in female local prisons compared with most male establishments. This may be related in part to the measurement issues mentioned above, but shows that violence and assault are features of almost any prison (see Mandaraka-Sheppard 1986). Table 4.3 shows prison assault rates over time including general and serious assaults on staff. The table shows some increase.

There are numerous studies of assault rates in prison. Many of these are concerned with prisoner-on-prisoner assault rather than prisoner-on-staff assault. Broadly, it is possible to conclude that both social factors (the particular prisoner or prison officer involved) and situational factors (for example, the design of the prison wing, the time of day or levels of overcrowding) have parts to play in determining assault rates in general. YOIs have traditionally had very high assault rates (the younger the prisoners, the higher the rates, on the whole), which is attributable in part to the impulsiveness of young prisoners and the different relationship staff may have with them. It is interesting to note that within these overall high levels, some YOIs will have relatively low assault rates.

In his thorough statistical study of assaults on staff in male closed establishments in England and Wales, Ditchfield (1997) found that

Table 4.2 Assaults on prison officers, 2008

Function	Serious assaults on staff	Average unified staff	Proportion of assaults per unified staff member
Category B	1	1,300	0.08%
Category C	29	6,448	0.45%
Dispersal	7	2,402	0.29%
Female closed	1	368	0.27%
Female local	6	1,032	0.58%
Female open	0	57	0.00%
Male closed YOI	38	3,115	1.22%
Male juvenile	3	685	0.44%
Male local	45	9,525	0.47%
Male open	0	537	0.00%
Male open YOI	0	125	0.00%
Semi open	1	532	0.19%
Grand total	**131**	**26,126**	**0.50%**
Annualised	**175**	**26,126**	**0.67%**

the age of prison officers emerged as the most important predictor variable – that is, the older the prison officer, the less the likelihood of assault. Ditchfield observed the sharp increase in the rate of staff assaults by prisoners between 1989 and 1993 in England and Wales and attempted to correlate this rise with many different variables over the same period (staff age, prisoner age, type of offender, ethnic group, remand/sentence status). Only staff age changed to any great extent during the period. As we saw in Chapter 2, the distribution of staff ages changed quite considerably over this period, after the influence of Fresh Start. Only 16.6 per cent of officers (2,485 of 14,990) were under 30 in 1989, but 28.1 per cent of officers (6,284 of 22,431) were under 30 in 1993. The population has fallen back to 16 per cent in 2006, as the large numbers of officers recruited in the 1990s begin to move into the 30–45 year age group (see Chapter 2).

Ditchfield notes that it is probably better to speak of an 'age/ experience factor' rather than an age variable. This would comprise such things as maturity, length of previous experience, a lesser need to be aggressive, 'the fact that social skills tend to improve with age (as in all walks of life)' (Ditchfield 1997: 1), and so on. Ditchfield also notes that other changes brought about by Fresh Start – most notably the buying out of overtime which means that officers are no longer

Table 4.3 Prison assaults* summary statistics (England and Wales)**

	2000*	2001*	2002*	2003*	2004*	2005	2006	2007	2008
Population									
Males and females	*64,602*	*66,301*	*70,778*	*73,038*	*74,657*	*75,979*	*78,127*	*80,216*	*82,572*
Males	61,252	62,561	66,479	68,613	70,209	71,512	73,680	75,842	78,158
Females	3,350	3,740	4,299	4,425	4,448	4,467	4,447	4,374	4,414
Assault incidents									
Male and female establishments	*9,423*	*10,695*	*11,515*	*11,835*	*12,558*	*14,406*	*15,054*	*15,231*	*15,847*
Male establishments	8,865	10,061	10,773	11,032	11,702	13,317	13,893	14,227	14,942
Female establishments	558	634	742	803	856	1,089	1,161	1,004	905
Three-year rolling average assault incidents per 1,000 prisoners									
Male and female establishments	–	–	*156.62*	*162.01*	*164.31*	*173.28*	*183.50*	*190.72*	*191.49*
Male establishments	–	–	155.87	161.22	163.17	171.23	180.48	187.46	189.11
Female establishments	–	–	169.56	174.53	182.17	205.90	232.44	244.80	231.88
Three-year rolling average assault incidents per 100,000 prisoners									
Male and female establishments	–	–	*15,662*	*16,201*	*16,431*	*17,328*	*18,350*	*19,072*	*19,149*
Male establishments	–	–	15,587	16,122	16,317	17,123	18,048	18,746	18,911
Female establishments	–	–	16,956	17,453	18,217	20,590	23,244	24,480	23,188
Serious assaults									
Male and female establishments	*792*	*795*	*953*	*1,156*	*1,217*	*1,371*	*1,403*	*1,484*	*1,481*
Male establishments	745	755	914	1,091	1,134	1,305	1,344	1,434	1,438
Female establishments	47	40	39	65	83	66	59	50	43

Assaults on staff

Male and female establishments	2,189	2,694	2,843	2,884	3,194	3,500	3,529	3,267	3,198
Male establishments	1,941	2,406	2,545	2,585	2,887	3,065	3,006	2,857	2,846
Female establishments	248	288	298	299	307	435	523	410	352

Serious assaults on staff

Males and females	172	181	196	266	272	300	280	284	283
Male establishments	160	169	188	246	246	278	255	265	264
Female establishments	12	12	8	20	26	22	25	19	19

* Prison violence can be measured in a number of ways. This table focuses on assault incidents including fights. A new Key Performance Indicator for serious assaults was introduced in 2003/4 and as a result reporting of all assault incidents improved. Reported incidents before 2005 are therefore not directly comparable with later figures. In particular, although figures for 2000 to 2002 have been included they are under-reported by modern standards. It is now expected that all assaults, including fights, should be reported whether or not there was an injury. As this was not the case in the past care needs to be taken when interpreting changes over the years.

In prisons, as in the community, it is not possible to count assault incidents with absolute accuracy. In prison custody, however, such incidents are more likely to be detected and counted. Care needs to be taken when comparing figures shown here with other sources where data may be less complete.

** *Data sources and quality.* These figures have been drawn from administrative IT systems. Care is taken when processing and analysing returns but the detail is subject to the inaccuracies inherent in any large-scale recording system. Although shown to the last case, the figures may not be accurate to that level.

present at the prison for as long, making relationships more difficult to establish and maintain – may be responsible for the rise in assaults. The introduction of integral sanitation may have (paradoxically) resulted in less prisoner–officer contact. Longer hours out of cell may have increased opportunities for assaults to occur. Ditchfield's work supports earlier research by Davies and Burgess (1988) in a local prison, and by Rasmussen and Levander (1996) in Norway. Each study found less experienced officers at a higher risk of assault.

Chapter 2 showed that the distribution of prison officers shifted in recent years, first towards a larger proportion of slightly older and more experienced officers and then toward a younger age-group. At the same time, assault rates have fallen and then risen somewhat. It is possible that, among other things, this changing structure of age and experience among prison officers might be able to explain both the drop and the rise in assaults.

More qualitative explorations of assault lend credence to this idea. For example, Fleisher's (1989) research at USP Lompoc in California led to this observation:

> A Lompoc staffer's only offensive or defensive 'weapon' is his ability to elude trouble with talk. A skilled staff-talker can usually get himself, other staffers, or prisoners out of a 'tight spot'. The mark of a good staff-talker is getting a prisoner, even an aggressive one, to do as the staffer wishes. An inexperienced staff-talker or an overly aggressive one might find one or both of his eyes swelling and turning black. (Fleisher 1989: 174)

Assault is an ever-present risk to staff who work with prisoners. As the next chapter will show, the potential threat of physical harm to prison officers by prisoners provides some of the 'energy' for prison officer culture.

The role of female staff in male prisons

The introduction of female officers into male prisons (and of male officers into female prisons) is one of the moves that has been made to help 'normalise' the prison environment. Most of the research exploring the introduction of female officers into male prisons considers integration problems between colleagues, that is the problems female officers face working within a masculine subculture found among male prison officers. Very few studies have considered the impact of female staff on prisoners or on the prison environment, or the relevance of female officer integration to shaping the meaning of prison work (but see Tait 2008a and Crewe 2006). Those that have looked at the impact on the prison find beneficial effects of increased female staff on assault rates, suicide rates and staff–prisoner relationships (e.g. Rowan 1996).[3]

Studies of female entry into male prisons have been carried out principally in the US, Australia and the UK – those jurisdictions which have most recently legislated against sex discrimination. Perhaps the most important and consistent finding is that there are more similarities between male and female officers in the way they carry out their work and in the attitudes towards and expectations of the job than there are differences (see, for example, Wright and Saylor 1991). The main differences found between male and female officers is that there is a lower incidence of marriage and dependent children among female officers and a higher level of education. Male officers are more likely to have a trade or technical qualification (Enterkin 1996). There are assumptions (supported by evidence from US studies) that the introduction of female staff into male prisons has a 'calming effect' – that is, the introduction of female staff reduces the incidence of violence. Assault rates are found to drop against both female and male officers in those prisons achieving at least a quarter of female staff in their establishments (Rowan 1996). This is thought to be due to differences in styles of interaction, based on women's greater interpersonal skills, their avoidance of confrontation or resort to force, and the 'protectiveness' of men.

Female staff use adjudication procedures as frequently as male officers, suggesting that they are not being unduly lenient (Rowan 1996). It is difficult to determine how far stereotypes of male and female officer behaviours are reflected in reality – as prisoners (and staff) tend to judge each individual staff member regardless of sex when asked; they discriminate within the sexes.

Studies carried out in the US and Australia show that the introduction of female staff into male prisons created some resistance from some male staff due to the perceived emotional and physical vulnerability of female officers to male prisoners, and the privacy and decency requirements associated with strip searching. A key reservation shared by many male officers is the need for reliable physical back-up in times of violence. Female officers are sometimes thought to confuse already dangerous situations by evoking 'protective' instincts from their male colleagues in situations which require guaranteed solidarity:

> Oh shit, I've got three males and one female. That means that I'm two down because it means someone has to watch out for you. (Officer, cited in Farnworth 1992: 290)

Fears expressed by male officers about female officers being sexually assaulted can serve as both an expression of concern and a mode of intimidation. Male officers have been found to resent perceived positive discrimination in favour of women promotionally, or to believe that women can use their sexuality to achieve favoured treatment (Farnworth 1992: 288).

Several studies have investigated the early (perceived) difficulties of female staff integration (Crouch and Alpert 1982; Enterkin 1996; Stohr *et al.* 1996; Pogrebin and Poole 1997). One of the most interesting issues arising out of studies seems to be the question of whether the work of prison officers is 'really a man's job'. Female officers in non-UK studies report harassment, gossip, set-ups and exclusion from 'acceptable male social behaviour' of 'going to the pub to unwind after a stressful day' (Farnworth 1992: 292) because of the likely consequences. Female officers who dealt effectively with the sexist behaviour of their male colleagues had to be confident and secure in their approach and be capable of answering back. They needed to 'maintain their dignity without losing the support of male officers'. Recent expansion of the traditional role and changing perceptions of appropriate prison officer behaviour together with the growing acceptance of the presence of female staff, the evidence of clear benefits and long-standing experience in other countries (for example, Sweden and Denmark) suggest that some of the 'trademarks of prison work' must include good interpersonal skills, dealing with prisoners on a personal basis, resolving conflict without resort to violence, etc. Few problems appear to emerge in relation to female officers working with prisoners and many notable benefits have been found.

Prisoners are generally positive about the presence of female officers (Liebling and Price 1999). They are seen as bringing a 'human touch' to prison, and are sometimes felt to be easier to talk to than male officers. They are also felt to 'slow the macho bit down on the male officers' (Prisoner).

However, some long-serving male officers see female officers as bringing some difficulties:

> I can't understand what they get out of it, working in a male establishment. I certainly wouldn't want to work at Holloway.

It's basically male oriented here – 500 odd male prisoners. But the initial reaction to female staff at Frankland was that we had to watch their backs as well as our own! The narrow corridors, very dark and dingy – it wasn't a good environment. There was always a chance that a female would get dragged in a cell or in the showers. There are some who have done very well, and who are good staff and I do enjoy working with some of them. They are good officers, you can forget that they're females. But when you see a pretty little thing trotting in at 21 years old who wants to be a prison officer for the next thirty-nine years? – I don't think so … (Officer)

The worries most often expressed about female officers are about boundaries rather than about physical safety. Some female staff feel safer in prison than male officers (although not all do). Prisoners were generally cautious:

If you do talk to a member of staff – especially to a female – there's a hundred eyes on you. Attractive women seen talking to prisoners – they will stop it – they are that paranoid. If an officer and a con form a relationship of any sort. They are so afraid of scandal. It does happen. (Prisoner)

Female staff were just as aware as male officers of the dangers of the wrong kind of relationship with prisoners:

Are you aware of having learnt ways of dealing with prisoners? (Interviewer)

Yeah – a lot of prisoners will say something because they're trying to wind you up. Especially when I first joined, being a female you got the odd comment and stuff. And if you bit back, that's what they wanted. (Officer)

What sort of things would they say?

Just silly remarks – I was only 21 when I joined so there would be things like 'Oh, does your mum know you're out? Have you got a curfew?' And then it would be 'alright darlin', what's a girl like you doing in a place like this?' But you just don't bite to it.

So how do you handle them now if they say something?

It depends. You get a few, but it's mainly all done in jest. If they're like 'oh, you'll be all right,' and constantly go on, you just warn them that these keys and these epaulettes show you that I'm in charge, not you. But I don't take offence. I don't believe it, either. (Officer)

Some prisoners talked of finding the experience of talking to any woman without 'the complications of sex' was actually a new and valuable experience. The extra 'risk factor' of being female appeared to heighten awareness among female staff of the need for strict boundaries, of the need for a line over which prisoners could not go.

Some prisoners (and staff) suspected that female staff were deployed tactically to disarm prisoners – and felt (often from experience) that women could be as effective as men in control and restraint teams. The majority of staff, prisoners and senior managers, felt that the deployment of female staff in male prisons was a successful and normalising feature of the prison.

Exploring diversity: role differences in England and abroad

Prison officers who work in Young Offenders Institutions may differ in several respects from staff in adult and/or local prisons. Many of the officers interviewed expressed a preference for working with young prisoners, commenting that there was more 'hope' with the youngsters, that they were still amenable to change. (Liebling 1992: 196)

One of the interesting outcomes of a day discussion with staff from several types of establishment about their role was the consensus expressed among staff that the essential role of the prison officer was the same. Different situations may require a particular blend of skills, but it was impossible to generalise about one type of establishment next to another. 'Having bottle' (confidence), patience, flexibility, a sense of humour and the ability to be decisive even in 'grey areas' were felt to be key attributes, whatever type of establishment officers worked in. Officers who worked in women's prisons expressed the same need for patience, fairness and diplomacy as officers working in local prisons, with young prisoners or in training prisons. The ability to 'not bear a grudge' was a key survival trait (Wilson 2000).

Some women prisoners demanded higher levels of support. Long-term adult males expected efficient 'service delivery'. Juveniles needed 'significant others' who modelled boundaries and who could liaise effectively with families. The tasks differed by degrees: officers in local prisons processed (received, discharged and classified) large numbers of short-stay, 'unknown' and known prisoners; officers in juvenile establishments did more casework, and came under new and complex legal pressures such as the Child Protection Act; officers in therapeutic communities had to keep a careful eye on boundaries. But the key skill of any officer was knowing how to read a million different situations and personalities accurately – and to draw on the right blend of skills for the moment.

Internationally, we are struck by the generally much longer periods of training required for officers (up to two years, for example, in Denmark and Norway, and one year under a mentor followed by three months' training in Slovenia). In the US, officers receive 160 days training when they begin their service, then 40 days 'annual sustainment training' after their first year (personal communication). Officers are required to take an examination every five years in Slovenia in order to continue in employment. There are lower and upper age limits in many jurisdictions (for example, an upper age limit of 37 in the US). There are many similarities between jurisdictions also – such as the type of 'statement of purpose' to which officers work.[4] Australian states have the most similar training and pay structure, ratio of staff to prisoners, statements of purpose and models of staff–prisoner relationships to those in England and Wales.[5] Queensland Department of Corrective Services, for example, has longer than average shifts (12 hours), but generous long-service leave provisions and regular six-day breaks following each six weeks' work (Rynne, 2007: personal communication).

The role of personal officers

Many prisons have personal officer schemes whereby named officers have special responsibility for a small number of prisoners (usually around 5–10 prisoners to each officer). Some schemes are more developed and formal than others, and the duties involved normally include interviewing, report writing, attendance at relevant review boards and generally getting to know the prisoner for 'welfare' purposes (in the old-fashioned language of the earliest schemes). Personal officers can 'help to influence a prisoner's future behaviour

77

by example and guidance' (*The Personal Officer*, booklet produced by HMP Risley 2000) and they tend to work more closely with the probation service (and other specialist and outside agencies). They have a formal and an informal role (providing 'casework on the hop') and are expected to encourage prisoners to engage in the regime and in activities on offer which may be of benefit to them. They provide a focal point for prisoners and a personal relationship through which constructive work can be developed and progress can be discussed. Sometimes they become involved in family matters, for example resolving family problems or mediating between prisoners and their families. Personal officer schemes do not always work well, either for practical reasons (personal officers do not work regularly enough in one area of the prison) or because prisoners and staff develop relationships with some individuals rather than named others. Where they do, it is often because of strong management (and staff) support for such a scheme, and a tradition of shared working with probation and other services. Personal officers can have a very significant role with, for example, life sentence prisoners and young prisoners, and in relation to particular aspects of prison life such as IEP boards. But, ideally, all prison officers should be 'personal officers'.

Conclusion: the role of the modern prison officer

> There is reason to believe that the correctional officer role is much more demanding, broad and rich than is generally believed ... Correctional staff are engaged in guiding, mentoring, facilitating, developing, and watching prisoners. If a prisoner needs assistance with a job, getting along with others, programming, interacting with staff, or obtaining privileges, then correctional officers are their more likely resource, given their proximity and frequency of contact. (Hemmens and Stohr 2000: 327)

We have tried to identify in this and the previous chapter some of the characteristics of role model officers and some essential features of the prison officer role. Prison officers are necessarily confident in action and in communication with others. They represent – and use – authority. Officers are more confident than they used to be at 'reaching for their pens' (see Liebling 1992). Much of their daily work involves the accomplishment of routines: unlocking, delivering meals, counting, moving, receiving, discharging, observing and locking up. We use the term accomplishing (rather than 'operating') the regime advisedly: officers achieve the routine, each day. Crucial to the 'smooth flow' of this routine is the 'regime'. This rests on the ability to talk, assist, steer and manage prisoners:

> Prison officers deal daily with prisoners' welfare – from providing them with their basic entitlements, through teaching them how to wash and dress, to saving their lives. This they do from the moment the prisoners wake up, throughout every part of their day, and to some extent, their night. With the assistance of various specialists within establishments, a prison officer's job is to 'look after' prisoners ... Custody, care and control ... are the key features of a prison officer's job. (Liebling 1992: 197)

Officers describe their best days as follows:

> The best day? So long as we have no friction. If we have some sense of achievement, where you've helped somebody ... job satisfaction. Ninety per cent of the problems here are solved by listening. You needn't take any action, as long as you listen, have a sympathetic ear, that's the great part of it. (Officer)

> When you unlock in the morning, lock up at night, no problems, no confrontations, we've had a bit of a laugh with each other, kept a reasonable atmosphere to the day and when I walk out of that gate, I'm not taking the job home. (Officer)

> Things are at their best when we can all communicate. (Officer)

> When I get a sense of achievement. One of my personal inmates, for instance, he's coming up for release in about eighteen months and he's been trying really hard to move on, get closer to home, but they won't accept him until he's done an anger management course and a relationships course, and there aren't any. But I've worked with him and with the wing psychologist and she's doing them one-to-one now. So that's good. He's really pleased with that, really thankful and grateful. And I feel like I'm glad that I've managed to wangle it for him, help him. Because obviously without these courses he's still going to get released but hopefully with these courses we won't see him again! (Officer)

Officers describe how casual conversations might lead to prisoners taking an Open University course, making a decision to change their behaviour or making a change in the nature of their relationship. They expressed pride in their ability to talk prisoners through unwelcome changes, bad news or an awkward moment:

> A good day ... it could be, if something's gone wrong and we've sorted it out correctly; on other days nothing at all might happen but that could be a really good day – we expected something to happen and it didn't. It's then a good day because it didn't happen. (Officer)

They liked to be busy, to face challenges, to solve problems and to be working with other officers who offered, 'yeah, I'll do that'.

Although it is impossible to arrive at one version of the 'good' prison officer it is possible to identify role model prison officers and some of the common characteristics that these officers share. They have 'bottle', or personal strength. They are resourceful, multi-skilled, loyal and proud. They can deal effectively, at their best, with challenging, unpredictable individuals who others have turned away.

Whatever the personality or role of any officer, they have had to adapt to greatly changing circumstances in the last decade or more. Official depictions of the role of imprisonment, and the role of the prison officer, have swung from Woolf's vision of prison officers delivering justice, fairness and respect, to the post-Woodcock/Learmont view of the officer as a tool of procedural security (and potentially a danger to his or her organisation), towards the more recent stress on balance and the achievement of positive, offending behaviour work with prisoners. But this type of work does not always place the officer at its centre (in the way we feel it should). These are important shifts which have occurred in quick succession. When asked, staff express a desire for more and better training on conflict avoidance, on how close to or distant they should be from prisoners, on how to resolve the apparently paradoxical need for consistency and flexibility (see Chapter 6) and on the management of difficult behaviour (see Hay and Sparks 1991; Liebling and Price 1999). Staff yearn for clearer recognition of these best aspects of their work. Staff 'wishes for their prison' vary according to each establishment's circumstances, role and style of leadership, but in general, staff wish for accessible, visible and strong management, a sense of purpose and direction (for individual areas of the prison as well as for the establishment as a whole) and, most often of all, a constructive role with prisoners. They want to be trusted and respected, and yet prefer to be closely (if 'appreciatively') managed, to high standards. They often feel undervalued and, most of all, unknown and sometimes stereotyped by their senior managers. While prison staff express considerable discomfort with modern management demands, prison officers also express exasperation with their minority 'underperforming' colleagues and want their establishments to be 'flagships', to be unique in some way or to excel at something in particular. They want to use and develop their skills, be valued as part of a team and to occupy a primarily public service role[6] with confidence and professional skill. Their greatest wish is to be fully involved and to make a difference (Liebling et al. 2001).

Notes

1 The main results from the research can be found in Liebling (1992), Liebling and Krarup (1993) and Liebling (1995). See also Harvey (2007).
2 The Key (the Prison Governors' Association magazine, January 2001) reported a 140 per cent rise in governor grade sickness.
3 Studies of sex differences using standardised personality tests indicate that women score more highly on scales of 'tendermindedness' and males sometimes score more highly on scores of 'assertiveness' (Stohr et al. 1996). Women are considered to be more 'relational', emotional and verbally skilled than men (Gilligan 1986). Interestingly, developments in the role of the prison officer towards a 'new interactional style' have resulted in a shifting profile of the desirable officer including more of the typically female methods of communication and interaction.
4 In Slovenia, officers must give the following pledge: 'I solemnly pledge that in the course of performing tasks of protection and supervision, I will carry out my tasks in a conscientious, responsible, humane and legal manner, and will respect human rights and basic freedoms'. In the US: 'It is the mission of the Federal Bureau of Prisons to protect society by confining offenders in the controlled environments of prisons and community-based facilities that are safe, humane, cost-efficient, and appropriately secure, and that provide work and other self-improvement opportunities to assist offenders in becoming law-abiding citizens'. In Queensland: 'Our purpose: community safety and crime prevention through humane containment, supervision and rehabilitation of offenders. Our vision: a world class corrective services system. Our organisational values: we value integrity (am I acting ethically and honestly in this matter?); learning (am I learning from what I am doing?); social responsibility (am I acting in the

best interests of the community?); and accountability (am I prepared to be held publicly accountable for this action?).'

5 The custodial recruit course in Tasmania runs full-time for seven weeks, with practical application and testing of skills during the first year of work. In Australian Capital Territory and South Australia the course runs for eight weeks. In Queensland it runs for nine.

6 As stated at the outset, we are conscious that we have not included a separate discussion of the role of prisoner custody officers in contracted-out or privately managed prisons. Some evidence suggests that there are important differences (see James *et al.* 1997; McLean and Liebling 2008) as well as some similarities. We are investigating them in ongoing research.

Chapter 5

Staff–prisoner relationships: the heart of prison work

It is difficult to define what corrections officers do, let alone assess how well they have done it. Nevertheless, it is clear that the direct work product that these officers produce is not security, control or safety but personal interactions between themselves and prisoners. The affective nature of these interactions directly influences the level of tension between officers and prisoners and indirectly influences the safety, security and control within the prison. (Gilbert 1997: 53)

In the control of prisoners, officers shall seek to influence them through their own example and leadership, and to enlist their willing co-operation. (Prison Rule 6(2))

At the end of the day, nothing else that we can say will be as important as the general proposition that relations between staff and prisoners are at the heart of the whole prison system and that control and security flow from getting that relationship right. Prisons cannot be run by coercion: they depend on staff having a firm, confident and humane approach that enables them to maintain close contact with prisoners without abrasive confrontation. (Home Office 1984: para. 16)

It is a well-established maxim that staff–prisoner relationships matter. The impact of staff–prisoner relationships and of staff behaviour more generally on the quality of a regime is crucial:

> Whatever statements of the policy may promise, it is the local staff who are ultimately responsible for putting policy into effect. Introducing changes in programme activity may be an essential first step in changing the nature of a regime but the way in which staff supervise new activities will be a major determinant of the trainee's [sic] experience. (Thornton et al. 1984: para. 3.3)

In his review of prison regimes, HM Chief Inspector of Prisons, Judge Tumim found that:

> the prison officer needs to be skilled in specific areas of prison work, and there is considerable job satisfaction to be gained from this. One of the problems facing prison staff over the years has been a lack of clear job specifications or an appreciation of the skills needed for prison work ... Despite the development of management techniques which emphasise the diversity of prison work, we found few examples of prison staff working flexibly or with a high expectation of the job. (HMCIP 1993a: paras 8.2(1) and 8.7)

Despite the centrality of staff–prisoner relationships to the running of prisons (Home Office 1984; Sparks et al. 1996), few satisfactory analyses of the nature of the staff–prisoner relationship have been conducted.[1] There has been wide recognition of the significance of staff–prisoner relationships to order (see, for example, Home Office 1984; Ditchfield 1990; Sparks et al. 1996), to justice (Home Office 1991), to security (Home Office 1995) and to constructive regimes (Dunbar 1985). However, it is likely that different models of the staff–prisoner relationship are implicit in these different visions. A lack of clarity about what the 'right' relationship might be and how this might be achieved has become particularly evident in the light of recent reports exposing the dangers of conditioning, the under-enforcement of rules relating to security and the effects of under-management on staff behaviour (see, for example, Home Office 1994, 1995). Staff–prisoner relationships can go wrong in several different ways – they can be too close, too flexible, too distant and too rigid (see Sparks et al. 1996). As Lucas demonstrates in relation to justice (Lucas 1980), it is easier to identify wrong relationships (injustice) than to specify right relationships (justice). There is a need for clearer thinking about what 'a right relationship' is.

The term relationship can mean 'alliance', 'association', 'connection' or 'dependence'. There is a flow of interaction and dependence in two directions (e.g. see Shapira and Navon 1985), although, in the coercive environment of a prison, relationships are invested with an unusual amount of power (the ability of one party to influence or determine the behaviour of another party). This power is 'held in reserve' most of the time, so that day-to-day interactions take place without explicit reference to it, but both staff and prisoners are aware of who has how much power and prisoners may try to challenge it, overturn it or keep it to a minimum. Because of the power-laden nature of interactions in a prison, both staff and prisoners are sometimes uncomfortable with the word 'relationship'. When we use the word 'relationships' in the prison context, we mean how staff relate during sustained periods of interaction, including interaction of a non-rule-enforcing – or rule-resisting – nature. Relationships are made up of social practices, of some rule-enforcing and many non-rule-enforcing encounters. In a prison, these social practices exist around the 'tasks' of the prison day – and 'relationships' can develop as a result. This distinguishes them from family relationships where power flows between members but within a much more affectual context and the relationship has an independent value, or from social relationships, where interaction is more voluntary, or from work where power also flows but less overtly and relationships evolve and may merge into friendship. We considered using the term 'relations' (which has a slightly more restricted meaning – interaction around a task). In general, however, we concluded that only the word 'relationship' could adequately describe what we have observed. The dimensions of the term staff and prisoners are sensitive to are its associations with voluntariness and with families. We agree that there are important limits to 'relationships' in prison and we shall discuss them later in this chapter. But in the end, we have found no satisfactory alternative to the word.

In general, perceptions of staff–prisoner relationships are often quite favourable in prisons in England and Wales (see White *et al.* 1991; Relationships Foundation 1995; Liebling *et al.* 1997). They are generally characterised – and contrasted with relationships between staff and prisoners in some other jurisdictions – by relatively high levels of respect, relaxation and good humour. It is part of the 'British tradition' that relationships between staff and prisoners provide the glue which hold prisons together. These are commonly held perceptions, with the proviso that serious complaints are sometimes voiced by individual prisoners relating to staff attitudes or behaviour in particular establishments. So within this overall picture, there may be significant variations between types of establishment and between individual establishments in relation to the kind of relationships which exist. Flexibility on rule enforcement is one important dimension on which relationships can differ (as argued in Chapter 6) but other variations are closeness and distance, staff confidence and mutual trust, which may be related to rule enforcement.

Goffman describes an 'involvement cycle' whereby staff move from distance to 'warm interest' to being 'burnt' and to 'retreat'. Once removed from the dangers of contact, the cycle begins again. There are special difficulties in handling this cycle when the population concerned is capable of behaving destructively towards themselves as well as towards staff. There are awkward reverberations if involvement transgresses certain boundaries – reverberations almost as powerful as 'the incest taboo' (Goffman 1961: 75).

The job of being a prison officer is carried out in 'a special moral climate', in which staff are faced with 'hostility and demands', and yet are expected to meet the prisoner 'from a rational perspective'. How is this achieved? Clarification of this complex feature of prison work can only be achieved through detailed and long-term studies of the nature of staff–prisoner relationships in a number of establishments. We have carried out one such study (Liebling and Price 1999) and a detailed review of the literature (Price and Liebling 1998), and will draw on these and other sources here.

Key questions, which we address as far as we can in this chapter, are:

1 What is the nature of staff–prisoner relationships? Is it possible to describe them accurately and to explain the various models of staff–prisoner relationships identified in different establishments? What accounts for the existence of these differences? Are there models of good practice? What fosters and what undermines 'right' relationships? How, and to what extent, do relationships hold prisons together? How and why do staff–prisoner relationships (relationships involving considerable dynamics of power) become dysfunctional?

2 What are the roles of 'trust', 'respect' and 'fairness' between staff and prisoners, and between staff and management, in the special environment of a prison?[2]

We have not answered all of these questions fully, but we consider them an important framework through which to think about available, ongoing and future research.

Striving for 'right relationships'

To answer questions about what 'right relationships' are and what drives them, we need to be able to describe their nature. What is required and what is possible may differ substantially between different types of establishments and over time. Certain common themes emerge, however. Among the 'ingredients' necessary to positive regimes and relationships are: staff empowerment, high morale, the existence of clear aims, 'a proper induction for staff in order to inculcate them in the values of the establishment', high expectations and the presumption of an 'active role' to be played by staff in the life of the prison (e.g. Deighton and Launay 1993). At one establishment, praised for its outstanding staff–prisoner relationships, 'staff were encouraged to use as much discretion as possible in the way they worked. Thus many chose not to wear uniform and rarely resorted to formal disciplinary procedures' (Deighton and Launay 1993). The Inspectorate found high morale, good teamwork, positive staff attitudes towards prisoners (and vice versa) and an unusually high level of discretion used by staff, with very few complaints. They found that 'prisoners dropped their defensive barriers' and that 'this presented opportunities for positive work' (HMCIP, 1993b: 49; see also Cooke 1989 and 1991).

The question of how far 'liberal' staff–prisoner relationships are acceptable or advisable in the special environment of any prison – particularly since the security lapses of the mid-1990s – needs careful consideration. Are good staff–prisoner relationships intended to secure order, control and compliance, or are they linked to other aims such as tackling offending behaviour? How real are the conflicts between officers' 'welfare' and security tasks? As we saw in Chapters 3 and 4, officers have three essential tasks: security, rehabilitation (or tackling offending behaviour) and care, and 'getting through the daily routine'. All three overlap and support each other.

In 1970, Emery published a review of the impact of the so-called 'Norwich Experiment' on the local prison at Bristol (Emery 1970). Before the introduction of the altered regime, Bristol prison had the highest rate of reported prisoner offences of all local prisons (Emery 1970: 22). Not only did the prison suffer greatly from overcrowding, but its staff were divided (Emery 1970: 33–4). The Norwich Experiment, developed in the 1950s, relied heavily on building a closer relationship between staff and prisoners. More association, improved prisoner–staff relationships and more work were all central to the scheme (Emery 1970: ix). By keeping the boundary between prisoners and staff clear, through a clearly articulated system of punishments and rewards, the experiment aimed to reduce the divisive sense of unfairness that arose from the use of staff discretion (Emery 1970: 12).

Despite initial staff resistance to an increase in their hours due to the growth of time that prisoners were allowed to spend out of their cells, and despite some resistance from a minority of prisoners to greater amounts of association, both sides ultimately came to value the changes in the previously restrictive regime. Increased association reduced tension, and reduced the symbolic and actual centrality of staff to prisoners:

> With this went a significant decline in prisoner hostility to officers, a lessening of mutual distrust, and the virtual disappearance of the schism in the officer ranks between 'activists' and 'passengers'. (Emery 1970: 91)

As Emery shows, however, the question of how involved it is advisable to ask staff to become is complex. Genders and Player's review of the therapeutic regime in operation at Grendon illustrates the significance of 'close' and 'treatment-oriented' staff–prisoner interactions (Genders and Player 1995). The staff play a significant role in Grendon's aim to have 'no more victims'. On an unannounced short visit to the prison Judge Tumim was particularly impressed by the variety and scope of problem-solving and conflict resolution (HMCIP 1993c). Despite all the positive findings of Inspectorate Reports, there is a tension between Grendon's dual role as a therapeutic community and a prison (Genders and Player 1995: 96–8). As Genders and Player explain:

> Grendon's primary identity is that of a prison and, as such, it is subject to the same formal rules as the rest of the system. In consequence, whatever level of co-operation the prison extends to the therapeutic community, it must reserve the right to step in and seize control whenever the security and discipline of the establishment is perceived to be under threat. Thus, within the communities, the staff team, amongst whom the uniformed officers form the majority, retain the ultimate authority to make or revoke decisions in the name of the prison. (Genders and Player 1995: 97)

In order for the balance between prison and therapeutic community to be maintained along with order and control, Grendon is almost entirely dependent upon the degree to which the officers and prisoners are able to modify their traditional prison roles, in order to break-down the social divide between the 'keepers' and the 'kept' and to facilitate co-operative relationships and alternative working practices. (Genders and Player 1995: 98)

According to Genders and Player, the staff–prisoner relationships in Grendon 'tended to be characterised by three specific qualities: individualism, permissiveness and trust' (Genders and Player 1995: 98). Furthermore, relations within the staff community were different from other prisons as

there was a flattening of the formal staff hierarchy, a bridging of the usual divide between the civilian and uniformed groups, and an emphasis upon democratic teamwork. (Genders and Player 1995: 99)

The ideology of treatment within Grendon has a significant impact on the mode of maintaining discipline and control. Despite the underlying fact that persistent non-cooperation is not tolerated, Genders and Player reported a different approach to many forms of prisoner behaviour which in other prisons would normally result in adjudications. That is

[a] key feature of staff working practices at Grendon is the high level of tolerance which officers extend toward behaviour which their formal training in prison discipline requires them to define as insubordination. The use of abusive language to an officer and the refusal to obey an order are amongst the most common disciplinary charges recorded against prisoners in other prisons. Yet at Grendon such behaviour rarely results in formal proceedings … alternative means of controlling it are used. In essence, officers are expected to exercise control through therapeutic means and to interpret such behaviour as the manifestation of a man's problems and thus, as material for discussion rather than as an offence requiring a formal hearing. (Genders and Player 1995: 101)

Although Genders and Player reported that almost all of the staff they interviewed (94 per cent) thought that, in some respects, working at Grendon was more difficult than working elsewhere, 'more than three-quarters of the officers stated that they found their work at

Grendon to be rewarding and fulfilling' (Genders and Player 1995: 102).

Hay and Sparks comment at some length on the nature of staff–prisoner relationships in their study of control problems in dispersal prisons. They note that:

> Much of prison officers' activity is taken up in talking to prisoners and coping with the contingencies of daily events ... the question of approach to prisoners is open to particular disagreements about the appropriateness of different kinds of relationship and practice. Views on this issue vary in respect of the degree of closeness or distance which is right for staff to adopt vis à vis prisoners and on problems of flexibility vs. consistency. This, in turn, varies in relation to the kind of regime which they are expected to run, and hence the particular demands which the managerial philosophy of the prison makes upon them. (Hay and Sparks 1991: 83–4)

Hay and Sparks argue that these issues are 'very much a matter of concern and debate among staff'. Prisoners also express concern about 'boundaries' and knowing where they are. The 'key issue' of staff–prisoner relationships is highly significant and complex.

In studies of small units, it is noted that staff continuity (including continuity of governor grades and an effective and integrated management team) and personal officer schemes are identified as two of the key components in securing 'right relationships' (Home Office 1987: para. 52; see also Bottomley 1994: 35). Lack of continuity leads to 'low morale', a poor 'sense of cohesion and purpose' and 'poor communication' (Bottomley 1994: 34). It makes personal officer schemes unworkable (McAllister *et al.* 1992; Bottomley 1994) and creates undue pressures for staff.

A good personal officer scheme can be 'one of the best means to achieve close staff involvement with prisoners' (Home Office 1987: para. 52) and could potentially be 'the lynch pin of a successful policy of control and containment' and also 'facilitate behavioural change in prisoners' (Bottomley 1994: 35). Evershed and Fry concluded that the personal officer scheme was 'possibly the most important aspect of the (Parkhurst) unit's regime' (Evershed and Fry 1991: 31). Martin argued, in his evaluation of Parkhurst Special Unit, that the personal officer scheme 'undoubtedly enhanced the role of the officers' but that it was at the time of his research being 'jeopardised by too rapid moves of staff' (Martin 1991: 130; see also Needs 1993: 11).

One of the main aims of the (now defunct) Control Review Committee (CRC) special units was 'for staff to attempt to reduce the level of unacceptable behaviour in prisoners by employing their skills as prison officers' (Bottomley 1994: 22 describing Parkhurst). A 'high degree of staff involvement' was seen as one of the key ways in which prisoners' behaviour could be managed and where necessary, challenged. High staff morale and commitment facilitated by continuity and training was seen as vital (Bottomley 1994: 26). An important principle was allowing staff to 'volunteer' for specialist posts. It may also be important to offer incentives for staff to get to know (particular groups of) prisoners well and to feed into any review system (Bottomley 1994: 37). Needs commented in his review of the operation of the Hull Special Unit that:

> There has been much constructive, and some outstanding, work by involved individuals who bring to bear a down-to-earth good sense combined with skill at communicating. There are others who are less involved, to the frustration of their colleagues who must shoulder more than their fair share of the burden of demands. (Needs 1993: 11, cited in Bottomley 1994: 38)

Similar conclusions were drawn from evaluations of the Close Supervision Centres which replaced the CRC small units (see, for example, Clare and Bottomley 2001).

Staff–prisoner relationships in general are likely to be the key determinant of the success or failure of any policy. In an evaluation of the Hollesley Bay structured incentives regime carried out in 1967, it was found that the experiment was partially sabotaged by staff on one of the 'control' houses surreptitiously introducing an incentives system with review boards and enhanced facilities in order to compete with the 'experimental' houses. Staff eagerness to be 'the best' made it impossible for them to 'hold back' on schemes which appeared to have a positive impact on prisoner behaviour (Williams, 1999, personal communication). This shows a commitment to 'achieving results' which is one of the Service's greatest strengths. Staff are the vital medium through which such a scheme can operate. Staff frequently become committed to 'their' wing or unit, wanting their area of the prison to function smoothly and without confrontation.

In Joe Pilling's influential lecture, *Back to Basics: Relationships in the Prison Service*, Pilling, a former Director General of the Prison Service, identified the high standards and expectations characteristic of 'the finest Borstal tradition of care for and belief in the individual and his potential' (Pilling 1992: 2). He reminded the Service that the basic tenets of good relationships between prisoners and staff are about 'knowing, respecting and caring for prisoners as individuals' (Pilling 1992; see also Dunbar 1985). He argues

> a well ordered and safe environment is still characterised by open, relaxed relationships of mutual respect between staff and prisoners. (Pilling 1992: 3)

This 'tradition' faced a loss of confidence at the time of the escapes from Whitemoor and Parkhurst in 1994 and 1995 (although arguably one of the reasons the escapes occurred was precisely the absence of such relationships). One learning point for the Service has been that the (vague) term 'good' may be better replaced by the term 'right' relationships. Pilling's five key concepts of respect, fairness, individuality, care and openness should still underlie all that the Service aims to achieve. This, Pilling goes on to show, depends upon the ability of staff of all grades to 'work with' prisoners, allowing them to participate in decisions about their personal development while in custody. Staff should be empowered, valued, trained, supported and encouraged – and the Service should 'recognise and reward those values' in its promotion procedures and in other ways. 'Good relationships can be preserved in spite of the inevitable frictions of prison life' (Pilling 1992: 10) and this is as relevant to staff–staff and staff–management relationships as it is to staff–prisoner relationships.

Our own study at Whitemoor was intended to 'fill the conceptual gap' left by previous research on staff–prisoner relationships and to provide clearer thinking about what 'right relationships' might be. In the remainder of this chapter, we try to explore why staff–prisoner relationships are so important to prison life and what this tells us about the nature of prison work.

There were certain key questions that we wanted to answer, such as what was the quality of staff–prisoner relationships? What did officers and prisoners want from these relationships? Could the quality of staff–prisoner relationships be measured and improved? Key performance indicators (KPIs) do not measure 'intangibles' such as the quality of staff–prisoner relationships, the usefulness of activities provided or the social climate of an establishment, which are much harder to translate into service delivery objectives for staff to follow.[3] Are there ways in which staff can be motivated and encouraged to work constructively with prisoners and with management to secure the delivery of 'positive and just regimes'?[4] Are there different kinds of officers, and are variables such as length of service, age, experience, etc. of major significance (as indicated by research on assaults on staff: see, for example, Sparks *et al.* 1996: 234; Ditchfield 1997)?

In general, we found that staff–prisoner relationships at Whitemoor at the time of our study were good and, considering the frictions of prison life, they were quite close. Most prisoners felt that 90–95 per cent of their interactions with officers were civil and polite, although it was notable that officers generally had a more positive view of relationships on their wing than prisoners did. Relationships operated within fairly clear frameworks of expectation. Staff wanted compliance and acceptance of their authority. Prisoners wanted to experience themselves as agents, as individuals, and to resist 'indifferent' or overbearing forms of coercion. The flow of power was negotiated in this space: only legitimate power generated the sort of consent prison officers required.[5] There were 'mind games': staff described sometimes feeding misinformation or trying to manipulate desired outcomes:

> It's a game of cat and mouse. We're trying to catch them out, they're trying to get one over on us. (Officer)

Prisoners preferred officers to be 'straight', even if they were giving unwelcome news or instructions. Officers who 'gave it the verbal', 'wound prisoners up' or overreacted to provocation lost their authority and encountered disrespect. Prisoners felt entitled, by the fact of their imprisonment, to feel frustrated, disgruntled and aggressive. Prisoners assumed that staff should avoid becoming caught up in this transference, and should be capable of maintaining a professional 'distance' in the face of their frustration.

The boundaries of staff power were constantly under pressure from prisoners:

> I just will not do what I'm told. I'll be: 'but why? if you do it like this it'll be much better.' I put it right to a screw the other day – he's not so much offensive as sneaky on how he's been using it, he's been over the top with all the petty rules. He wants promotion and so on. And so I said, 'look, I'm unemployed, I've been banged up for six months with no job and the reason I lost my job was because of a bad back.' I said 'You don't have to lock that door. I'll go out for a bit of a walk, I'll come back. There's only an hour left until unlock. You don't have to lock

that door, it's down to landing discretion. You personally don't have to do it but you do. What is it about you that makes you want to go around locking people up?' He said, 'They're the rules.' I said, 'no, it's down to landing discretion.' 'Well, I can't let one out without letting others out.' 'No, that's not right, you can let the people out that cause no problems. I won't run around the landing. Fine. I'm not a nuisance. You don't have to lock me up. I'm not refusing to work. There must be something psychologically wrong with you if you're insisting on banging me up.' And he just slammed the door and left me locked up. But I've had my little pop at him. That's how he is, he's one of those nasty little fuckers that won't. This morning I've been left open all morning, because the screw on the landing was very relaxed, he knows I won't cause him any grief. I'm in my cell, lying on my bed reading my book. What's the difference between the door being shut and the door being open? It used to be that you got left open. Now it's 'bang 'em up, bang 'em up.' Why? There's no real trouble. (Prisoner)

Prisoners expressed ambivalence about staff being in control. On the one hand, many prisoners tested every space to see where there was room to push officers back. On the other hand, the majority were uncomfortable if staff did back off:

One time, I brewed up thirteen weeks solid on the trot, two litres every week. They missed it every single time. I was a very nervous prisoner with it sitting around … ! If someone shouted 'DST on the wing!'[6] – I'd stick it on the window sill; stand there ready to knock it out. It does make you nervous because you know that the DST will cause you grief. As long as you're not doing anything major, I think they should leave you alone. Some of them do, some are really good. I mean, I used to smoke dope on the landing. A couple of new staff come in, I sat at the 1's playing pool, rolling a joint sat at the table. I lived here, as far as I was concerned, and this is what it used to be like. New officer saw me skinning up, ran to the centre – 'he's taking drugs down there!' The SO came down, so I put the matchbox over the joint and he says 'you're rolling a joint? Don't do it on the landing.' I said, 'hang on, I live here, get back in the office.' This is my way of conditioning them. If they see it done openly, it forces them back to leave you alone more. He said, 'off the landing with it, in your own cell.' He threatened me basically, said that if you don't go to your cell to smoke it, he'd lock down the landing and spin everyone. So he put it right on me then. So I said, alright, I'll do it in my cell. So it stopped me walking round with a joint. Which is fair enough, because I was taking the piss. (Prisoner)

One of the curiously under-discussed features of staff–prisoner relations was the impact of major incidents: hostage-taking, fires, disturbances, serious assaults, witnessing violence – the risks of these, officers' worst experiences of them – and the capacity individual staff members and prisoners had to absorb these experiences and to 'go on'. The evidence suggests that overexposure to these kinds of incidents, without support, can damage and dehumanise staff, with dangerous consequences (Tait 2008c). There was an acute awareness of the potential for danger among staff (and many prisoners). There was also an honest acceptance that in some situations, individual prisoners 'lost control' and could not be relied upon to remember 'credits' in any relationship built up over time:

Do you think prisoners make distinctions between officers when there is violence? Do you think they avoid officers they have got relationships with? (Interviewer)

I don't know really, to be honest, because when it reaches a situation where they think the only option they have is violence, I don't know whether they have got the control or the awareness to differentiate, really. Because I have seen situations where somebody that I have known quite well has turned round and smacked me, then smacked the PO, and I've restrained him and it's somebody who I knew quite well, who I have known previously ... I knew he was violent but I didn't think he would do that really. There's ... it might be a chemical thing, but there's a stage where a certain part of the brain shuts off and, you know, it's a panic reaction. (Officer)

Officer and prisoner views of each other

Officers and prisoners worked with different visions of each other, and these visions informed the type of relationships that developed. For prisoners, the 'role' that officers played in their lives was illustrated by their characterisations of officers: broadly, prisoners saw:

- a small but significant number of 'good' officers who would do things for you and go out of their way to help you;

- a larger number of 'neutral' officers who were in the job for the money but would usually treat prisoners like human beings; and

- a small number of 'bad' officers who would not try to help prisoners and who could be vindictive or pick on prisoners they didn't like, enforcing 'petty' and 'sneaky' rules.

Often, the prisoner's view was reduced to a simple dimension: 'good' or 'bad'. However, some prisoners could produce a much more detailed characterisation of officer 'types':

> You've got the ones who really aren't interested, are purely in the job for the money and will tell you that ... I'm certain there are some in the Service that are here for the power, and would probably do the job if they were only on six thousand a year. There are others who have some weird interest in being around criminals and notorious people. You have others who genuinely want to try and do something, and I have met them and spoke to them about it; there are officers who feel that they have something to offer. You have career people who are doing it for their career; if they weren't prison officers they could be working in companies. (Prisoner)

Sarah Tait proposed on the basis of her recent empirical study at two prisons that officers can be divided into five types, based on their orientation towards prisoners. Her typology of officer approaches to care was developed by comparing officer views and practices with the desired type of care described by prisoners. Approach to care was related to officers' views about prisoners as a group, their preferred basis of power, and their emotion management style. Officers' sense of personal security shaped their interaction with their environment and their ability to empathise with prisoners. *True carers* held a prisoner-led philosophy and practice of care and experienced the highest level of reward in their work. *Limited carers* and *old school* officers drew on similar professional identities but from different eras; they offered a pragmatic form of care and limited their use of authority and affective involvement. *Conflicted* officers expended considerable energy on a 'deserving few', but their caring was conditional and was often conflated with control. A further group of officers were identified as *Damaged*. These officers had minimal involvement in caring largely due to sustained trauma in their work. Some avoided work, while others were aggressive towards prisoners. Conflicted and 'damaged' officers were the most alienated, and struggled to make sense of their experiences and emotions. The gender and proportions of officers of each type constituted wing and prison cultures, which were related to institutional levels of care. Tait argues that care is a meaningful construct with which to conceptualise prison officer work, and is of vital importance to alleviating the pains of imprisonment and offering prisoners hope for the future (see for example, Tait 2008b).

At Whitemoor, views of prisoners were far more differentiated (by both prisoners and officers) than those of officers:

> There are those who get on with it, who'll just do it, and basically put up with whatever the system is. At times they might have a little outburst because we all do. You'll blow off steam and then a couple of hours later you'll be better. There's prisoners who sometimes because of their connections you feel work it different. Let's play the game a little bit. Because there is the thought in the back of your mind that someone could be at your house, somebody could follow you. It's not the best thing to be worrying about … But most of these aren't that influential. And then you've got your gobshites and your arseholes who are just swine. Buck the system, buck any form of authority because it's authority. Doesn't matter who it is. Totally anti-authoritarian and will be so for a long time. And you've got to work them different. You've got to side with them, but make it clear to them that what you say goes. (Officer)

Some resisted 'typifications':

> I know it's a real cliché, but they're just human beings. Take them as you find them … You can't be judgmental. They're just human beings, and the majority are absolutely fine. (Officer)

> I don't think you can see them in general. You tend to react and treat people in the way that they're reacting and treating you. I tend to give most prisoners a fair chance. Quite a few times you see prisoners who start off with an aggressive attitude, but once they get used to you they calm all that down – and some of the 'worst' prisoners on here, if you take time to speak to them, then most of the time they're not that bad. They may be

feeling frustrated, but if you talk to them and listen to them you can break down a lot of the barriers. (Officer)

Both officers and prisoners were aware of the difficulty of placing trust in any individual officer or prisoner. Officers acknowledged that their basic security and control role and the need for safety meant that some wariness (or even mistrust) of prisoners was necessary. Often, the lesson of replacing trust with caution had been learned the hard way:

I've had one threaten to rape me. He got moved. Also there was one female someone attempted to take hostage and I was actually on leave that day – it was my landing, and another prisoner said that he was actually going for me. How true that was I don't know.

How does that sort of experience affect you? (Interviewer)

Umm – that one at first, the thought that it possibly could be true was a bit of a shock because of the prisoner – it shocked everybody. He'd have been the last person, if you had to put in order all the prisoners on the wing as to who'd be the first to last to take a hostage, he'd have been very near the bottom. But really, you can't dwell on it. … (Officer)

It's constant learning, because they will try anything and everything to get their own way. It's hard to trust somebody and not trust somebody at the same time. You've got to look into their eyes and wonder if they're telling the truth or not, which winds a lot of prisoners, who are telling the truth, up. And you can't get across to them that it's because you've been had over in the past so many times by so many other prisoners – 'but that's not me!' – 'But that's what they said to me last time!' (Senior officer)

Prison officers and prisoners traded in *gradations* of trust. Again, this was a finely balanced exercise, where experience, without grudges, was necessary. In their interactions, prisoners were constantly aware of the many different roles officers played – particularly in relation to any reports that might be written about them. Prisoners played a role too:

You can't be yourself with officers. There are times when I have said something and then it's been thrown back in my face four years later ... in a report. (Prisoner)

Yet, despite this wariness, and despite all the inevitable problems of life in a prison, almost every prisoner and every officer had at least one or two good relationships with members of the other group:

Some you can get on with better than others – my personal officer is as good as gold. I can't spell too well, and if ever I wanted anything like that done, and I've only got to go to him, and he don't say, 'oh, later' – what he usually says is, tell me what you want, and he'd go away and the next time I'd see him he'd have written it all out for me ... If I wanted something properly, good as gold he was. (Prisoner)

I suppose there's one, [X], I'm always pulling his leg – he's on a constant diet and yet he's always got a Snickers or a Mars Bar in his hand, so I'm always pulling his leg. He was sitting there yesterday looking at his toenails and I said 'I bet you haven't seen them for a long while, have you?' Just banter like that. And he calls me his favourite officer. I think it's the jokey rapport I have with him. At the end of the day, he respects me as an officer. If I ask him or tell him to do anything, he'll do it. I never get any problems with him. (Officer)

Why were relationships established in the first place, when officers were in a position of authority over prisoners and were responsible for the enforcement of rules, and prisoners were often trying to avoid those rules and were in a place they would rather not be? What was important and significant about them?

The significance of staff–prisoner relationships

Officers and prisoners at Whitemoor both agreed that relationships were important on many levels. They were significant for:

- instrumental reasons (as officers, 'we need them to make the prison run smoothly, and to gain intelligence'; as prisoners, 'we need them because officers write our reports and are gatekeepers to a lot of things we want'); and

- normative reasons (good relationships are a humane and pleasant thing; they make prison work/life in prison easier; good relationships are an end in themselves).

Prisoners were more likely to concentrate on the first of these aspects – the strategic and material reasons for establishing relationships, although many did note that reasonable relationships made prison more bearable:

> It's important in a lot of ways – if you want something done, or if you're having a bad day over something, you could go to an officer and say, look, this is what's happening and, you know, that officer would go all out to solve it. That's what I like with the officers in here, because whenever I have any problems I can say to them that something isn't right, and I have to say that ten out of ten, they've solved it. I'm glad to say that I can say that. It's true that they do sort my problems out. (Prisoner)

Officers relied on their relationships with prisoners to achieve order and safety (one senior officer astutely described the value of relationships as 'quiet power'). Prisoners wanted relationships that would achieve justice (and this notion of justice included some reference to 'care').

Relationships were the 'oil' which smoothed the flow of a prison day, but in a way that implicitly meant more power (or a more effective utilisation of power) for officers. Officers were aware, as were many prisoners, that a good knowledge of prisoners led to increased power:

> You can tell if they're up to something because some of their attitudes change, they try and distance themselves from you. It's one of the things that helps us monitor them – their reaction to us. (Officer)

> When you're on your own wing, you know the prisoners ... and when a prisoner passes a comment, you know whether that is normal for that prisoner or might be causing trouble. You ... pick up the vibes ... you can weigh things up. (Officer)

As we noted in the previous chapter, one of the most significant aspects of staff–prisoner relationships was that they constituted the framework within which decisions were made (and discretion exercised) by prison officers, and the context in which those decisions were assessed and evaluated by prisoners. Relationships were the route through which everything else was achieved, and through which prisoners perceived the delivery of fairness, respect (see later in this chapter) and justice – see Figure 5.1.

There was an important link between the relationships officers developed with prisoners (and the relationships they wanted) and rule enforcement:

Has there been an occasion where you might have placed a prisoner on report and you chose not to? (Interviewer)

Yes. Instead, I put an SIR[7] in and the security department said I should have put him on report, but in my opinion, I didn't think he warranted it. It was one of the orderlies … There are two of them, and one had just quit. The other asked who had applied for the job, and I said, no one as yet. The prisoner said that was good because he wanted to choose who worked down here, and that he wanted one of his mates. I said that wasn't appropriate, and he said that he didn't want no black people down there. He became – not aggressive – but intimidating. I

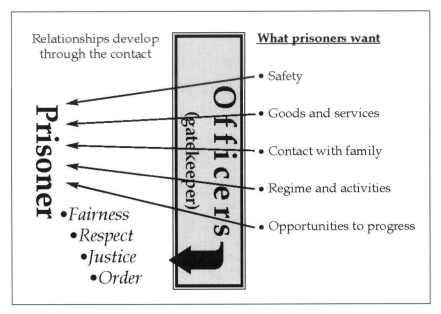

Figure 5.1 The significant role of prison officers

put it on an SIR and they said I should have put him on report for racism, or for intimidating me. *But because I work as a cleaning officer, I wanted to keep some kind of relationship.* I'd already had a word with him, told him I wasn't happy with what he'd said, but I thought that if I'd put him on report for it, it would have broken the relationship, and it didn't warrant that. I'd spoken to him and told him that I didn't agree with racism and with what he's said, and in the end he apologised and shook my hand, which I thought was a result really. (Officer – emphasis added)

This is a modern illustration of the argument made by Sykes (1958) that we will encounter in the next chapter. Here, we can examine how these accommodations are made. There is a continual tension between the intrinsic, caste-like gap separating staff and prisoners, and the bridging of that gap that is necessary if the task of 'getting through the prison day' is to be accomplished smoothly (Ben-David and Silfen 1994). This tension is not – and cannot be – controlled by formal rules and structures but by informal structures that lead to the development of mutual understandings between officers and prisoners.

The decisions made by officers were commonly embedded in knowledge gained through relationships – not just about what was happening on the wing but, most importantly, about the personalities of individuals. Officers constantly framed their decision-making with regard to the individual prisoner in front of them, seeking the best way to calm the situation and achieve their goals. With the knowledge gained through relationships, officers' observations became meaningful, their judgement could be informed and they knew how to handle potentially dangerous situations. As one officer put it, 'part of a prison officer's job is to get people to cooperate with them, and relationships are crucial in that'. The most refined skills possessed by prison officers were in managing complex human behaviour:

If you know who's who, who's jostling for what position, who has what kind of hold on which prisoners, who's beginning to lose his cool … then, you know what you are doing when you take one out. You can front it, intervene, nip it in the bud. You can pull one of them aside and say, 'look, let's get this sorted out; we're both adults, let's find a route which saves face'. Otherwise you risk playing into a potentially explosive situation. (Officer)

Through relationships, prisoners (and officers) became individuals. Officers and prisoners sometimes knew truths about each other which others did not know (the bad mornings, the fiery tempers, the second girlfriend, the impending divorce, the parole rejection, and so on). Staff could use this information to deploy their authority more wisely and carefully with the complexities of their population in mind. Officers did not often (according to the accounts we heard from prisoners) use their power in coercive ways. The relationships officers had with prisoners could help them effect positive change in the prisoner, or aid them in dealing with difficult personal problems. In this aspect of their work, prison staff often won our admiration. Indeed, officers were at times working not with the idealised abstractions of specialists, visitors or researchers, but with the worst and most difficult aspects of the human spirit, head on. In this sense, they could be more liberal, accepting and honest in their practical and daily encounters with prisoners than any of their critics.

Prison officers develop in their work what Giddens (1984, 1990) has termed 'practical consciousness'. By this, Giddens means all the things that we know about our work or what we do in our lives, but which we cannot easily explain in words. This aspect of knowledge enables us to make decisions without necessarily being able to verbalise how and why each decision was made. Prison officers can thus often achieve what might seem the impossible without being able – or required – to explain how it was actually accomplished, from the maintenance of the day's routine to the ending of a tense encounter. This is what experienced officers mean when they refer to the sorts of knowledge experience brings. They often regard this working knowledge or practical consciousness as 'common sense':

> We were doing MDT.[8] He was in the seg. on seven days loss of tobacco and I knew that and he wouldn't pee for me, so I said, hurry up I'm dying for a fag. He said, 'Do you smoke, Gov? I haven't had a fag for days'. I said, would you like one? 'Oh, I'd love one'. Then pee in that bottle and I'll give you a fag. 'You'd better'. If I say you'll get one, you'll get one. He peed. I gave him a fag. That started that relationship off. But he's come to the wing and he's really trying to get on with it. We have a laugh. (Officer)

What did prisoners consider important in relationships with officers?

It was important to prisoners that they remained moral agents in their dealings with prison officers: that is, persons with some uniqueness. They wanted to be treated as individuals, despite their imprisonment, and despite being subject to a tightly run regime. Prisoners also wanted officers to recognise when petty injustices and frustrations occurred, to understand how important these might be to prisoners and to agree that they were unfair – and to allow some space in which these frustrations could be expressed. Prisoners needed officers to be predictable (not necessarily as a group but certainly as individuals) so that they did not feel subject to whim, and so that they could build up trust in particular officers. Most officers were aware of these ideas (if only on the level of 'practical consciousness') and would treat prisoners as rational beings:

> If you're not sure, tell them you're not sure, but be straight with them. It's important because they will come to rely on what you say then. X asked me to sort something out about his diet. I checked it out, he was right, he wasn't getting something he should. I made sure he got it, and I'd said, if you're right I'll get it for you ... He was right and he got it; he said thanks very much. Because I get on well with him now, because I've demonstrated to him that I'm straight with him, and on a couple of occasions I've told him (no), and then I've gone the other way and done something for him (as well) – now, if there was a problem, and I was to say to him 'just be quiet and listen to what I'm going to say,' he's going to listen to me, and trust me when I say, 'if you go behind your door now, I'll get you out as soon as I can.' [...] I sorted out his visit for him – we as a Service had messed up his visit. It wasn't his fault. The attitude of the visits staff was, stuff him, he's only a prisoner – but that's not right. He'd followed the rules; he'd done everything correctly, and we'd screwed it up. I made sure he got a visit. That's not doing him a favour, it's doing what I feel is right. [...] We have a duty, if they've obeyed the rules and regulations themselves, to do right by them. (Senior officer)

'Doing right by them' was precisely what prisoners wanted staff to care about.

Table 5.1 shows the terms prisoners used when they were describing the best officers on their wing. Perhaps most important, prisoners wanted the prison officer to be a human being – regardless of the authority they held, the orders they were giving out, the bad news they might hold, prisoners wanted officers who could be themselves and be human:

They should be good judges of when to use other parts of their personality ... [But] this is a serious place we're in; it's a warehouse of suffering; the home to a lot of people, and they should treat that with a little respect. But that doesn't mean that there has to be no sense of humour ... I think if they could get a prison officer with all those qualities ... Someone that is aware of other people's needs. It's happened before when a prison officer who's had a go at me has come back and said he was sorry about it. I wouldn't just respect that, but I'd get a lot out of that – human communication. Someone who isn't perfect, but tried to be as good as he can be, and isn't afraid to apologise if he makes a mistake. (Prisoner)

Table 5.1 The best officers

• a listener	• motivated
• a controlled sense of humour	• intelligent
• mature	• capable of using authority
• someone who'll keep an eye on you	• careful
• someone you can talk to	• compassionate

The importance of fairness

The word 'fairness' is heard frequently in prison. Research has shown how important fairness is to prisoners, and how prisoners closely relate perceptions of fair treatment by officers to perceptions of the fairness of the regime as a whole (Ahmad 1996; Liebling, assisted by Arnold 2004) – that is to say, if officers treat prisoners fairly, prisoners will generally consider the prison regime to be fair as a whole (see also Sparks *et al* 1996).

Fairness was generally a one-way process[9] – officers were judged by prisoners on whether they were fair or not. Fairness was strongly related to distribution, and it was officers who held the distributive power. Officers did not expect to be treated fairly by prisoners (indeed, officers would expect the typical prisoner to act self-interestedly).[10]

Officers were aware that their relationships with prisoners were often grounded in their position as 'gatekeepers' and distributors:

> I think most relationships start off being bad anyway, because you've got a white shirt on. So initially, with the reputation that Whitemoor has, you are the enemy. And then it's a case of breaking down those barriers, making yourself known to that prisoner on that spur, letting him know that you are an individual, and that you may be an officer and hopefully a well-respected officer.

> *How do you do that? Break down the barriers?* (Interviewer)

> It's a case of being fair, I suppose. Giving him information that you know he's going to need, rather than just ignoring him. (Officer)

Officers and prisoners gave different reasons as to why prisoners should be treated fairly. Officers usually saw fairness as important for instrumental reasons, for making the job easier, with fairness defined as equality of treatment – if one prisoner gets something, then all prisoners should. The significance and the meaning of fairness were usually tied together in an officer's thinking:

> *What do you mean by fairness?* (Interviewer)

> That nobody gets anything that they shouldn't really have. And if one person gets it, and another person says 'he's got it, why can't I have it?', there's got to be a bloody good reason, whether it's a mistake or he's entitled to it and you're not. Because once you start doing one thing, that favour or little perk … that becomes the thin end of the wedge. And what was a small perk is the norm, and then it's the accepted norm, and then it's automatic right. And a lot of prisoners don't realise that a lot of things that are allowed in prison are actually privileges, and they can be taken away. But because they've had them so long, they're apparently entitled to them by law. (Senior officer)

Fairness for officers was consistency in distribution and in rule enforcement. Fairness was tied up with the formal and material aspects of prison life. The concerns of prisoners for fairness were twofold: first, a feeling that fairness was right *per se*; and second it had an important symbolic role: if prison officers were not fair, then the criminal justice system (and the law) could not possibly be fair:

Can you describe what fairness is? (Interviewer)

What you have to remember is that people come from outside to prison. They're in prison because they broke the law, and being here is their punishment, being taken away from society. In prison there are certain rules and regulations, you're told what you're allowed and what you can do. Whilst you're in prison, if the prison officers break the law themselves, don't give you what you're entitled to, and be very aggressive to you – it just teaches people that all this obeying the law, going by the book, staying out of trouble is just pure bollocks. So that when they get out, they're even more ... rules and regulations aren't going to mean anything to them. (Prisoner)

Prisoners often described a sort of fairness that could be regarded as *consistency in process*. Such consistency was often valued for the security it brought – even when the outcomes of such consistency could be unfavourable (see Tyler 1990):

Well a friend of mine tried to take [governor X's] eye out ... he didn't like the answer he was given – but at least he would give you an answer. Any other governor would lie to you, fuck you about, lush you, anything at all. But [the governor] (a) he was fair, (b) he was honest. So if you went with something and you weren't getting it, he would tell you 'no you're not getting it and you're not getting it because ...' He'd tell you fair, where others would say 'oh I don't know, I'll have to ...' and fuck you about ... He was straight, I thought he was okay. He was blunt, but personally I prefer that to someone saying 'I'll have to see him, and I'll have to see him and ...' (Prisoner)

Many prisoners, however, realised that equality of treatment could result in unfairness of *outcome* and perceived injustice. To reach the goal of equality of treatment, individual needs were sometimes sacrificed. This was a difficult area, and some prisoners verbalised the complex moral position of the officer very clearly:

Fairness is paramount. Sometimes they just can't be – their hands are tied and they can't make a decision. Prisoners think the one

107

who opens his door is the one who can solve his problems. But it doesn't work like that. What is fairness? It is ... to have compassion. I think that is what it is. If you have compassion for people, then everything else will follow. You are not closed-minded; if someone is distressed, you ask questions, get the guy out of his cell. Make a phone call to the hospital. (Prisoner)

A prisoner who had recently lost his job after an adjudication put it this way:

You come to terms with the fact that it's happened, but at the same time you're looking for some sort of fairness at the end of the day, and when you find that you don't get any, you sit down and you think 'boy, it's not just that prison's a rough ride, but they try and make it rough everywhere in the system for you.' Especially when you're getting out of jail soon. There's no compromising. If there's compromising in fairness, then I think people would get on better. By not having any *compromise in fairness*, people don't get on and it makes a bad situation even worse. (Prisoner – emphasis added)

Prisoners were asking for flexibility within a framework of consistency. They were asking that their individuality, their own needs, be attended to when rules were enforced or decisions taken. There was thus an understanding that straight consistency in rule enforcement could lead to unfair treatment. The prisoners were asking for discretion to be exercised in their cases. This was the apparent paradox that led us to the moral philosopher Harrison (1992). The prisoners were asking for 'mercy' (a decision not to enforce a rule) to be granted. As we argue in this chapter and elsewhere, officers did exercise 'mercy' in many cases.

The granting and receiving of respect

Like the concept of 'fairness', the word 'respect' is heard frequently in prison. It is clearly an important feature of relationships between officers and prisoners, but the word is used with different meanings. What does 'being treated with respect' mean?

We identified at least three different examples of the term 'respect':

1 respect as fear/power;
2 respect as individuality;
3 respect as moral strength (or legitimacy).[11]

The first kind of respect relates to power or status. In this case, if I say that I respect a person, I acknowledge the power held by this individual and their capacity to wield that power to do damage to me (or indeed to help me). This is the typical 'gangster' or 'Mafia' notion of respect. It does not necessarily denote admiration or liking of the individual concerned but these ideas can be included. Some prisoners at Whitemoor talked about their time in the military producing respect from ex-military officers. Officers frequently mentioned the need to be respectful (wary) of the potential for danger in certain situations with individual prisoners. This was not the most common notion of respect but it seemed significant.

The second and more common use of the term respect was earned by stepping out of role – that is, by an individual stepping out of the stereotypical role adopted by virtue of being 'a prison officer' or 'a prisoner'. This notion of respect is linked to negative expectations – as a stereotypical prisoner, I expect the stereotypical officer to be untrustworthy, deceitful, power-hungry, abusive and lazy, and to nick me for any minor thing I do wrong. As a stereotypical officer, I expect the stereotypical prisoner to lie, cheat, intimidate, shout and act selfishly at all times. When an individual steps out of that stereotypical role and, for example, promises a prisoner something and comes through with it promptly, or treats me politely and asks me to do something rather than delivering an impersonal order, or a prisoner obeys my request quietly and without dispute, or debated a point with me without threatening violence – then I respect that person and see them as an individual. This idea of respect has as a main tenet the notion of *individuality*:[12] the knowledge that *I am not a stereotypical prisoner or prison officer*. By responding to me as an individual – by doing what I asked without complaint, by demonstrating a little care and humanity – you have recognised this fact. One prisoner gave an example:

> I give them their dues, because I've been acquitted of hostage taking and that ... and I've been acquitted of stabbing their colleagues before, assaulting them and ... they haven't been malicious towards me ... The SO said to me that he'd like to think of me as one of his successes, because I've changed in the way I go about things. He's seen me in situations, and tried

to make sure there are no obstacles in my way, and I can only respect someone like that. He saw I was going through mental pressures, and he didn't bring any physical harm towards me, he tried to help me out so I could go through even further. And this lady [officer] as well, she saw what I was going through and she came through and 'you alright?' People like that, I can't help but respect. They haven't brutalised me, they've only tried to help me. (Prisoner)

Officers who went out of their way to help prisoners, who wrote letters for prisoners who were illiterate or who came in during their spare time to help out the prison bands, were recipients of this second kind of respect. They stepped out of the 'them and us' characterisation.

The third notion of 'respect' may be specific to those who hold power or authority. This notion is something of a combination of the first and second and applies in prison exclusively to prison officers (and occasionally to some governors). This is respect for the officer who has what one prisoner described as 'moral fibre'. In our research, it was respect for the officer who had a firm but consistent line but enforced that consistency in a flexible manner. One prisoner described one such officer:

He was very by the book – he'd do things like come along and tell you, *'If I catch you again, you're nicked.'* He'd tell you straight. Anything to do with security he'd nick you for immediately. He's not a man I would have smoked a spliff in front of, you know? Not that he would have objected in his own personal view of things, but it would be like you were taking the piss. Some officers just don't give a fuck. That's different of officers you respect ... You've got a prisoner who's right stroppy, they're not going to get intimidated, they're going to stand there and go, 'uh-huh, uh-huh, okay, I hear what you're saying. I accept that ... but this is how the prison runs, and that's how it has to be.' They'd tell you straight. I like that. (Prisoner)

This respect applied to officers who did their job 'properly', officers who were not afraid of the rules they had to enforce, but who were willing to debate and engage in dialogue with prisoners over those rules. These officers would listen to a prisoner's argument but not be swayed from their position. Further (and this was very important) such officers were prepared to explain why they could not be swayed, and why they held the position that they did. These were officers who knew the rules, but who saw a consistent 'bigger picture' to their work and were prepared to bend rules when they did not match that bigger picture (and be able to explain to prisoners and to managers why those rules were bent). The respect held for these officers lay in an acknowledgement of the power held by them and the careful manner in which it was used.

Respect could be earned or lost. Prisoners generally talked of officers 'earning' respect through their actions; officers more frequently spoke of prisoners 'losing' respect through their actions. This meant that more work at relationships was required by officers to enjoy respect than by prisoners. Without contact with prisoners, respect could not be earned by officers; however, if this contact was handled in the wrong way, respect was in jeopardy.

Respect was a key concept that arose out of and affected relationships. While staff and prisoners often began with a mistrust of the other deeply embedded in cultures, memories and structures, it was possible to break through those barriers and to build trust and respect for the quality of the human individual on the other side. Cultures, memories and structures are not binding. Individual agency shaped the prison world. Examples of humanity and individual feeling were possible – and important – in this coercive environment.

These differences in the meaning of the term respect are important. Officers should respect the prisoner as an individual, but should not 'respect' the power of prisoners to the extent that they underenforce or avoid the rules glibly. Which differences are legitimate and can be 'allowed'. Is underenforcement ever 'just'? (see further Liebling: assisted by Arnold 2004).

> The bigger picture is saying, this jail is a complex place, there are always exceptions to things, and people should be treated as individuals. And these people who struggle and say, 'no, they're not, they're all prisoners and we treat them all the same,' isn't the case. Ninety per cent of what we do, we have to treat prisoners the same. We can't give them all individual meals, we can't give them individual visiting times, but in reality people are individuals and act in different ways. (Officer)

Boundaries, relationships and corruption

The discussion of 'boundaries' and possible corruption inevitably arose in this piece of research. In some respects, this is precisely the difference between 'good' relationships and 'right' relationships. This was a particularly pertinent issue at Whitemoor, where relationships had been (arguably at one point) too lax or too blurred and had been partly responsible for the escapes from the SSU in 1994 (Home Office 1995).[13]

The vulnerability of officers at Whitemoor to corruption was felt to be low, principally because of the traumatic history of the prison and the resulting boundary-conscious prison climate. However, both officers and prisoners felt that if the wrong officer was caught at the wrong time by the wrong prisoner, then something might develop:[14]

> *How vulnerable are prison officers to corruption?* (Interviewer)

> Depends on the personal make-up and personal life at the particular time. It could be a mixture of the two – a rough personal time with debts or something. Officers seem prone to it [debts] – maybe it's the stress that means that they need lots of holidays or something, go therapy shopping to make them feel good. But you've got a lot of powerful men in here with a lot of money who are very persuasive. And if someone's vulnerable, then yeah ... (Senior officer)

There was an assumption among officers that when we mentioned 'corruption', we were talking about the hard end of the scale – trafficking (particularly drugs and mobile phones) or aiding an escape. Both of these things were unanimously deemed 'corrupt'. However, at the lower end of the scale, things were much more opaque. Was swapping cigarettes corrupt? Was betting on the football for chocolate bars? There were significant differences between officers on these issues, and doubts about the ability of managers or others to draw a clear and satisfactory line:

> It's very difficult to see when someone's being over-friendly to you. Because it happens over a period of time – prisoner Bloggs gives you a cup of coffee one day and the next day he's got a biscuit – it's difficult to see it happening until the point at which it's 'I gave you a cup of coffee, could you perhaps bring us in X and Y?'

> *Where is the line? A cup of coffee?* (Interviewer)

> Yeah – it's difficult, isn't it? Not until you were doing something against the prison rules, I think. Which is pretty obvious – it's

written down what you don't and you can't do. It's difficult that, definitely. But I wouldn't say I was being corrupted until I was doing something against the prison rules – but you're being corrupted before then, aren't you? (Officer)

The dangers of corruption sprang from the need to maintain relationships with prisoners and from the difficulty of saying 'no' if it might cause harm to that relationship. As one prisoner put it, 'Everybody likes to be liked, don't they?' Each officer's personal boundary came from their own personal view of what was and what was not corrupt, which was mainly related to where they as individuals felt comfortable 'drawing the line'. For some officers, betting small amounts on football matches was fine; for others, it was not. A few officers, particularly some of those who had worked in the SSU, were unwilling even to use first names with prisoners.

The issue of boundaries between officers and prisoners was clearly a vexing one. Figure 5.2 illustrates some of the dynamics of staff–prisoner relationships. Generally, relationships and life in

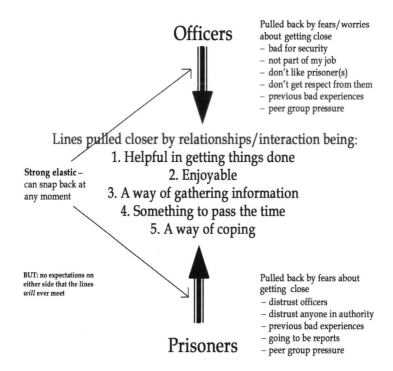

Figure 5.2   The dynamics of the officer–prisoner relationship

prison carried on without explicit reference to them. However, when a boundary was suddenly called into question, or when an event occurred that affected boundaries, difficulties could arise. It was at these points – a lockdown search, for example, or an assault – that officers stepped firmly back into their roles as *officers*. It was a sudden reminder that this was prison, and that these relationships were artificial and had limits. These situations were like the cinema projector breaking down in the middle of a film: for a while, you can be immersed in the story on the screen, but when the picture breaks and the lights come on, you remember that the screen was showing only a superficial fiction, and you are brought back to reality. In the same way, relationships between officers and prisoners could often carry on until a boundary was crossed. It was at this point that the 'lights came on' and the reality of the situation (of the 'keepers' and the 'kept', of officer and prisoner) rudely interrupted the (temporarily forgotten) artificiality of the interaction. Such a moment placed the limitations of the relationships between officers and prisoners in sharp focus.

Limits to relationships

> There are 512 prisoners here; there are 700 staff on the books. That's an enormous amount of relationships, and not all of them can be good or will be good. A good prison officer will understand the limits of his relationships with prisoners, will accept that with some prisoners, they will not have a good relationship, but can still manage that relationship in a very professional sense. Bad prison officers (a) try to treat all prisoners the same, and that doesn't work; or (b) simply hide behind, 'it ain't my job, it's far too difficult, I'm not prepared to think for myself'. You just have to be able to talk to people. (Senior manager)

Relationships between staff and prisoners were constrained by the realities of human coexistence, and by their context. The prisoner culture (values and beliefs, shared unevenly among them but present nevertheless) placed limits on the extent to which prisoners could 'be seen' to have close relationships with staff. Prisoners who were perceived as too friendly with staff were labelled 'grasses', disloyal to the distance required for dignity among fellow prisoners. Some resistance by prisoners was probably natural – people rarely accept authority unquestioningly. Relationships were also limited by the vision staff and prisoners had of each other (see above). Sometimes officers and prisoners disliked each other – or in some cases, simply disliked what the other represented. For some officers, prisoners represented a lack of self-control, greed or amoral activity; for prisoners, staff could represent the injustices of experienced authority. There were limits to what 'relationships' could achieve in a prison. They could not replace decent regimes and the possibility of hope for the future, but they could support such things, soften the impact of losses of privileges and bring a more human touch to the realities of prison.

Relationships were also important in the delivery of justice at a micro level. Prison officers could embody their prison (or at a wider level, the criminal justice system) every time they spoke to or approached a prisoner (see Tyler 1990). The best examples of relationships we observed – relationships that included fairness, respect and dialogue between officers and prisoners – could be seen as instruments of legitimacy. Actions of prison officers matter – they can generate trust in the prisoner, the establishment, the criminal justice system and authority in general. In this sense, prison officers 'embody' a prison's regime. More is said about this important aspect of prison life and work in *Prisons and Their Moral Performance* (Liebling, assisted by Arnold 2004).

The overuse of power

We have concentrated in this chapter on the use of discretion for legitimacy.[15] Clearly there are overuses of power and uses of discretion (including discrimination) which are *against* legitimacy.[16] The questions of how staff resist the overuse of power, avoid holding grudges and retain relationships in the face of constant challenge have been inadequately considered in research and in training. Cultures can develop in whole establishments or (more often) in parts of establishments where staff are careless and occasionally brutal with the power they hold. Or staff may have all their pride invested in very high levels of security and discipline, and almost none invested in activities or relationships (Liebling *et al.* 1999).

The (controversial) Milgram and Zimbardo experiments demonstrated some of the dangers of power, and there are enough examples of staff violence against prisoners, or uses of intimidation to illustrate the real possibilities of staff having or using too much power of the wrong sort.

Motivated by curiosity about the cooperation of thousands of Germans with the systematic destruction of the Jews and others during the 1930s and 1940s, Milgram conducted a series of experiments intended to investigate readiness to obey morally wrong or physically dangerous acts. He called his experiments 'the effects of punishment on learning', and persuaded duped volunteers to administer shocks of increasing severity to a 'student' who gave wrong answers to a series of tests. The experiment was conducted under the strict guidance of the experimenter, who encouraged the subjects to continue. Many showed signs of severe distress and some eventually refused to go on. Sixty-five per cent of the subjects gave shocks up to and including 450 volts, apparently endangering the life of the actor who masqueraded as the student. When the experiments were repeated at a less prestigious university, the number of subjects willing to reach these levels in the experiment fell to 50 per cent. When the subject was in the same room as the 'student' instead of being the other side of a glass partition, obedience levels dropped to 40 per cent; when subjects had to force the hand of the learner back onto the shock plate, obedience levels dropped to 30 per cent. When other 'teachers' left the room during the experiment in protest (providing social support for refusing to obey), obedience levels dropped to 10 per cent. When another person delivered the shock, obedience levels rose to 95 per cent. When the experimenter left the room, obedience dropped to almost zero. Other related obedience studies show that ordinary citizens are more likely to obey an instruction if it is given by someone in uniform, even if they subsequently leave the scene, and that nurses will deliver dangerous levels of drugs to patients if instructed to do so by an unknown doctor over the telephone (Hofling *et al.* 1966).

These studies argued that abusive behaviour is best viewed as a product of transactions with an environment that supports such behaviour, and that social institutions contain powerful forces which can make good men engage in evil deeds (Haney *et al.* 1973).

Haney *et al.* (1973) conducted an experiment in which subjects role-played prisoners and guards in a simulated prison. The aim of the experiment was to 'assess the power of ... social forces ... in this situation'. Subjects were carefully selected after careful diagnostic testing of a large group of volunteer male college students. The sample were randomly assigned to play either prisoners or guards. The experiment was intended to last two weeks. Behavioural interactions were observed and video-taped, and the participants were asked to complete questionnaires, self-report scales and interviews.

The authors concluded that the simulated prison became a 'psychologically compelling environment', eliciting unexpectedly intense, realistic and often pathological reactions from the participants. The prisoners experienced a loss of personal identity and reacted to the arbitrary control of their behaviour. This resulted in a syndrome of passivity, dependency, depression and helplessness. Most of the guards experienced a gain in social power, status and group identification, which made their role-playing rewarding. The coping behaviour resorted to by half the prisoners was the development of acute emotional disturbance. A third of the guards were judged to have become more aggressive and dehumanising than predicted. Few of the reactions could be attributed to pre-existing personality traits. The authors concluded that imprisonment destroys the human spirit of both the imprisoned and the imprisoning. They argue that the brutality of prison stems not from the characteristics of individual guards and prisoners (the 'dispositional hypothesis'), but from the 'deep structure' of the prison as an institution.

To test this hypothesis, they controlled for the characteristics of guards and prisoners by elaborately creating a simulated prison setting which aimed to reflect the social-psychological milieu of existing prisons. They aimed to create the functional equivalent of activities and experiences characteristic of the prison: feelings of power and powerlessness, of control and oppression, of satisfaction and frustration, of arbitrary rule and resistance to authority (Haney *et al*. 1973: 72). Twenty-one subjects were selected from 75 respondents after screening for emotional stability and maturity. There were 10 prisoners and 11 guards. A cell block was designed in the basement of Stanford University psychology department. The guards believed the experiment was intended to study the behaviour of prisoners only. Uniforms were given (to an extreme specification) and the guards were given police night sticks to carry. Once participants had signed up to the experiment and its terms and conditions, they were 'unexpectedly' arrested at their places of residence. Their exposure to the simulated prison was extreme, with the guards quickly abandoning the prescribed rules and routines.

The authors claimed to have acquired clear, consistent and reliable results: a huge and largely negative impact on the affective states of guards and prisoners. The characteristic nature of interactions was negative, hostile, affronting and dehumanising; prisoners quickly developed passive modes of response. Five prisoners had to be released early due to extreme depression, crying, rage and anxiety (Haney *et al*. 1973: 81). One developed a psychosomatic rash. The experiment was terminated early, after six days. In contrast, most of the guards were upset by the decision to stop the experiment and were enjoying their roles. One guard reported being distressed by the suffering of the prisoners and considered requesting a transfer from the role of guard to that of prisoner. They all arrived on time for work and some remained on duty over time. The reactions of the prisoner group and the staff group are described by the authors of the study as 'pathological'. Some prisoners coped better than others and not all the guards became hostile. Personality and attitude dispositions accounted for some of the variation in reactions and adjustments to imprisonment. There were slight differences between prisoners who demanded early release and those who stayed until the end of the experiment. Prisoners who remained scored higher on conformity, conventionality, extroversion, authoritarianism and empathy. Prisoners were rarely addressed individually, whereas prisoners did refer to guards individually. Over time, guard behaviour became more insulting, with some variation between three shifts, the evening shift being the most harassing. In interviews, prisoners expressed negative feeling, outlook and negative self-regard. Ninety per cent of the conversation between prisoners was about prison matters and their regard for each other deteriorated over time. Both guards and prisoners reported negative affect, but prisoners reported twice as much. The guards observed, after the experiment, that they were surprised by how much fun being authoritarian could be and the prisoners expressed surprise that they had felt so out of control of their emotions. They had begun to act in ways which helped to sanction their victimisation by the guards. Follow-up suggested that all the negative effects (passivity, dependency, depression, helplessness and self-deprecation) were temporary. The authors were surprised by how easily sadistic behaviour could be elicited in 'non-sadistic types' and how easily emotional breakdown could occur in stable types:

> In less than one week their behaviour in this simulated prison could be characterised as pathological and anti-social. The negative, anti-social reactions observed were not the product of an environment created by combining a collection of deviant personalities, but rather the result of an intrinsically pathological situation. (Haney *et al.* 1973: 90)

The study has been severely criticised on methodological grounds (the experiment was too extreme and the results were actively sought: see Jones and Fowles 1984). But there are important warnings here, and some resonances with some real situations observed in contemporary prisons (see, for example, Sparks *et al*. 1996; Liebling *et al*. 1999; the accounts of unhealthy cultures described in some Inspectorate reports and reports of US military prisons at Abu Ghraib and Guantanamo Bay). Zimbardo revisited these themes in his recent book *The Lucifer Effect: How Good People Turn Evil* (2007), arguing that we should always be on the alert for the darker side of institutional life.

Conclusion

The role of staff–prisoner relationships is crucial to prison life. Relationships can 'go wrong' in many different ways. Right relationships can provide security, order, legitimacy and social support. According to Biggam and Power (1997), 'social support could be considered as an important psychological and social variable that contributes to adjustment in prisons and the amelioration of stress' (214). In their study of 125 young offenders in Scotland they administered the Hospital Anxiety and Depression Scale, the Beck's Hopelessness Scale and the Significant Others Scale (SOS). The young offenders, having identified important relationships under the SOS, then rated each of these relationships in terms of 'actual' versus 'ideal' support. They found that 'prisoners displaying psychological distress expressed a desire for more support from their fellow prisoners' and more emotional and practical support from officers. Indeed, 'vulnerable prisoners show a desire for a more "therapeutic" relationship with staff'. Perceived deficits in support from officers 'were the major predictors of anxiety, depression and hopelessness' (Biggam and Power 1997: 225–6; see also Liebling and Price 1999). Staff–prisoner relationships mediate levels and types of order, and they may mediate levels and types of prisoner distress (see further, Liebling and Tait 2006). At their best, relationships between staff and prisoners both constitute and help to support the finest work accomplished by prison staff.

Notes

1 There has been some pioneering 'audit' work on relationships between staff and prisoners carried out by the Relationships Foundation, which has some interesting points to make about the state of staff–prisoner relationships. This work, although of interest, is not sociological in

its analysis. For a more sociological and staff/prisoner-led analysis of relationships, see Liebling, assisted by Arnold (2004).

2 For example, routinely, what space is shared and what is not shared? What effect does prolonged contact over time have on staff–prisoner views of and interactions with each other?

3 The MQPL survey, operational since 2002, is based on research intended to achieve this; see Liebling, assisted by Arnold (2004).

4 During our many conversations with staff throughout previous projects we were informally told of a research project carried out at Onley, which found that prisoners were more likely to be actively engaged in activities when one shift was on than when the other shift was working.

5 In practice, prison officers were not too concerned about the type of consent they achieved as long as they achieved behavioural (as opposed to attitudinal) consent. On the importance of this point, see Sparks *et al.* (1996) and Liebling (2008b).

6 Dedicated Search Team.

7 Security Information Report.

8 Mandatory Drug Testing.

9 In this, it differs from the notion of respect, which we discuss below.

10 Officers, in their turn, expected to be treated fairly by management.

11 There were other ideas of respect (like respect as liking or as friendship), but we have tried to restrict this discussion to the three most frequent and relevant ways in which they were used.

12 A Kantian notion: 'respect for persons'.

13 We do not deal here with abusive treatment of prisoners by staff – a different form of 'corruption' that can have institutional as well as individual causes.

14 It is significant that only one respondent (a prisoner) mentioned that any wrongdoing would have to be on the initiative of the officer rather than the prisoner – the assumption was that officers were actively coerced or attracted into corruption by prisoners.

15 Arguably we have concentrated in this book on the best aspects of prison officer work and very little on the 'dark side'. This is consistent with our aims. There is a case for more contemporary empirical work on poor performance, abuses of power, and 'when things go wrong', but this is not our present task.

16 Public and media interest has tended to focus on 'the dark side' and some aspects of centralised management aim to control this facet of the prison officer's world.

Chapter 6

The centrality of discretion in the work of prison officers

[S]ome level of human interaction between officers and inmates beyond that of keeper and kept is an essential aspect of inmate management. It is the collective force of thousands of daily and hourly personal interactions between inmates and officers that drives up tensions and hostilities or quells them, fosters resistance or compliance, and engenders confrontation or co-operation in any prison. The 24-hour-a-day treatment provided inmates by routine interactions with line officers should be recognised as the primary and most influential treatment programme offered by any prison. (Gilbert 1997: 59)

[Discretion] is inevitable because the translation of rule into action, the process by which abstraction becomes actuality, involves people in interpretation and choice. Law is fundamentally an interpretative enterprise in which discretionary behaviour is compelled by ... 'the vagaries of language, the diversity of circumstances, and the indeterminacy of official purposes'. (Hawkins 1992: 11)

The policy of Incentives and Earned Privileges (IEP) brought the issue of discretion to the attention of those interested in prison work in England and Wales. The IEP policy essentially required governors of every establishment to draw up and introduce a system of encouraging and rewarding 'good' behaviour by prisoners and deterring 'bad' behaviour. It was based on the use of three levels of privileges: basic, standard and enhanced. It was a popular policy within establishments, but it was poorly and speedily implemented, with no training, in about 30 establishments in mid-1995, and extended progressively to the rest by early 1996, with limited opportunity to learn from and apply early experience of the policy's operation. Staff could now allocate prisoners to basic, standard or enhanced levels of privileges, based on their behaviour (that is, staff judgement about their behaviour based on each establishment's local IEP scheme). The Cambridge Institute of Criminology was invited to carry out a two-year evaluation of the operation and effects of this new policy (Liebling *et al.* 1997). In one of the five prisons we studied over the two years of the evaluation, very different numbers of prisoners were allocated to the basic level of privileges on different wings. Our study was both a before and after (outcomes) study, and a 'process' study of how the policy was implemented. During the process part of our work, we noted these variations in the 'resort to basic', particularly in one of our establishments. We looked more closely. Differences between prisoners could not account for these variations. Using our before and after data, we were able to link this finding about the disproportionate use of 'basic' to aspects of life on each wing. What we found was that staff, on the wing where relationships with prisoners were poor, resorted to the formal procedures at their disposal far sooner than staff on wings where reasonable relationships were found. They were less likely to warn prisoners first, to engage with them about their behaviour or to intervene in situations brewing on the wing. Instead, they retreated more into their offices and used formal disciplinary and quasi-disciplinary tools to manage prisoner behaviour. Linked to this distance between staff and prisoners were higher levels of fear among prisoners, more trade and higher stakes. The wing where this 'standoff' pattern was most marked subsequently went on to experience a major disturbance towards the end of our research (Liebling 1999). Staff were rigorously resisted by prisoners because they used too much power of the wrong sort.

Staff practices, particularly in the way they use their formal and informal power, differ. These differences have important effects on the life of establishments. So, this was an empirical illustration of the maxim that 'staff–prisoner relationships matter' (Home Office 1984; and Chapter 5, this volume). When we looked at the responses to our question from the before and after study about the quality of staff–prisoner relationships, we were no wiser. A simple question: 'How would you describe relationships between staff and prisoners?' got simple answers: 'good', 'OK', 'poor'. The word 'good' could mean anything, including, 'it's good that we never see staff', or conversely, 'it's good that they never stick to the rules'. Out of this research, then, grew our question: what is the nature of staff–prisoner relationships, which we have addressed in Chapter 5. In addressing the question of staff–prisoner relationships, we were (inevitably) drawn into a study of the use of discretion: how do staff go about their work; *why* are staff–prisoner relationships important, and in what ways? In this chapter we consider this key feature of prison officer work.

The enforcement of every rule in a prison by prison officers is impossible – or at least makes life very uncomfortable for prisoners and staff, as we shall see below. This sociological reality means that, somehow, prison officers must choose which rules they do enforce, which rules they do not and which rules they 'bend' and when. In short, officers must use their *discretion*. Officers use much more discretion than they think, or report to strangers and probably governors. A senior officer at Albany perceptively put it like this:

> We're governed by rules, and there is a saying that exceptions prove the rule. The most important thing is to know when that exception should be used. The good prison officer will bend the rules for good reasons, for the right reasons. (Sparks *et al.* 1996: 155)

But what are the 'right' reasons for bending rules and under what circumstances should rules *not* be bent? How, in practice, do officers decide? This question lies at the heart of officers' daily work:

> I can normally get them to do what I want them to do without having to resort to putting them on report. In my opinion, you can't be doing the job that well if you're having to place them on report all the time … There are ways of getting them to do what you want. They know the rules and regulations, and we know them. If an inmate is refusing to go to work, nine times out of ten I'll be able to get him to go to work without having to place him on report, just through communication skills. If he doesn't, then he goes on report, but normally I can get them to go … I just explain to them – you're being stupid here. Just because you got out of bed the wrong side this morning …get yourself up, washed, dressed, go to work, then you'll be able to get your canteen on Friday. If you don't do that, you know I've got to place you on report and you'll lose your wages. It's up to you, it's your choice at the end of the day. I'll leave you

to get on with it. I'll close the door, and within a few seconds the bell will go off. And they do just go to work. I just explain the situation to them. You don't normally need to explain it. They know, it's just a case of bloody-mindedness – 'I can't be bothered today.' (Officer)

Few studies have looked explicitly at the use of discretion in prisons. The Arizona Department of Corrections recognised the significance of the use of discretion in its formal training, and outlined the 'value-based ends' to which prison staff could apply their discretion:

- to maximise cooperation among all participants in the correctional setting – inmates and staff alike;

- to promote interaction between inmates and staff which demonstrates how individuals should interact in their communities and homes;

- to harmonise, as much as possible, the need for security with respect for human dignity; and

- to develop a consistent scheme of rewards and deterrents which lead inmates to view the use of your (the officer's) discretion as fair and just. By 'fair and just' we mean that the use of rewards and deterrents requires that you balance fitting rules and regulations to the individual with assurance that like situations require the same response. (Arizona Department of Corrections, 1982: 4, in Gilbert 1997: 56) We shall return to this important point at the end of this chapter.

However, there is an extensive literature on the use of discretion in other contexts (see, for example, Dworkin 1977; Goodin 1986; Gilligan 1986; Hawkins 1992; Dixon 1997; Holloway 2000; Padfield and Liebling, with Arnold 2001; Grounds *et al.* 2003). We will discuss a number of studies that examine how the police employ their discretion below.

The literature states that the inevitability of discretion springs from three sources:

1 *The wording of rules themselves* – 'vagaries of language' mean that words can never perfectly describe a situation, action or continuum. As Hart (1958) puts it, rules are 'open-textured' (see also Twining and Miers 1991):

First: Words are vague; they have only a settled core of meaning, but beyond that a penumbra of borderline cases which is not regimented by any conventions ...

Second: Words are ambiguous; that is, have more than one relatively well settled use. A testator leaves his vessels to his son. If the question is whether this includes his flying-boat, it is the vagueness of 'vessel' which is the source of the trouble; but if the question is whether the bequest refers to the testator's boats or his drinking-cups, *ambiguity* is responsible.

Third: We are tempted, when we are faced with words, to look round for just one thing or quality for which the word is supposed to stand ...

Fourthly: For any account descriptive of any thing or state of affairs, it is always possible to substitute either a more specific or a more general description ...in answer to the question 'What did he do?', we may say 'He killed her' or 'He struck her', or 'He moved his arm', or 'He contracted the muscle of his arm', all of which may be true, but only one of them may be appropriate.

2 *The situations to which the rules will apply* – the 'diversity of circumstances': no two situations are ever exactly alike, and rules cannot be written that will cover every imaginable situation. Some interpretation will therefore be required by those working on the 'front line'.

3 *The official purposes* guiding an organisation. There is often, in any organisation, a potential lack of clarity in organisational aims, but also confusion or contradiction between different aims and objectives. The governmentality literature (for example, Rose and Miller 1992; Barry *et al.* 1996) alerts us to the way in which political rationalities (broadly, the wider ideas that lie behind policy) and political technologies (the ways to achieve these rationalities) are liable to subversion by interested groups and individuals. Even with clear aims and objectives and clear ways to reach these objectives, outcomes can be different from those desired. The aims and objectives of the Prison Service have received attention from many sources (Home Office 1979, 1991, 1995; King and Morgan 1979; Bottoms 1989), with many critics accusing them of being vague, in conflict with each other or too numerous.

Discretion, then, is inevitable; it is also, in Goodin's (1986) un-comfortable term, ineliminable. Wherever there are rules, there will be discretion. In the prison context, this is especially true.

Prison officers and the 'defects of total power'

As Gresham Sykes argued, in his 1958 study of a maximum security prison in New Jersey:

> The rulers of this society of captives nominally hold in their hands the sole right of granting rewards and inflicting punishments and it would seem that no prisoner could afford to ignore their demands for conformity ... The custodians have the right not only to issue and administer the orders and regulations which are to guide the life of the prisoner, but also the right to detain, try, and punish any individual accused of disobedience – a merging of legislative, executive and judicial functions which has long been regarded as the earmark of complete domination. The officials of the prison, in short, appear to be the possessors of almost infinite power within their realm; and, at least on the surface, the bureaucratic staff should experience no great difficulty in converting their rules and regulations – their blueprint for behaviour – into a reality. (Sykes 1958: 41–2)

Prison officers cannot enforce every applicable rule if the prison day is to maintain any kind of worthwhile flow:

> If the rulers of any social system could secure compliance within their rules and regulations ... it might be expected that the officials of the maximum security prison would be able to do so. (Sykes 1958: 41–2)

However, despite the rules, officers constantly have to work at the maintenance of order. Officers know that the use of physical coercion has severe limits on a day-to-day basis, and in seeking compliance from prisoners they have no very effective system of rewards or punishments (although arguably IEP has helped a little). Rule-breaking and non-compliance is common among prisoners, but there is more to enforcement than the rules:

Systems of power may also fail because those who are supposed to rule are unwilling to do so ... The 'corruption' of the rules may be far less dramatic than the insurrection of the rules, for power unexercised is seldom as visible as power which is challenged, but the system of power still falters. (Sykes 1958: 53)[1]

This observation is now something of a penological commonplace. To the newcomer, the prison seems a place of rules, limits, uneven power and clear standards. As we illustrated in Chapter 2, prison officers constitute a substantial 'custodial force' and about two-thirds of the officers employed in an establishment will be directly involved in the supervision and control of prisoners. Prison officers have a monopoly on the use of legitimate force. There is a clear pyramid of authority – with prison officers 'at the coalface' responsible for the translation of policy into everyday practice. The problem is:

The objectives which the officials pursue are not completely of their own choosing and the means which they can use to achieve their objectives are far from limitless. The custodians are not total despots, able to exercise their power at whim, and thus they lack the essential mark of infinite power, the unchallenged right of being capricious in their own rule. (Sykes 1958: 42)

Prison officers are not free from laws, norms and observable outcomes – and these considerations place limits on how they achieve their (and others') ends. In practice, despite the availability of coercion, the surveillance, the searches, the cameras and the rewards and punishments available, the actual behaviour of prisoners 'differs markedly from that which is called for by official commands and decrees' (Sykes 1958: 42). Despite the fact that 'the prison' is generally regarded as the ultimate sanction and the ultimate tool for the control of deviance, violence, theft and drug use persist in the prison and prison staff have to manage their existence and effects:

Far from being omnipotent rulers who have crushed all signs of rebellion against their regime, the custodians are engaged in a struggle to maintain order – and it is a struggle in which the custodians frequently fail. (Sykes 1958: 42)

Gresham Sykes and the late-modern prison officer

Sykes was writing in the 1950s. Some of what he observed in New Jersey State Prison has altered in the modern prison, as new designs, technologies and penal practices have developed. But his key argument is important: that staff do not hold total power. Just as in crime figures generally, there exists outside the official figures a 'dark figure' of unrecorded offending: the unobserved assault, the threat, the possession of weapons and contraband. McDermott and King, in a classic study of English prisons, described some of the 'mind games' of prison life: hide and seek, call my bluff, the magic roundabout (McDermott and King 1988). Staff have considerable (and arguably in recent years increased) power, but:

> If power is viewed as the probability that orders and regulations will be obeyed by a given group of individuals, as Max Weber has suggested, the New Jersey State Prison is perhaps more notable for the doubtfulness of its obedience than its certainty. (Sykes 1958: 45)

The late-modern English prison has seen a clear 'return to power' for staff, particularly after the Whitemoor escapes, which were linked to a power imbalance between staff and prisoners and the neglect of formal rules. But prison staff have also become less numerous, as careful management practices have resulted in a more precise and limited deployment of prison officers on wings. Prison staff have gained both coercive and legitimate power since the early 1990s, and they have lost some of their (potentially inflammatory and also coercive) 'power of presence' since the introduction of Fresh Start in the late 1980s and privatisation and market testing in the 1990s. We shall consider this 'reconfiguring' of the power base of staff further below.

First, we need to explore some of the forces which 'undermine' the power position of prison staff. Sykes argues (as others have subsequently) that the power of the custodians is not based on authority. What does he mean? Authority is a 'complex social relationship' in which an individual or group is recognised as possessing the right to issue orders and those who receive these orders feel a duty to obey:

> In its pure form, then, or as an ideal type, power based on authority has two essential elements: a rightful or legitimate

effort to exercise control on the one hand and an inner, moral compulsion to obey, by those who are controlled, on the other. In reality, of course, the recognition of the legitimacy of efforts to exercise control may be qualified or partial and the sense of duty, as a motive for compliance, may be mixed with motives of fear or self-interest. But it is possible to think of power based on authority in its pure form and to use this as a baseline in describing the empirical case. (Sykes 1958: 46)

The second of these elements of authority (the sense of duty as a motive for compliance) supplies 'the secret strength of most social organisations' (Sykes 1958: 47). Authority is accepted as legitimate for reasons relating largely to internalised morality but also relating to the nature of these social institutions. In the prison, Sykes argues:

Power must be based on something other than internalised morality and the custodians find themselves confronting men [sic] who must be forced, bribed, or cajoled into compliance. (Sykes 1958: 47)

As he goes on to say, this does not mean that prisoners do not recognise the legitimacy of prison staff power. In fact, prisoners are astute judges of the legitimacy of a prison regime and the evidence supports a strong relationship between their perceptions of a regime's legitimacy and their willingness to comply with it (see later; see also Sparks et al. 1996). As Lord Woolf found:

A recurring theme in the evidence from prisoners who may have instigated, and who were involved in, the riots was that their actions were a response to the manner in which they were treated by the prison system. Although they did not always use these terms, they felt a lack of justice. If what they say is true, the failure of the Prison Service to fulfil its responsibilities to act with justice created in April 1990 serious difficulties in maintaining security and control in prisons. (Home Office 1991: para. 9.24)

The point made by Sykes is that the normal 'bond' between the recognition of the legitimacy of staff power and the sense of duty has been 'torn apart' (Sykes 1958: 48). Prisoners recognise that the prison has a certain validity, but their subjugation 'is not complete'. There is, inevitably, resistance. Sykes puts the argument thus:

Whether he sees himself as caught by his own stupidity, the workings of chance, his inability to 'fix' the case, or the superior skill of the police, the criminal in prison seldom denies the legitimacy of confinement. At the same time, the recognition of the legitimacy of society's surrogates and their body of rules is not accompanied by an internalised obligation to obey and the prisoner thus accepts the facts of his imprisonment at one level and rejects it at another ... It is in this apparent contradiction that we can see the first flaw in the custodial bureaucracy's assumed supremacy. (Sykes 1958: 48)

Once the use of force is rejected as a means to secure obedience, for it is inefficient as well as the least legitimate mode of power, then other means must be sought:

In short, the ability of the officials to physically coerce their captives into the path of compliance is something of an illusion as far as the day-to-day activities of the prison are concerned and may be of doubtful value in moments of crisis. Intrinsically inefficient as a method of making men carry out a complex task, diminished in effectiveness by the realities of the guard–inmate ratio, and always accompanied by the danger of touching off further violence, the use of physical force by the custodians has many limitations as a basis on which to found the routine operation of the prison. (Sykes 1958: 49–50)

Coercion is sometimes used (the development of sophisticated control and restraint techniques and changes to the physical design of establishments have made these forms of coercion more effective in many ways). But rewards and punishments constitute 'a better means of persuasion' although these have to be genuinely perceived as such and must be seen by prisoners as significant enough to encourage reasonable behaviour. Sykes argues that the punishments available in prison are limited because they 'do not represent a profound difference from the prisoner's usual status' (Sykes 1958: 50), and they may have counterproductive status-enhancing effects (this is often seen in segregation units and 'special handling' units such as close supervision centres). The rewards on offer may be too limited, and they have tended over time (until recently) to be granted all at once upon entry to the prison. Prisoners tend to see 'rewards' or 'privileges' as 'rights', sometimes arguably for good reason (for example, decent visits facilities and provision to help ensure proper access to their families).

The IEP study carried out in 1995–7 found that increased use of incentives and punishments did not result in significant improvements in prisoner behaviour overall (although there were some important examples of its successful use; Liebling *et al.* 1997). Instead, it seemed to lead, along with other policies introduced at the time, to losses in prisoners' perceptions of the legitimacy of prison regimes, and in the quality of staff–prisoner relationships, which are, in turn, both related to the maintenance of order, the main aim of IEP. There were dangers in an oversimplistic conception of IEP and in the use of discretion in the granting and taking away of privileges. Prisoner behaviour is complex and difficult to assess as much of it is invisible, and there are unclear conceptions of 'good' and 'bad' behaviour, with very different thresholds within and between prisons. The importance of process and of decision-making generally cannot be overestimated. Further elaboration on this research can be found in Liebling (2000; 2008b) and Bottoms (1999).

The 'un-exercise' of power

So, the prison officer is operating without (Sykes says) the moral duty of his or her charges, without coercion and with limited, albeit significant, rewards and punishments which are difficult to distribute fairly. There are other forces at work which weaken this already fractured monolith of power. Staff may be unwilling to impose the rules:

> The un-issued order, the deliberately ignored disobedience, the duty left unperformed – these are cracks in the monolith just as surely as are acts of defiance in the subject population. (Sykes 1958: 53)

The 'un-exercise' of power in prison is hugely significant – and may constitute both 'the best' and 'a worst' form of practice, as we shall argue later. Sykes calls these practices 'corruptions'; Sparks *et al.* call them 'accommodations' (Sparks *et al.* 1996). We want to argue that, deployed in an appropriate manner, the underuse of power constitutes 'the best' form of prison officer work: what we (and others) have called peacekeeping. This best work consists of the diligent and skilled use of discretion. Used in the wrong way, the underuse of power can be regarded as unprofessional and, at worst, a form of 'conditioning' or omission of duty.

Let us look first at the underuse of power as omission – Sykes' loaded term, 'corruptions'. Three structural features of the prison bring this about:

- the close nature of the contact or 'lack of social distance' between staff and prisoners throughout the day;
- the claims of reciprocity and goodwill; and
- the involvement of prisoners in some 'formal' duties (orderlies, library staff, hotplate servers, listeners, etc.).

The first arises from the most basic feature of prison life. It is staff who unlock prisoners, who bear the brunt of their resentments or who pass on bad news. Their working style is the subject of commentary and sometimes rebuke by prisoners on a daily basis. Staff may come to share some of the irritants of the 'unreasonableness of authority' and they may come to like and respect certain of their charges (sometimes more than they like and respect their own managers). Prisoners become individuals – and this delicate and at times uncomfortable position is actively advocated by those who design and manage the prison from afar.

The second arises from the dependency of staff on the consent of the prisoners in order to 'get through the day'. Prisoners move from the wing to work, because they are prepared to, and staff ability to 'handle' prisoners in a basically cooperative way demands the generation of goodwill. The prison officer is often judged by the atmosphere on a wing: is it clean, are prisoners amicable and cooperative, and are relations reasonable? To achieve this, goodwill matters.

The third arises from the practice of 'trust', as trusted prisoners ('trustees' or red bands, listeners, and so on) are given small duties and responsibilities (powers) which they deploy in different ways. Such positions may bring influence beyond the strict definition of their role – and in this sense, the staff have 'given away' a certain degree of power and may not be fully aware of how it is being used.

All of these practices are necessary and appropriate aspects of the legitimate prison. A certain tolerance is necessary so that compliance can be achieved 'where it counts' (Sykes 1958: 57). But such practices need to be self-consciously policed; they can cross important thresholds. Staff, very occasionally, become emotionally entangled;

they make deals; they often tolerate, and sometimes collude in, rule-breaking behaviours. They may fear prisoners and let power go for this reason. Their power, once given away, is hard to regain. One officer may find it difficult to exercise power in an area where another officer has given it away.

So, prison officers:

[F]ar from being converted into brutal tyrants, are under strong pressure to compromise with their captives, for it is a paradox that they can insure their dominance only by allowing it to be corrupted. (Sykes 1958: 58)

As others have argued, you may have to 'lose control in order to gain control' (Sykes 1958; Sparks *et al.* 1996; Liebling and Price 1999). Existing studies tend to emphasise distance and antagonism between staff and prisoners – although a few recent studies (and of course some of the classics) have looked at cooperation and accommodation (see Liebling and Price 1999; Liebling 2000). A study by Shapira and Navon in Israeli prisons found that contrary to the picture of total institutions painted by Goffman and others after him, the apparent 'gap' between staff and prisoners is often narrow, linked as officers and prisoners often are by common interests, by cultural and social values and experiences and by common deprivations (Shapira and Navon 1985; see also Morris and Morris 1963). This narrowing of the gap can render officers vulnerable to corruption, for example bribery, malign under-enforcement, yielding to unreasonable demands, or even 'romantic ties' (Shapira and Navon 1985: 136–9), as Learmont was at pains to argue following the escapes from maximum security custody (Home Office 1995). Staff and prisoners live in a state of mutual dependence within prison, and may share extra-institutional pressures (such as political or religious affiliations, neighbourhoods, family problems, etc.) which serve to moderate the 'basic split' so often assumed by commentators on the prison. These personal hesitations, tensions and conflicts which shape policy and resist attempts made to enforce compliance (for example by training, audit and inspection) constitute a key and underestimated part of a prison officer's working role.

These 'corruptions', if they are 'corruptions', are rooted in flaws in the social system of the prison itself (Sykes 1958: 60), and mean, in practice, that 'the job requirements of the guard's position are not technical skills' but rely on 'matters of character such as courage, honesty, and so on'. Sykes' argument that the rulers are reluctant, on a day-to-day basis, to enforce their total power, but instead make a series of 'accommodations' to keep the 'smooth flow' of prison life going, is critical to any satisfactory understanding of prison life. A gap between staff and prisoners must exist, so the prison can work as a prison, but the gap must be narrowed, so that the prison can continue to function – at any rate, once the option of total isolation has been rejected. There is thus a continual tension between the intrinsic, caste-like gap between staff and prisoners, on the one hand, and the bridging of that gap that is necessary if the task of 'getting through the prison day' is to be accomplished smoothly. This tension is not – perhaps cannot be – controlled by formal rules and structures, but by informal structures. Mutual understandings develop whereby staff and prisoners 'establish tactical agreements and unofficial arrangements enabling them to carry out their work'. Staff must use the largely underestimated discretion they have to do this, but there are no explicit principles or guidelines which can aid them in their decision-making. Again, we shall return to this point later.

Sykes draws the conclusion that a 'brief period of schooling' can familiarise the new officer with the routines and procedures of the prison, but that prison staff cannot be fully prepared for the realities of their role with 'lectures and discussions' alone (Sykes 1958: 61). Prison staff often argue that the training they need most is 'what to do in the event of trouble' (Sykes 1958: 45). They may also value training in the development of courage, honesty and integrity.

The power base of prison officers

Much of the work of prison officers involves the use of power: seeking to influence the behaviour of others. According to Hepburn (1985), staff draw upon six types of power base in a prison to achieve this:

- *coercive* power (for example, the use of segregation, searches, transfer, the disciplinary system);
- *reward* power (for example, the distribution of privileges, prized jobs, favourable reports);
- *legitimate* power (formal authority, the 'rule of law');
- *exchange* power (the informal reward system, under-enforcement and accommodation, as outlined by Sykes, above);
- *expert* or *'professional'* power (expertise – for example, in resolving conflicts, competence); and

- *respect* or personal authority (officers' manner of working with prisoners, their leadership skills).

Prisoners may be more likely to comply with or prefer some modes of power over others (Hepburn 1985: 147–9; see also Sparks *et al.* 1996), for example legitimate and expert power. Deficiencies in some power bases lead to the establishment of others – so that insufficient coercive power may lead to the establishment of reciprocity or 'exchange' (accommodations). This move from a mainly exchange to a more coercive power base might be a helpful way of characterising prisons, and in particular the fluctuations seen in recent history. Individual officers may tend to use some power bases over others – and this has been shown to vary with their overall attitudes towards their work and with experience (Hepburn 1985: 150).

Arguably, prisons and prison systems vary over time in the types of power bases that are in favour. Views changed about what the most appropriate combination of power bases might be. For example, in the opening years of the high security prison HMP Whitemoor (1991–3), caught up in the ideals of 'liberal optimism' that followed the publication of the Woolf Report, staff had been encouraged (or in their view, had been abandoned) to negotiate with prisoners in the interests of order on the grounds that security was virtually guaranteed by modern design techniques. It was thought, for good reason, that long-term prisoners required 'a liberal regime within a secure perimeter' (ACPS 1968; Liebling and Price 1999; see also Bottoms and Light 1987; Liebling *et al.* 1997). Following a dramatic set of escapes in 1994, as well as problems of disorder, negotiated 'appeasement' practices fell out of favour. Other 'liberal regimes' were also 'reined in' (for example, Long Lartin; see Sparks *et al.* 1996), as they became regarded as having abdicated control and a form of authority which staff and prisoners needed. After 1994, the senior management team at Whitemoor, and other prisons, began deliberately to reshape the power base of staff: from mainly 'exchange' power – the power of accommodation and negotiation – to a much more explicitly 'coercive' power – the increased use of segregation, transfer, privilege removal, disciplinary punishments and lock-downs. A 'reward' power base (the granting of privileges) also became a 'coercive' power base (the *removal* of some privileges; see Hepburn 1985) with the introduction of IEP. Interestingly, the other power bases Hepburn identifies: 'legitimate', 'expert/professional' and 'respect', did not decrease, and some evidence suggests they may have increased, at least in the early stages, as prisoners traded in relative freedom, fear and chaos for restraint, order and security, and the knowledge that staff (and not other prisoners) were in control. The risk, once staff established their new confidence, is that the significance of legitimate, expert and personal power is forgotten, if coercive power becomes too easy to use (see Drake 2008).

This transition from one form of power to another, and prisoners' basic consent to it under reasonable conditions, has been witnessed in other establishments (e.g. HMP Highpoint over the years 1995–7; see Liebling *et al.* 1997). But this is a complex process. Our observations were that coercive power could increase compliance, but not on its own (see Liebling and Price 1999) and not if it becomes too raw (Drake 2008). In this new regime, prisoners also felt the 'depth' (Downes 1988) and 'weight' (King and McDermott 1995) of imprisonment as never before, and described one of these prisons as 'safer, in a tense sort of way' (Liebling and Price 1999).

Staff were sometimes careless with their increased power and prisoners were aware that so-called relationships between staff and prisoners were there to oil the smooth flow of the prison: the higher the control quotient, the more 'oil' was needed. Relationships were – in this context – instruments of control as well as instruments of justice. They were described as a sort of 'quiet power'.

Our argument so far is that staff have, on the one hand, less formal power than they need at their disposal. However, they also have a wide range of *different* types of power available to them. Legitimate power and expert power seem to be the most effective in securing compliance (see Bottoms 1999; see also Home Office 1991). Coercive power is most effective when it is 'always available but rarely used' (Hepburn 1985: 160) and combined with other more palatable kinds. This type of analysis has been more common in studies of policing. We shall look next therefore at the use of discretion in policing.

Police discretion

There are significant similarities between the work of a police officer and that of a prison officer, beyond their functions within the criminal justice system. Reiner defies 'policing' as 'the whole craft of governing a social order' (Reiner 1997: 997). This is one of the key problems of the prison – how, successfully, to keep a community in order. Prison officers 'police' the prison in a similar way to police officers policing a community. Both possess the 'powers of a constable', which derive from the concept of a 'peace' officer – someone who kept the King's or Queen's peace.[2] A certain amount of consent is required to achieve the task. Over-policing threatens this consent.

> The central concept underlying police research has been discretion, the recognition that the police do not automatically translate law into policing practice. (Reiner 1997: 999)

Studies of police use of discretion have examined the significance of non-law-enforcement, peacekeeping work and the dependence of formal upon informal modes of control (Banton 1964; Bittner 1967; and Smith 1986, for example).[3] Underlying all police practice is the potential use of legitimate, state-granted, physical force – although this potential remains unused for the vast majority of the time. Police practice has complex and often contradictory functions, and most examples of good policing rely on verbal skills rather than physical coercion. All of these observations are true of prison work. Both the task of policing and the task of 'policing' prison behaviour require the use of power and authority, the use of discretion, the pursuit of order and an opposition to lawlessness.

Of course, there are important distinctions to be made between policing and prison officer work. First, prison officers are more continually in contact with their charges. Officers in local prisons have observed that they often see offenders 'from cradle to grave', even when they each move between establishments. As a result of continuing contact, relationships are formed with prisoners and authority is often deployed through these relationships. Secondly, prison officers are more visible to their immediate line managers than police officers. Thirdly, the formal legal power held by a prison officer over a prisoner is probably greater than that held by a police officer. Prisoners are no longer free citizens, and there are many powerful rules available to the prison officer.

Prison officers and prison rules

If discretion is about the choice to enforce or not to enforce a rule, it is first necessary to outline the many different kinds of rules and instructions which structure the work of prison officers. As Loucks (2000: 6) points out:

> To the observer, regulations governing the minutiae of prison life often represent an impenetrable bureaucracy. In order to

uncover management policy, one has to unravel layers of rules upon rules.

There are many levels of rules within the prison system. First, there are the Prison Rules and the Young Offender Institution Rules: the statutory instruments by which the Home Secretary regulates the operation of prisons and YOIs by virtue of authority given him by section 47 of the Prison Act 1952. The Prison Rules as a whole were most recently updated and approved by Parliament in 1999 and have been slightly amended since then.[4] Second, as most of these broad Rules 'leave a great deal of discretion to the prison authorities' (Loucks 2000: 6),[5] the Service issues instructions to give guidance as to the interpretation of the Rules. These instructions, now published in the form of Prison Service Orders (commonly referred to as 'PSOs'), cover every conceivable aspect of prison life from sentence planning and segregation, for example, to zoonotic infections and flag-flying duties. One of the difficulties the Service had, to which Woodcock (Home Office 1994: recommendation 60) drew particular attention, was the fact that the Service had too many instructions, some dating back many years. It was this that prompted Woodcock to comment famously that: 'It could be said that what the Prison Service needs to do most of all is to comply with its own written instructions' (para. 9.27). Since Woodcock reported the Service has attempted to rationalise its instructions but there are still a great many Circular Instructions (issued before 1993) and Instructions to Governors (issued 1993–7) in addition to the never-ending flow of new PSO instructions. Little wonder that discretion is an intrinsic part of the officer's role.[6]

The legal status of the Rules, Prison Service Orders and circulars is complex. Loucks points out that the Prison Officers' Training Manual states that the Rules have the force of law. Prison Service Orders and circulars have 'no legal status whatsoever despite the fact that they contain massive detail relevant to the conduct of daily life in prison' (Livingstone and Owen 1998: 1.39). Prisoners can appeal to the courts – for example, through an application for judicial review of a decision – but the judicial route is a difficult and time-consuming process. Yet the involvement of external checks on the use of rules is increasing: courts are now more willing to intervene in prison life on standards of fairness than they once were; the Prisons Ombudsman acts as an 'avenue of complaint' for prisoners, independent of the Prison Service (Prisons Ombudsman 2000 and subsequent Annual Reports), and can make recommendations about decisions. The Human Rights Act 1998 provides recourse through the UK courts on European Convention on

Human Rights issues, and is likely to increase the understanding of prisoners' rights among prison officials. Prison officers and governors are now more aware of these external checks and balances when they are taking decisions.[7]

Despite the vagueness surrounding the legal standing of the various types of regulation, officers are faced with a situation where they:

- have a great many rules at their disposal;

- are responsible for the maintenance of security and order, and for helping prisoners lead a good and useful life (and additional goals of their own prison or wing) and are meant to do this mainly through the application of the rules;

- know that the total enforcement of the rules is:
  - impossible (there are too many rules);[8] and
  - highly undesirable (the prison would not function, prisoners would become frustrated, other officers would resist, etc.); and so

- must choose which rules should be enforced and which should not, and to what extent.

Although full enforcement of the rules is impossible, prison officers are also well aware that a lax under-enforcement of rules can, in many circumstances, produce other undesirable results. Under-enforcement is justifiable when it is intended to achieve their effect or end informally, that is without recourse to the exercise of formal authority. The tone of voice used in conversation or the use of humour are often effective substitutes for formal 'orders': here, for example, rules are still enforced, but tacitly. Under-enforcement can render officers accountable and their jobs vulnerable to prison managers rightly requiring high standards of security and probity. This is an extremely difficult tightrope to walk. Officers complain that the use of 'banter' – so central to their work – is sometimes made risky by increased attention to potentially racist or sexist language and behaviour. Staff must be at the right place on many dimensions (see Figure 6.1).

When do officers choose to enforce rules and when to relax them? What principles do they employ to help them decide? How far can their reasoning be explained? What is good practice? We discuss below what we learned about prison officers and discretion during our research at Whitemoor.

Staff must be in the right place on several dimensions:

too little power	←	**use of power**	→	used too often/too much
too little used	←	**use of discretion**	→	used too often/too much
fear	←	**confidence**	→	arrogance
weak boundaries	←	**relations with prisoners**	→	distant
friendship	←	**personal feelings**	→	hatred
deference	←	**respect**	→	disrespect
appeasement/collusion	←	**communication**	→	ignoring
complete openness	←	**contact/consultation**	→	authoritarian
over-involvement	←	**involvement**	→	lack of concern
too flexible	←	**fairness**	→	too rigid

Figure 6.1 The 'right place' for prison officers

Prison officers and the use of discretion

With the exception of officers in the SSU,[9] there was a consensus among all prison officers, governors and prisoners at Whitemoor that prison work consisted mainly of 'grey areas' with only small areas of clarity, despite the existence of an increasing number of rules and guidelines. There were constant tensions between what 'the rule book' would say and what 'common sense' suggested. This has been observed in studies of policing and other areas of 'law in action' (Smith 1986; Hawkins 1992; Dixon 1997):

> They say to be a good police officer, you need to use common sense. But when the shit hits the fan, they say you should have used the rule book. (Australian police officer, cited in Dixon 1997: 5)

The policing literature suggests that officers frequently enforce their *authority* rather than 'the law' or 'the rules'. This was very much in line with what officers at Whitemoor said to us and with what we often observed them do. There were significant non-legal factors which influenced decisions to enforce the rules, just as in policing – for example, whether an officer was treated with respect or not by the prisoner in question (see the next chapter), or whether the safety of the environment was threatened (Sykes and Brent 1983). Sykes and Brent suggested that the police operate with an *asymmetric deference norm,* that is they adjust their level of deference/respect to just below that of a civilian. Police officers expect civilians to acknowledge that this asymmetric status norm governs their relations – in effect, the police assume a slightly higher status than the status of civilian. 'Negative police conduct is directed towards citizens who refuse to defer to their authority' (Sykes and Brent 1983: 101). Police officers are also problem-solving, and often do so with long-term objectives in mind. They are not simply choosing between arrest and non-arrest, but between different typifications of the situation, of the 'situated identities' of the civilians and between many alternatives in addition to arrest/non-arrest (calming the situation down, for example).

We found prison officers – just as police officers – making judgements about interactions by considering demeanour, gestures and language (whose content and tone is continually interpreted; Rorty 1989). Negative interaction could be a substitute for a formal sanction. Thus prison officers under-enforce the rules but may still enforce their authority – in many different ways. Prison officers reach a solution to the situation in front of them that does not necessarily draw upon the rules at all.

It was through the use of discretion that staff structured their own and prisoners' activities, and that they managed (usually) to maintain order and (some level of) compliance. So, to return to the question posed at the beginning of this chapter: what were the 'right reasons' for a prison officer to 'bend' the rules?

To begin with, it was simply not considered politic or efficient to resort to the rule book at every opportunity. It was fairly consistently felt, by both prisoners and staff, that the 'decent thing' was to be reasonably sparing with the rules, unless there was a good reason not to be:

Has there been an occasion recently where you were expecting to be placed on report and weren't? (Interviewer)

Yeah – I've [expletive] off a few screws and thought that I'd gone a bit far, but didn't get a nicking sheet that night.

How does something like that then change the relationship you have with that officer you swore at?

It actually improves your attitude to that officer. The screws can earn respect. If a screw comes in and finds booze and pours it down the toilet, they've got my instant respect, because I know they're told to nick us. I've lost, because I've lost the hooch. That's enough of a punishment for me. The officer's been sensible – if I had bucket after bucket, then fair enough, nick me. But a little bit, if they ran out and nicked me for it, no respect at all. They get instant respect, they've behaved in a humane manner. (Prisoner)[10]

The important question of boundaries is addressed in the next chapter. Officers and prisoners recognised that rules were resources upon which to draw rather than templates to be applied at any opportunity. Rules were one source of power that ensured one sort of order and were not always (or even frequently) the best way of achieving order. Less coercive methods of power often achieved a more sustainable form of order.[11] It was all a question of balance. While formal punishments such as those following adjudications or loss of incentives status were not meaningless to prisoners, they might not have the desired impact if prisoners had 'friends who would sort them out' if privileges were lost (or if prisoners gained status among their peers for 'going down to basic').

The consent of prisoners (and most prisoners consciously felt that they were consenting to or granting order to the prison rather than being controlled) was crucial to whatever type of 'order' was established. This was just like the concept of policing with consent. Animosity could quickly develop if staff took a hard line over detail or approached prisoners with 'the wrong attitude':

[Prison Service] college is a little bit like learning to drive a car. Once you've passed your test at the end of college, and you're put in a prison, that's when you really learn to drive. You take things a little bit further, you learn where your line is … can I go a little bit faster round this corner? And the next day, a little bit faster … and then you nearly lose it and you think, whoa … I'll pull back a bit there … I went to a YOI and I learned the job there and so it was quite difficult coming here, from a place where I was shouting and screaming … if you holler at some of these, it doesn't get you anywhere. (Senior officer)

Clearly different styles are required in different types of establishment. One of our most important findings concerned the reasons whereby officers justified their decisions to enforce a particular rule or not. While it was widely recognised by staff and managers that rules were often bent or under-enforced and that situations were sometimes best not handled in the strict and inflexible manner of the rule book, we found little evidence of any explicit principles guiding the exercise of discretion. While senior managers confidently communicated their vision to us, this vision, about moving from 'control' to 'order' and about safely granting prisoners some agency, was not clearly understood by prison officers. Each prison officer had their own principles, their own 'bigger picture' of what prison was about and of what their particular role was in the prison. This in turn informed how they handled specific situations. We give an example below.

One question we asked a lot of officers during interviews was about what they would do if they came across a prisoner who was 'wired up' during a regular cell check (drawing a wire to his stereo from inside the cell light to avoid having to pay for batteries). Officers gave us a range of responses, each of which was shaped by the individual's own 'bigger picture' of prison work. For example:

- Officer A (just out of the SSU) answered immediately: 'Close the cell, call the Works Department to safely take down the wire, and place the prisoner on report'. His reasoning was that wiring up was against the rules of the prison and was also a potential safety hazard. His 'bigger picture' centred on the enforcement of the rules as a route to safety and order. While the officer was willing to 'bend' some rules, this incident was serious enough to warrant a formal adjudication. Any repercussions for his relationship with the prisoner or with others were not considered – or were sacrificed to the need to maintain the rules.

- Officer B said that he would 'Take down the wire and confiscate it, and have a word with the prisoner when he came back on the wing'. The prisoner would be 'warned that wiring up was a dangerous thing to do and could end up with him being placed on report or electrocuted'. This officer recognised the expense of batteries to prisoners and appreciated that some of them might resort to wiring up. He did not want to place the prisoner on report (but would do so if the prisoner was caught again) and chose to reach the same overall result as Officer A (stopping the prisoner wiring up) but in a less formal manner. He also felt that this method of resolution had the added bonus of granting the prisoner a favour. Strictly, the prisoner should have been placed on report. In this way, the prisoner was placed in the officer's debt, and the favour could be called in at an opportune time in the future. The 'bigger picture' of this officer was centred on long-term wing order and the maintenance of relationships.

- Officer C took a different view. He said that he would take the wire down, but leave it in the prisoner's cell. He would let the prisoner know that he'd found the wire and that he'd put the prisoner on report if he found him wired up again. ('You don't leave a wire up when an officer's coming round, do you? It's taking the piss. He should know that someone's going to get annoyed at that' – Officer.) As with Officer B, he felt that this action meant that he was granting the prisoner a favour. His reasoning for leaving the wire in the cell was pragmatic: prisoners are going to wire up, whether we like it or not; they have to get the wires from somewhere. If I take this wire away, then the next time the hair clippers (or another electrical item) are signed out from the office, they'll eventually reappear without a lead; the wing will then be without hair clippers for a week while Works fixes them. The wing runs more easily when officers are able to let prisoners have access to all the items they are entitled to. This officer's 'bigger picture' was all about keeping the flow of the wing going; ideas about enforcement, related to wider principles of rule-breaking, were subordinated to the principle of 'smooth flow'.

Here, each officer did actually 'enforce' the rule about wiring up, but in different ways (to different degrees). The decisions of prison officers were informed by interpretation and choice. Decisions were embedded in meaning, knowledge, experience, values and relationships. Each wing of the prison and each spur within that wing and each particular officer on each spur tended to have an 'ethos' or 'way of working' that was different (at times, only subtly so) from all others. To some extent, these different ways of working were differences in the exercise of discretion – differences as to which rules would be enforced and to what extent, and in which times and places. Senior managers were aware that officers enforced or did not enforce rules for different reasons and were concerned about how to ensure that the reasons for staff behaviour were the correct ones:

This is what we are trying to get at – where the boundaries are; and these questions, 'do you play pool, don't you play pool?'; 'do

you take a biscuit, don't you take a biscuit?' – they divide the staff.
(Interviewer)

The answer is in your head; the answer is the kind of person you are as an officer. And if you are playing pool because you feel that you need to ingratiate yourself with prisoners, then playing pool is the worst thing you should do. If playing pool is simply a vehicle for communicating at a more significant level with prisoners about issues of order, control, responsibility, ownership, drug dealing, whatever it is you want to legitimately discuss – if doing it over a game of pool is the way to do it, then that's absolutely the right way to do it. (Senior manager)

There was a lot of talk about the boundaries of rule-bending and relationships, about where these boundaries were and about how prison officers and prisoners knew when they were crossing them or when they had to be 'policed'. In this sense, the job of being a prison officer was likened to the job of being a parent. It was important that staff were in charge of the boundaries rather than prisoners. By the nature of their position, prisoners were compelled to challenge these boundaries and frequently did so. But like parents, prison officers had different personal thresholds, just as they had different 'bigger pictures'. Yet unlike parents, prison officers also had to bear their professional 'line' in mind:

We've got quite a volatile mix at the moment, so every day you get through, you think, we've done OK there. When you get someone talk to you ... prisoner X was here two days ago and we had a confrontation on the hotplate about fruit. And he didn't get what he wanted. We then had another confrontation three days later about visits. He knew I was new on the wing, and he was really trying to see how far he could go. So I just put my official head on – 'you ain't getting nothing. They're the rules and you'll obey them'. I did that for about a fortnight. He actually approached me about a week later, said this and that, is there any chance you can sort it out? I said I'd have a go, did it, and we now get on very well. (Officer)

Prison work as peacemaking

A wider interest in the use of discretion among law enforcement officials has often been linked to the potential abuse of power (Liebling *et al.* 1999) rather than its underuse. Perhaps the primary role of prison officers is in peacekeeping. We found that prison officers underused formal power more often, and to better effect, than they overused it. Under-enforcement, the movement from tension to peace without incident, the use of language rather than action to avert the requirement for force, was far more common. Managers did not often recognise or reward this kind of professional conduct. There is a gap here between what could be seen as a post-Learmont view of a prison, where rules are there to be enforced (and *should* and *can* be enforced), and the sociological facts of imprisonment, where rules are only resources on which officers draw. Arguably, before Woodcock and Learmont, the Service was regularly failing to enforce rules, exercise authority and use power. The tightening up which followed has had benefits, some of which are related to 'better rule following'. The question is all about balance.

In practice, staff use their judgement, experience and sensitivity to the specific context of the wing:

> When you first come onto a new area, as a new officer, you basically say 'what happens here' and they say 'it's done like this'. So you do it like that, but the regular staff do it their own way, which is the relaxed way and you say 'no it's like that' – then you get abuse. A few times I got that. I remember a con had a go at me once here, shouting, and the whole wing watched. I didn't shout back, I didn't lose my temper, and nobody got hurt. (Officer)

As an officer, what you could do was limited not as much by the formal rules governing prison life but by an officer's confidence, their credibility on the wing and the relationships they had with prisoners and other officers:

> You can't walk straight in as a new officer, because the prisoners will spot you a mile away, and start calling the shots and throwing your weight around. You can legally! But the cons don't accept that. You have to earn the respect of the prisoners. There have been quite a lot of new officers who have turned

up in the past few months, and they try to copy the old officers straight away – and this doesn't really work. You must develop your own style. You can be influenced by people to a certain extent – you've got to be as you do that in any job – but you must establish your own personality within the job. (Officer)

The positive and successful use of discretion was central to being a good prison officer. It involved not having to resort to asserting their authority formally and being willing not to use force (although that did not mean never using force) but attempting to solve situations peacefully and through talk before anything else, except in an emergency when physical force was required. Most officers found control to be more easily established without always using the rules and by first establishing relationships with prisoners. Through those relationships, and through the confident but sensitive application of discretion, 'peace' could be constantly accomplished and re-accomplished. This routine but central part of prison officers' work was highly valued among officers themselves – but was not often seen (or perceived as seen) by those who managed them. Relationships with prisoners, framed by and established through the discerning use of discretion, constituted some of the best aspects of prison officer work as we argued earlier. Below we consider ways of thinking about the use of discretion which can keep it within agreed boundaries: through the 'trained application of reason'.

Daily penal practices and the trained application of reason

This jail is a complex place, there are always exceptions to things, and people should be treated as individuals. (Senior manager, in Liebling and Price 1999)

Bottoms argues, in his critique of von Hirsch's desert theory of punishment, that mercy, or compassion, can be rationally exercised (Bottoms 1998: 67–8), that is that exceptions can be made. Consistency does not always lead to fairness – although parity (treating like cases alike) might, as Gilbert argues (cited earlier in this chapter). Bottoms is drawing on the reasoning of legal philosopher Harrison, whose essay on 'The equality of mercy' (1992) helps us to bridge the apparently irresolvable tension between flexibility and consistency, via the 'boundaried use' of discretion. Bottoms argues:

> Demands for mercy within a legal system especially arise when a given general rule seems likely to lead to an inappropriate (or unjust) result in a specific case; in other words, such demands 'are really often arguments about the need for flexibility' in the application of rules. (Bottoms 1998: 68)

There is an important distinction between 'the mechanical operation of rules' and 'the question of justice' in a particular case.[12] Rules are 'blunt instruments' which do not take into account the complexity or individuality of a particular case (Harrison 1992; see also Hawkins 1992). Real differences between individuals and situations justify differential applications of a rule, provided that the application of the rule – its enforcement or suspension – would be similar in any similar case. How can this sort of flexibility avoid becoming arbitrary decision-making? How can we be certain of 'what counts as a relevant consideration'? Harrison argues as follows:

> What it requires is the trained application of the reasons of law to individual cases ... If justice is to be done, the decision should be taken for reasons and be rationally defensible. Such a rational defence will include emphasising all the special features of the particular case ... Judgment is needed, but the best judgment is informed by, and sensitive to, reason. The best judgment is not just about one case in isolation, but is sensitive to the possible implications of that judgment on other cases. (Harrison 1992: 122)

What this means is that discretion should not be absolute, but should be 'boundaried' by guidelines which are 'flexible enough to be adaptable to meet the special circumstances of particular cases' (Bottoms 1998: 69). Such guidelines 'draw upon and yet also develop the *deep structures* of' (in this case) penological practice and thinking (in Giddens' language, the 'practical consciousness' of prison officers).[13] As Bottoms argues, and as we concluded from our research at Whitemoor:

> Bringing an occupation's 'practical consciousness' into the realm of formal discussion and deliberation may well be an appropriate way to begin to develop 'the trained application of reasons of law to individual cases', as Harrison puts it, precisely because the collective 'practical consciousness' often contains

some extremely useful pointers to good practice. But equally, in this process of explicit articulation of previous practice, it will very likely become apparent that appropriate good practice guidelines will need to go beyond the insights of 'practical consciousness' – which insights may at crucial points be overly vague …or even, on careful reflection, actually insupportable when critically considered. (Bottoms 1998: 70)

What this means is that open dialogue about detail – about boundaries, decision-making and the use of power, drawing on daily practice – is crucial to the development of 'the right' *deep structures* or practices. Staff and their managers should engage in conversations about detail: is it right to give biscuits to prisoners? To play pool? What are the reasons? This is what we witnessed in the SSU at Whitemoor – regular commentary by staff among themselves on each other's behaviour. We singled out this area of management practice as a fine example of best practice. Making the unconscious conscious, staff are encouraged to reason about their decision-making. Right behaviour is 'conduct for which reasons could be given' (Harrison 1992: 115). Actions are not justified by their source (because one has the power to decide) but by their content (can the decision be justified?). Without this constraint, we have 'power without accountability.' Harrison argues:

> Every use of power, of the power of states against citizens, should be subject to review. (Harrison 1992: 118)

Discretion, he goes on, cannot be eliminated; instead, it should be 'boundaried' and conceived as not 'arbitrary judgment' but 'rather, the ability to discern correctly' (Harrison 1992: 119). There is a need for flexibility, but also a demand for consistency that places a constraint on flexible decision-making, to the extent that there should be some means for dealing with 'exceptions' within a system, and so it should not be necessary (or allowable) to 'reach outside it to arbitrary judgment' (Harrison 1992: 120). If there are *principles* as well as rules, then judgment is guided and flexibility is possible. Discretion is legitimised by the fact that, first, a rule will always need to be interpreted, and secondly, that there are various ways of giving effect to that interpretation. Where disagreements arise, there is a need for dialogue and (Harrison says) reason:

> It's all to do with self-confidence, with seeing the bigger picture … There's some of it will be a skill, but most of it is development,

developing it in people and encouraging it in a positive fashion, not a negative fashion. This is where management come in ... at least (the officer) made a judgment and at least the lesson to be learned is, you did this, well done, but did you think of *this* best? So that you learn and grow, and that's done in a positive sense ... (Senior manager)

'Flexible consistency' sounds contradictory but it is a paradox which lies at the heart of keeping order and legitimacy in prison, and hence also at the heart of 'right relationships' between prison officers and prisoners. But 'flexible consistency' can only really work if there is a 'big picture' vision because it is this kind of 'understanding' which gives officers the values or principles to apply when making exceptions to rules and practices and the confidence to make those exceptions. It is the responsibility of senior managers (and governors within establishments), in consultation with staff, to provide this clearly focused 'bigger picture'. This is what appears to be missing from the formal training of officers (and governors) and from the considerations given to how best officers are enabled to perform their role. However, the wide interest shown in this book and in our appreciative inquiry work with staff in individual establishments, which has resulted in precisely these kinds of statements or 'visions', suggests that this need for a clearer 'bigger picture' is increasingly being recognised (see further Liebling *et al.* 2001).

Notes

1 'Corruption' is a pejorative term, perhaps in the current context inseparable from the term 'conditioning'. It hints that officers are failing in their work as a result of their under-enforcement of the rules. This analysis is too simple: the skill of order maintenance lies precisely in this delicate balance between enforcement and non-enforcement. The astute officer can discern between situations which require enforcement and situations which do not. We speak of non-enforcement, or accommodation.

2 A prison officer has the powers of a constable but does not hold the office of constable – see section 8 of Prison Act 1952. See, too, *Home Office* v. *POA* (*The Times*, 19 November 1993) and *Secretary of State for the Home Department* v. *Barnes* (*The Times*, 19 December, 1994). In February 2001 the Home Secretary, Jack Straw, replaced section 127 of the Criminal Justice and Public Order Act 1994, which made it unlawful for prison officers to take industrial action, with a reserve power and a voluntary industrial relations agreement (www.hmprisonservice.gov.uk/news).

Following the strikes held in the summer of 2007, the Brown Labour Government reversed this decision, once again making it illegal for prison officers to take industrial action. The Prison Officers' Association (POA) are challenging this position (see further, Chapter 8).

3 Keith Hawkins helpfully pointed out to us that the literature on regulation and enforcement may have relevance to prison work too, as enforcement takes place in the context of ongoing relationships, long-term compliance is sought in both negotiating and adversarial ways, and a mix of powers is used (see Hawkins 1984; Ayres and Braithwaite 1992; Baldwin *et al.* 1998).

4 This included the addition of the racially aggravated offences to Rule 51 and the addition of a definition of a close supervision centre at Rule 46(5). Changes have also been made to adjudication Rules requiring District Judges to hear cases where added days are awarded (Rule 42), to appeals procedures and to enable prisoners to be tested for alcohol use (Rule 50).

5 For example, the rule concerning classification (Rule 7) states that 'Prisoners shall be classified, in accordance with any directions of the Secretary of State, having regard to their age, temperament and record and with a view to maintaining good order and facilitating training'. The main and most comprehensive method of prisoner classification – security categorisation – is not mentioned in these rules; indeed, security, the prime purpose of modern imprisonment, is not present in the rule.

6 Finally, there are Prison Service Standards, whose purpose is to provide guidance as to process. Standards are not rules as such, but in practice strongly influence how policy is instituted. At the time of writing, there were 66 Prison Service Standards, which covered topics such as Education, Drugs Policy, Parole and the Use of Force.

7 The establishment of the post of Prisons Ombudsman in 2000 provides further evidence of the growing 'transparency' of the prison world in many respects.

8 Witness the fact that one form of industrial action that prison officers can take is to choose to 'work to rule'.

9 The Special Security Unit worked to very strict rules and guidelines and attempted to enforce them rigidly, feeling this to be the most efficient way to prevent a repeat of the 1994 escapes. Even so, after being reopened for just over two years, it was evident that officers and management felt that it would be valuable to bring back some limited amount of discretion and to relax standards somewhat in the Unit. It was closed in 2002 following the repatriation and release of Irish prisoners. Whitemoor had a unit for Dangerous and Severe Personality Disordered prisoners (DSPD Unit) and a Close Supervision Centre at the time of writing this edition.

10 Here, the prisoner is making a distinction between force and authority.

11 See Sparks *et al.* (1996) on the differences between 'situational' and 'social' approaches to order in Albany and Long Lartin in the 1980s.
12 Gilligan, Harrison and others have argued that 'justice', 'impartiality' and 'equality' may be abstract, cold virtues and that human beings want their interests treated mercifully, not impartially (see Gilligan 1986 and Harrison 1992).
13 This is prison officers almost unconsciously drawing on their experience, knowledge and skills.

Chapter 7

Prison officer culture and unionisation

If it ticks, why change it? (Prison officer)

Introduction

What sort of occupational culture exists among prison officers? Do they have a common way of thinking, based on identifiable aspects of their work? Is there a particular 'way' of working common to prison officers – and if so, what effects does this have on their approach to their work? Are different cultures found in different circumstances (including internal differentiation within establishments)? The concept of culture is useful to the extent that it helps us to analyse the impact of attempts to change or reform the prison (see Chan 1997) and to account for some aspects of prison officer behaviour. Reference is often made in official documents to organisational culture, 'institutionalised racism' and to a range of prison staff attitudes which are sometimes seen as impediments to modernisation and reform and which, at their worst, are linked to excessive use of force and other types of brutality and to corruption and other misconduct. What is the evidence for the existence of such cultures? Are they all necessarily negative? (We argue that they are not). Why do they arise and what are the implications of their existence for those working in and managing establishments? A professional, accountable and open Prison Service has a duty to be honest and self-critical about this complex aspect of its operation.

The term 'culture' tends to be used as shorthand for a range of negative values, attitudes and practices (Chan 1997). We would urge that the term be used more openly, so that positive as well as negative working cultures receive attention (see Waddington 1999 for an attempt to do this for policing). It can mean a set of 'craft rules' (Reiner 1992), or a language, a view about how things are done and some fundamental assumptions about why things are done in this way (Chan 1997: 113). These views are:

> ... socially constructed, and may be changed or perpetuated by organisational processes through repeated applications. In time, these cognitions are imbued with emotions and acquire degrees of importance; they become 'habits' of thoughts that translate into habitual actions. (Chan 1997: 113)

Critics of culture studies suggest that at least three working cultures exist: 'street-cop' (prison officer) culture, middle management culture and senior management culture. Very few studies have yet been conducted on the 'working personalities' of middle and senior managers in the Prison Service (although see Rutherford 1993 and Bryans 2007).[1]

Unlike the police, who have been the subject of many studies of their (so-called 'canteen') culture, the 'working personality' of prison officers has been neglected in research. One reason for this relative neglect was offered by Colvin:

> Prison staff have never appeared as glamorous heroes, for the containment of persons lacks the supposed elements of cleverness and excitement which have attracted novelists and film-makers to the police force. The main source of popular images of prison staff may well be the cartoonist's caricature of a stiff-necked, lantern-jawed martinet standing guard over a more obviously caricatured prisoner with shaven-head, broad-arrowed uniform, and ball and chain. (Colvin 1977: 2)

As many television series and film dramas demonstrate, prison officers do not have a positive public reputation, and sometimes the images projected can contribute to contradictory and stereotypical representations of prison officer work. This is something of which officers are generally well aware and from which they often suffer (as this chapter will show later on). But where does this negative image come from? Partly, perhaps, directly from these media and fictional portrayals: the sadistic prison officer is a mainstay of prison-set dramas (think of *The Shawshank Redemption*, *Escape from Alcatraz*, *Murder in the First* – or even *Porridge*).

However, there is also a problem related to the 'quiet' nature of successful prison work we discussed in our introduction. At one dispersal prison, the deputy governor had on his wall a poster featuring his desired (and, of course, never-to-be-realised) newspaper headline: 'Well Run Prison Has Quiet Day'. Though such 'success' in keeping an orderly and secure prison is highly valued by officers and managers within prisons (and also by many prisoners), it is not meaningful to those portraying the prison. In contrast to the police, there are few occasions when prisons attract the attention of the media for doing what they should.[2] While police officers are praised for catching criminals (widely perceived as their key occupational task), prison officers are not generally praised for preventing escape or retaining order – in wider society, this is simply expected of them. These are perceived as relatively easy tasks. Any 'failure' of the prison officer (an escape, unsanitary conditions, a suicide) is newsworthy.

There is one important similarity between media and fictional portrayals of prison and police officers: that is the issues important to the individuals who work within the organisations are often greatly simplified. The effects of this negative and disproportionate public image contribute to a prison officer culture that is insular, within which officers must justify their work to themselves and to other officers. Prison officers feel that they are doing an important job, whether this is generally recognised or not.

Studies of police culture

In contrast to the prison literature, there is a vast literature on the culture of the police, and particularly of police officers. According to Chan, author of *Changing Police Culture*:

> The concept of police culture originally emerged from ethnographic studies of routine police work, which uncover a layer of occupational norms and values operating under the apparently rigid hierarchical structure of police organisation. (Chan 1997: 110)

155

Waddington (1999: 287) argues that the study of police culture derives:

> from the discovery that police work is rarely guided by legal precepts, but that police officers exercise considerable discretion in how they enforce the law. That discretion and many other routine police practices are thought to rely upon the taken for granted beliefs and values shared by the police generally, but particularly by the lower ranks who are most likely to encounter members of the public in conditions of 'low visibility'.

As we have already argued, prison officers also regularly exercise discretion in their work. Studies of organisational culture are motivated by efforts to change organisations (and frustrations with corporate strategies which fail to achieve change) and, in relation to the police, with concerns about the delicate balance between the use of discretion *for* legitimacy and the use of discretion *against* it (discrimination, stereotyping and so on; see Liebling *et al.* 1999). A brief look at the literature on police culture is helpful in our effort to understand the prison officer's world, particularly as scholarly investigations of police culture and police uses of discretion are far more advanced and detailed than similar studies of prison officers.

Reiner (1992) sees the main constituents of police culture as follows:

- *a sense of mission* – the notion that policing is not simply another job, but is a job with a vital purpose. Police officers believe strongly in their legitimacy and 'worthwhile purpose' (Reiner 1992: 111);

- *pessimism and cynicism* – a 'hard skin of bitterness' (Reiner 1992: 113) is often developed by officers who see themselves as the 'thin blue line' standing between society and anarchy;

- *suspiciousness* – officers are constantly aware of their surroundings, watching for trouble and danger;

- *group solidarity (coupled with social isolation)* – officers may find it hard to mix comfortably with outsiders in social situations; there is a strong internal cohesiveness, partly linked to the need to rely on other officers in difficult moments;

- *conservatism* – the upholders of social order – this includes the political and moral views of officers;

- *machismo* – the 'alcoholic and sexual indulgences of the police are a product both of the masculine ethos of the force, and the tension built up by the work' (Reiner 1992: 124); and

- *pragmatism* – 'police officers are concerned to get from here to tomorrow (or the next hour) safely and with the least fuss and paperwork' (Reiner 1992: 124).

Others have suggested that police culture is characterised by a 'primary allegiance not to the organisation but to the job and ... to ... peer groups' (Chan 1996; Punch 1983). In Skolnick's (1966) well-cited formulation, the origins of police culture (what he terms their 'working personality') lie in two areas: danger and authority.

While many occupations are dangerous, police officers are 'unique in regularly being required to face situations where the risk lies in the unpredictable outcome of encounters with other people' (Reiner 1992: 110). The level of this danger may vary from force to force and from task to task, but its presence is a constant. The exposure to danger is generated by the fact that the police officer *has* authority and must enforce it. Whatever (possibly dangerous) situation is faced by an officer, the way to solve it is through the use of authority.

There are some similarities between the working norms of prison officers and those of police officers listed above. In particular, prison officers have a strong need to know that their colleagues will come to their aid when trouble occurs. They also demonstrate aspects of the sense of mission, cynicism and pragmatism suggested by Reiner.

The study of police culture is most often a study of what officers say, which authors then relate to what officers actually do (so that, for example, racist action is attributed to racist chatter elsewhere, such as the canteen). As Waddington (1999: 288) argues, 'this conceptual bridge looks decidedly rickety as it spans the obvious and frequently acknowledged chasm between what officers say and what they do'. This gap between expressed beliefs and action needs to be taken seriously. Waddington identifies several studies which did not detect racist behaviour in public incidents among officers who used racist language in private. He concludes:

> If there is little relationship between the privately expressed views of police officers and their actual behaviour on the streets, it appears that the concept of a police sub-culture contributes little to the explanation of policing. (Waddington 1999: 288)

Waddington believes that there is such thing as a police 'culture' (or cultures), but the existence of this culture should not be used for the purposes of explaining police actions. Waddington goes on to attempt an appreciation of police culture and talk, viewing it as a response to the structural conditions imposed upon the police. Other authors have made much more explicit links between culture and practice:

> Many of the complaints raised by minority groups against the police can be linked to aspects of the police occupational culture: the regular use of racist language, stereotyping of ethnic communities, unfair targeting and harassment of minorities, and in some examples the abuse of police powers or excessive force against suspects. (Chan 1996: 119)

The police tend to make clear distinctions between 'the rough and respectable', to take short cuts based on 'cues', to cover themselves and not 'rat on others' and to see themselves as defenders in the 'war against crime' (Chan 1996: 119–22). In a field characterised by wide discretion and lack of power among minority groups, stereotyping, harassment and apparent lack of accountability can easily result. Chan concludes that, in addition to legal and organisational regulation, cultural changes in organisations depend to some extent on structural (social, economic, political and legal) changes to the context – the conditions of policing – in which everyday decisions are taken (Chan 1996: 130–1).

Culture and the effects of prison work

The fact of being a prison officer and working day-to-day behind the walls of a prison with people who, on the whole, do not want to be there appears to produce some common effects. Furthermore, from what we have already argued in Chapter 4 about officers, it is clear that camaraderie, a cohesiveness which has features similar to those identified by Reiner, is central to the prison officer's role.

Kauffman (1988) spent time in a particularly 'hard end' maximum-security institution in the United States (and arguably one which differs markedly from the English high security prison). She interviewed a group of prison officers in the weeks before they started work at the prison and then interviewed them again four years later. She vividly sums up the effects that the prison had on them:

Most officers recognised the changes that had taken place in themselves and spoke of their changes with sorrow and bitterness in the interviews. Many of their young marriages were in trouble or destroyed. Some officers were so burnt out they could not go into supermarkets or take their children to the zoo. Others were so drug dependent that they had to get drunk before going to work on the 7 a.m. shift. Some were so angry and frustrated that they punched holes in the walls of their homes and abused those whom they loved. Most of all, they were desperately unhappy and despaired that life could ever seem good again. (Kauffman 1988: 212)

She quotes one officer:

[When] I started Walpole I had everything ... When I got out of Walpole I had nothing. No family, no morals, nothing. I don't give a shit about anything ... I like the way I was before. I was easygoing and I liked everybody and everything ... [Those] three years screwed up everything – don't feel the same about anything anymore. (Kauffman 1988: 212)

This is an extreme reaction to an atypical prison. Yet everyday exposure to conflict (however subtle) and argument, to the claustrophobia and enclosed nature of a prison, to the various tasks involved in trying to 'achieve quiet', clearly has its effects. At Whitemoor, for instance, officers gave the following examples:

People have said that since being in the Prison Service, I've definitely become more assertive and more confident. Without a doubt. Outside, you're more likely to complain about something or if there's something wrong with your food ... (Officer)

Well, it's changed me in a lot of ways – I'm much more cynical, my husband says I'm much more serious. You mature at an incredibly quick rate. I remember so powerfully my first six months in the Prison Service and being so overwhelmed by how depressing it was. I was at [large London local], maybe that's a variable [laughs], but I remember a lot of my friends who joined the Service at the same time as I did, feeling quite similar feelings to me, I think there is a big adaptation when you work somewhere like this. And I think part of it is a reaction to the people you meet – they're not happy people and their lives aren't happy and their lives are so full of horrible and nasty events, and that's bound to have an impact on people. (Officer)

When I first joined the Service, I looked at it like a large family. But as any large family, it has its little factions, and certain people in that family have certain nuances, and the way they are, they will drop you in it as soon as look at you. So within this large family, I suppose I'm very careful who I speak to, very careful what I say. I've become more diplomatic in my views, whereas before it would come out, exactly what I thought. I'm a little bit more reserved now. If I'm told to do anything that I think is a little bit suspect by anyone more senior, I'll ask for it in writing. It's about covering your own back, about making sure what you're doing is right and that if you don't think it's right making sure that someone is responsible for it. (Officer)

Beyond the rather broad term 'stress', research suggests other influences of prison work, including sleepless nights, difficulties relaxing, 'bringing the job home' (e.g. 'My wife says I shout more', Colvin 1977), heavy drinking and so on (see further Arnold 2005). The desensitisation produced by exposure to prison, mentioned above, is another important theme. Officers may become numbed to experiences which should trigger 'corrective' responses. Prison work demands of staff that they cope with brutality without becoming brutalised, that they experience feelings without being able to express those feelings legitimately or without the risk of being ridiculed or rendered ineffective. Genders and Player wrote of their experiences of long-term research in the therapeutic prison at Grendon (1995). It resulted in:

> ... a state of numbness ... Such desensitisation ... raised for us personal anxieties that we might become immune to 'normal' human feelings ... it was as if ... sentiments [of disgust, pity or shock] had shifted several points along a notional scale of tolerance.[3]

Prison officer culture

One US study generated a description of the content of a culture existing at one (perhaps atypical) prison. Kauffman set out a series of 'norms' (Kauffman 1988: ch. 6) which she felt constituted the 'officer subculture' at Walpole prison:

The prison officer code

Norm One: Always go to the aid of an officer in distress

> The obligation to go to the aid of a fellow officer is the most important positive responsibility of any officer. It is the norm on which officer solidarity is based, the foundation of their sense of brotherhood ... The strength of the norm lay in the very real sense that an officer alone 'can't last in a place like [this] a long time.' (Kauffman 1988: 86–7)

In the local language (argot), this became 'always respond to a slam' – that is, the slamming of the heavy metal door to a cell block, the sign of trouble. The 'norm' echoes the response to 'deuces' described by Fleisher (1989) and to alarms by Colvin (1977) in his study of Manchester Prison. Colvin (1977: 128) states that:

> Defining the prison as a conflict situation leads to a demand for unequivocal commitment and loyalty to the officer group.

At Walpole, 'more than anything else, a new officer was judged by his willingness to uphold this norm' (Kauffman 1988: 88). In Walpole, the camaraderie that came from knowing that support was there overcame the transgression of other 'norms' – an officer who was quick to any incident was allowed to maintain a softer line to prisoners than others, for example. The norm was not universal, however: some older officers, especially those on the 7–3 shift, did not adhere to it.

This idea, of the prison as an arena of potential conflict and violence where fellow officers may be the only people who can help, underpins the officer culture. It represents a reality of 'us/officers' against 'them/prisoners'.

Norm Two: Don't 'lug' (smuggle) drugs

> No norm of the officer subculture received more spontaneous endorsement than that against 'lugging' drugs ... Officers did not view 'lugging' as an unpardonable offence because of personal revulsion against the use of drugs ... The strength of the norm against 'lugging' lay in the potential danger to fellow

officers presented by prisoners on drugs or under the influence of alcohol. (Kauffman 1988: 91)

Suspicion of an officer 'lugging' was the only time most officers would violate the next norm, of not informing on another officer. Whatever else they may have taken part in as an officer, they would not smuggle in drugs for a prisoner. Most officers at Walpole were quite prepared to use violence against a prisoner, but would not place another officer in danger for any reason.

Norm Three: Don't rat

At Walpole, this norm depended to some extent on who was being 'ratted' on and to whom. An officer would never betray another officer to a prisoner; nor would officers cooperate in investigations or testify against another officer. The exchange below captures the complex dilemmas faced by an officer in informing on colleagues:

> – Let's say one of the prisoners were killed and you were there, you witnessed it ... What would you do in that situation?

> ... If somebody had died and I thought I should have done something, I'm sure – hopefully – I don't know. I don't know right now today what I'd do. Hopefully I would like to think that I would come forward as much as it would mean that I'd never be able to work in Walpole again ... If nothing else, you do believe that you need, you know that you need the rest of the officers in order to perform. And if you're alone, you can't last in a place like that for a long time.

> [The officer mentions he thinks some officers might be sympathetic to him if he came forward in such a situation. Kauffman asks him how many – ten in the whole prison?]

> No, I think it'd be a lot that would feel something for you. To what degree I haven't the slightest. But I would like to think it would be a lot ... But no one's willing to make the first move. No one's willing to make the first step because of that unwritten code that says that I violated them or I violated their code and I'm a correctional officer.[4] (Kauffman 1988: 97–8)

For Kauffman, to violate the confidence of a fellow officer is to lose all trust and all comradeship – vital tools for survival in Walpole.

Norm Four: Never make a fellow officer look bad in front of prisoners
Norm four, and the rest of the norms that follow, are those that govern routine behaviour. Criticising an officer with a prisoner present had two effects: it made the officer criticised lose some of his authority; and it dented the appearance of solidarity among the officer corps. A further point made by Kauffman demonstrating the extreme nature of prison life at Walpole was that this norm did not simply cover procedural or administrative matters (such as whether a prisoner is allowed a particular item, or how many visits he might be allowed). It also covered moral matters – such as whether an officer approved or not of the beating given to a defenceless prisoner, for example. Disapproval might be expressed at a later date, but not in front of the prisoner.

Norm Five: Always support an officer in a dispute with a prisoner
Again, this norm maintains the perception of strong officer solidarity. This was a 'positive' norm requiring action by the officer, so transgressions were not as strongly frowned upon as failures to hold up Norms One to Four.

Norm Six: Always support officer sanctions against prisoners
A more specific version of Norm Five, this covered informal as well as formal sanctions – most notably violent sanctions imposed by officers on prisoners. Many officers felt that the only right way to punish or attempt to prevent prisoner-on-officer violence was to return the violence. The pressure to become involved was strong, especially among new officers.[5] Officers who did not subscribe to this norm, who would refrain from getting involved in prisoner beatings, were subject to informal sanctions of their own – disapproval, loss of trust and so on. It certainly was possible to refrain from becoming involved, but retaliatory violence 'was a policy that was seen by officers and prisoners as having the endorsement of the vast majority of officers' (Kauffman 1988: 108).

Norm Seven: Don't be a white hat
A 'white hat' was the label given to those officers who would side with or express sympathy for prisoners. In practice, providing the officer had sufficient seniority and identified with and upheld the

other norms of officer behaviour, this norm could be (and was) often violated.

Norm Eight: Maintain officer solidarity versus all outside groups

Norms One to Seven were all concerned with officer–prisoner behaviour; this norm extends the antipathy felt to prisoners to anyone other than an officer. Cynicism and mistrust of the administration was common, as was mistrust of any individuals met outside the prison. Aware of their position in the media – both with regard to prison officers in general and Walpole in particular – officers were extremely wary of mentioning their work to anyone. This included, in some cases, their family. Partly this was to stop intimates worrying, partly because of the traditional plea that 'no one understands'. As Kauffman notes, this has the effect of furthering the isolation and increasing the dependency on the officer group.

Norm Nine: Show positive concern for fellow officers

Kauffman mentions this norm:

> not because it was widely obeyed ... but because it represented a behavioural ideal subscribed to by most officers. (Kauffman 1988: 112)

One main aspect of this norm was the maxim, 'never leave another officer a problem'. This ran into difficulties in practice, however, because of animosity between officer shifts, as well as *between* officers and everyone else. Specifically, the 3 p.m. – 11 p.m. shift would often complain that the 7 a.m. – 3 p.m. shift did not complete their responsibilities. On their part, the 7 a.m. – 3 p.m. shift would counter that the officers working 3 p.m. – 11 p.m. would annoy and harass the prisoners so much that, unlocking in the morning, the 7 a.m. – 3 p.m. shift received all the anger and frustrations of the night before.

This 'code' – although extreme – is a helpful summary of the 'culture' identified at Walpole (a problem prison). It may be interesting to reflect on how far some of the above 'norms' exist, and to what extent, in some specific prisons in England and Wales or elsewhere. What other or alternative 'norms' do prison officers share?

The value of prison work

Despite the challenges and potential problems of working in prisons, officers also find much of value in what they do, and often work in very positive cultures. (We have observed such cultures, for example, at Lancaster Farms, Blantyre House, Grendon Underwood and parts of Woodhill, Whitemoor, Full Sutton, Doncaster and Holme House, and we are aware that they exist elsewhere.) Officers at Whitemoor often mentioned the positive boost gained from advising or helping prisoners. This is something often missing from analyses of police or prison culture. Their sense of vocation is often linked only to the maintenance of order. Prison officers are often strongly oriented to doing their best to help prisoners:

> I met a prisoner at Butlin's, would you believe, and I suggested to him that as he'd worked in the kitchens he should go to some holiday camp, tell them he'd been silly and ended up in the Scrubs but worked in the kitchens and was cooking for over a thousand people there and he could use that experience. I wrote a 'to whom it may concern' letter stating that this person had done this, and my views on this person, and I was at Butlin's about two years later on ... I was there with my family, it was rather embarrassing – 'Governor, governor, governor, thank you very much!' So sometimes it's showing that you care, giving them that idea if you can. (Officer)

One of the themes already identified, and one of the attractions of the job for officers once they have joined, is the strong ties that bind officers together in moments of difficulty. Colvin reports:

> When that bell goes, you all go to help. Someone could be getting killed. (Colvin 1977: 127)

The ready response of officers to an alarm bell demonstrates (and is a function of) the tight camaraderie between officers in a prison. It defines the prison as a dangerous environment within which the support of fellow officers is required to survive. This close bonding and trust is very important to officers. The reality of serious physical violence upon an officer by one or more prisoners is relatively rare (there are also many examples of prisoners going to the aid of officers in dangerous situations). However, the fact that prison officers are outnumbered on any normal prison wing means that officers need to know that at any point in a working day help is no more than a few seconds away. The awareness of danger may be stronger in some areas of a prison than others – for example, in a segregation unit, where the potential for conflict with prisoners may be greater. It is one reason why cultures can differ from prison to prison, and from one location within a prison to another.

At Whitemoor, officers frequently mentioned how being a prison officer (whether other officers liked you or not) meant that you were potentially protected by everyone else working in the prison. For most, this was an accepted – but much prized – aspect of prison work. As an officer, you respond instantly and without question to someone in difficulty, knowing (rather than hoping) that they would do the same for you. What officers valued was the ability to work together, particularly in difficult times. The knowledge that, at busy moments or times of crisis, you could rely on your colleagues and come through a problematic situation was cited as a very positive aspect of being a prison officer, as we argued in Chapter 1.

The positive value staff gain from prison work is often missing from traditional accounts of the prison officer. Staff want to be involved in offence-related work; they want to be professional in their custodial work and in providing constructive regimes. They want the tools, the resources and the support required to carry out their tasks with a clear direction in mind. Even (sometimes especially) in the most difficult circumstances, their culture is characterised by willingness to 'give it a go'.

Kauffman demonstrates how working styles can alter between prisons, between wings or between shifts. Each shift had a distinct working 'style', produced to some extent by the responsibilities faced by each shift, but also a product of the direction and leadership available to each officer group. The 3 p.m. – 11 p.m. shift, the 'disciplinarians', were strictly controlled and managed by a single supervisor, a man with firm ideas about how his shift would be run. Hard but fair, the supervisor appeared devoted to his officers, who were more than prepared to return this loyalty:

He took us aside ... He introduced us to people. He told the [shift] to 'make these guys as comfortable as possible and give them all the knowledge you can.' And he asked us personal questions like he was interested. And he was. It was real.

– *Sounds like the basics of good management*

Definitely. That's all it was. He knew his job, and he was doing it sincerely, too. (Kauffmann 1988: 196)

Kauffman outlines how these officers were successfully managed:

He paid close attention to each officer's progress, offering both criticism and praise – the latter a very rare commodity at Walpole. And he systematically weeded out those who failed to meet his standards. He instilled a pride in his officers that they had desperately lacked in the preceding months. 'He made the job seem like it was a worthwhile job.' ... These were merely the basics of good management, but they were basics so sorely lacking in the rest of the institution that it gave this supervisor enormous stature in the eyes of his officers. (Kauffman 1988: 197)

Yet the 'standards' of this supervisor were often hard and forceful – 'not merely the show of force but ... the *use* of force [was] sanctioned and guided' on the 3 p.m. – 11 p.m. shift. The culture of the officers was easily shaped in this direction, (a) because of the officers' willingness to submit to any form of management and alliance (new officers were placed on the 3 p.m. – 11 p.m. shift after four weeks of the 'chaos' of the 7 a.m. – 3 p.m. shift); and (b) because of the ease with which control and discipline can be taught, especially if all officers are prepared to accept the problems that spring from it (violence and conflict with prisoners and others). 'It was', states Kauffman, 'a price most rookies were willing to pay. With rare exception, they saw no alternative' (1988: 198). She sums up the process of cultural and value change among the officers:

The typical Walpole recruit had entered the training academy sympathetic to prisoners. At the academy he had been taught to take the prisoner's perspective and had been imbued with the spirit of 'modern' corrections. He had been assigned to Walpole – often his institution of choice – where he had received cursory orientation before being flung alone into the most hazardous and difficult job in the institution.[6] There he had suffered deeply from his isolation from fellow officers and had learned to distrust the administration and hate the prisoners. His transfer to the 3–11 had offered him survival, acceptance and pride. The price he paid was surrender of old values, behaviour, and identification and adoption of those of the officer subculture as characterised by the 3–11pm shift. His socialisation was complete … But many of the officers grieved deeply over the changes they saw happening in themselves … Despite the rookies' adaptation to the 3–11, there were few 'true believers' among them. Furthermore, for all that it offered officers, the 3–11 was characterised by almost constant confrontation and crisis. Under the continuing stress, most officers rapidly burned out. (Kauffman 1988: 198–9)

Kauffman's research concentrated on a prison where working conditions were difficult. She provides a powerful account of the adverse effects of prison work. She links a strong culture to the difficulties of prison work. One of our arguments in this chapter is that the willingness of officers to 'pull together' can be a prison's strength and the source of more positive cultures (see Liebling *et al.* 2001). We have witnessed a similar but much more positive process, for example, in the Special Security Unit at Whitemoor, where a disproportionate number of our 'role model' staff had worked. When we considered what made this location 'special' and apparently effective at producing role model staff who were thought to work to high consistent standards wherever their next location, we concluded that staff working in the SSU developed in their confidence and skills; they became very clear about 'boundaries' and they worked to a united vision. They operated with a sense of purpose and were highly 'team-oriented'. The management model of this unit seemed to be the key to the positive working environment. It was close, supportive and demonstrated democratic staff–management relations. Team-building and the provision of an élite training course had contributed. There was close supervision (by colleagues as well as by line management), regular debriefings at the ends of shifts, a spirit of openness and dialogue, regular and purposeful staff meetings and 'reward by career planning'. It constituted a 'best practice' model of the management of staff. Working in such conditions empowered and motivated staff, and brought out the best they had to offer. Having a clear vision and a united team spirit undoubtedly contributed to high performance. The staff–prisoner relationships cultivated in the unit – distant, custody-oriented and coercive – may not have been suitable to men serving long sentences in conditions of maximum security; it was far too restricted. However, the culture generated among staff working in the unit was undoubtedly a positive one, and seemed to build consistency, confidence and self-awareness among them.[7]

Our interest in the shape and depth of prison officer culture and its impact on the quality of life for prisoners led to an attempt to explore its nature and, if possible, quantify the prevalence of positive and negative cultural attitudes, during an evaluation of a safer locals programme (of suicide prevention) at 12 prisons during 2001–4.[8] We were struck by the marked variations in officer attitudes towards prisoners and managers, and by the very different degrees of 'traditional cultural resistance' in different prisons (see further Liebling 2008a; Arnold *et al.* 2007). The presence of negative cultural attitudes among high proportions of staff had a negative impact on the successful implementation of the safer custody strategy at establishment level and on the provision of care for prisoners. A Quality of Life survey for staff was developed, arising from this study and other related work (the SQL), a copy of which is included in the Appendix to this edition. This survey assesses the quality of working life for staff, attitudes towards peers, managers and prisoners, towards rehabilitation and towards prison work. Results from several establishments suggest that officers' perceptions of the quality of their working life are an important indicator of the quality of care for prisoners. Significant variations are found between establishments in the nature (and fluidity) of staff culture. Changing a predominantly negative or resistant culture is difficult, but examples of positive inroads have been found (Arnold *et al.* 2007).

The camaraderie, the importance of prison officer culture and the unique context of the prison as an institution help to explain, at least in part, the significant role played by the prison officer's trade union in penal matters. No study of the role of the officer would be complete without a discussion of trade unionism, and of the Prison Officers' Association (POA) in particular.

Prison officer unionisation

During the sixties, the mines started to close; steel workers started to be thrown out of work; fishermen, and the trawling industry started to decline; the building industry started to decline. And what did the Prison Service do? We rushed into those areas and we recruited like mad, all gleefully patting each other on the back and saying 'You know, we are getting in some very good people' – and we were. We were getting in people who enjoyed a masculine environment, we were getting in people who had a kind of discipline that they had constructed

169

in their workplace. And they brought it to the Prison Service, and much of that was good. But – what they also brought with them of course were very different trade union attitudes that prevailed in the industries they came from. And they murdered us, for about seven years. They took us by the tail and they swung us around. And when they'd finished with the governor, they started on the Directors. (Former governor and regional director Bill Driscoll, from *Prison Britain III – Fresh Start*, BBC Radio 4, 5 August 1997)

How accurate is Driscoll's analysis? The legacy of heavily recruiting from the armed forces (which are arguably not union-friendly) and the fact that the Prison Service is not a disciplined Service in the military sense may qualify Driscoll's argument that recruitment patterns have led to the apparent militancy of the POA. Unionism has also been influenced by the growth of a 'rights-based culture' generally, and by the political risks of 'taking on the unions'. Two features of prison work may exacerbate the potentially volatile role played by the POA in the history of prison management: the requirements of the occupation for strong personalities; and the tendency for officers to trust 'what works today' rather than 'what others tell us might work better tomorrow'. Prison officer unions in different countries tend to have a similar role and style. Some of the robustness of prison officer union behaviour may be linked to the special circumstances of prison officer work (see Jacobs 1977; and Jacobs and Crotty 1978 on the emergence of prison officer unionisation in the US). The risk of violence, periodic 'favouritism' shown by administrators to prisoners, low prestige and low pay make prisons 'ripe for unionisation' (Jacobs and Crotty 1978: 6).

The POA has an unenviable reputation in some quarters and has been on the receiving end of considerable criticism (for example, Lewis 1997; HMCIP 2000; Laming 2000). Former Director General Derek Lewis (a more natural opponent of the POA than most) laid part of the blame for the 'poor record for security, humane treatment of prisoners and operating efficiency' in the Prison Service at the door of the POA. So far as Lewis was concerned, the negative public image of the prison officer is entirely the fault of the POA:

Its stubborn defence of restrictive practices, coupled with its belligerent and often threatening demeanour, resulted in deep public prejudice against prison officers, and an image of the service rooted in the past. (Lewis 1997: 130)

Lewis spoke of the POA as a dark malevolent force with the power to 'seduce' its leaders and members, spreading evil gossip about the future of prison employment, unsettling staff and making sure the Prison Service was run the way the Association wanted it, marching into governors' offices and scaring them into submission. Even if there are some truths here, this is, at best, only half the picture. The POA plays an important role in providing 'insurance' for its members, in keeping a careful eye on health and safety matters and in negotiating for pay and conditions. Their role must be considered in the light of criticisms made of the management of the Prison Service at both a national and local (establishment) level. Additionally, the tendency for senior managers to come and go from their posts means that a residual knowledge and understanding of managing any particular establishment on a day-to-day basis is found in the prison officer group and its union. There is, however, considerable evidence of POA 'intransigence' at particular establishments and nationally. There is also some evidence of dissatisfaction among members (or the need for a change of role) as the breakaway Prison Service Union (PSU) seeks (and, in many privately managed establishments, gains) recognition.

In terms of empirical research, little is known about the POA and its role.[9] Thomas (1972) relates the history of the Association until the late 1960s, and it is instructive to note that many of the complaints of prison officers, and hence many of the demands made by their union, have changed little during its history.

The origins of the Prison Officers' Association

As we have seen already, prison staff often feel aggrieved and neglected – and contrary to the views expressed by Derek Lewis – are quite able to feel that way without the persuasive power of a union official. Thomas (1972) demonstrates that prison officers have been feeling this way for most of the twentieth century:

> The question of a union for prison officers was mentioned for the first time, in Parliament, on 15 March 1906. The Home Secretary was asked about alleged grievances of warders, and whether he would allow them the right to 'federation' which postal employees enjoyed. As was usual with the Home Secretaries of the period he did not know of any grievances, and he deferred a decision on federation. (Thomas 1972: 143)

The end of the Boer War in 1902 had produced a sharp rise in unemployment and a similar rise in the number of people committed to prison. Prison warders (as officers were then known) found their workload increasing; they also found the prison environment becoming a home for other occupational groups – specialists, tutors and 'civilian clerks'. At the same time, prisoners began to receive certain privileges:

> From 1903 to 1911 impressive efforts were made to establish after-care facilities, educational provision was improved, diet was changed ... concerts and lectures were introduced. (Thomas 1972: 141)

Yet the discipline governing staff remained as tight as before, material conditions did not improve and pay awards were inadequate to keep up with living standards. In short, officers felt left out and undervalued, while attempting to cope with a rising prisoner population receiving more freedoms.

The grievances of prison officers spurred on the (then underground) *Prison Officers' Magazine*, which encouraged and helped form the 'Prison Officers' Federation', an unofficial trade union. The Federation published a list of eleven aims in 1916, the year it affiliated to the Labour Party:

- maintain contact with Parliament;
- throw more light on prison affairs through the press;
- improve pensions;
- abolish long hours in the convict service;
- increase pay;
- improve conditions in the Irish service;
- raise the level of pay in the local service to that of the convict service;
- fight for preference for civil guardsmen over outsiders for warder appointments;
- vigorously resist the appointment of army and navy officers to superior posts;
- abolish the confidential report; and
- afford a permanent means of protection for officers.

Some of the demands made were specific to the context at the time, such as the pay equalisation between the local and convict services. Others are common to most trade unions – increased pay, shorter hours and better conditions, for example. The current rules and constitution of the POA (revised 1996) lists the following as the Association's objectives:

(a)   to protect and promote the interest of its members;
(b)   to improve the conditions of employment of its members;
(c)   to regulate relations between its members and their employing bodies;
(d)   to provide and maintain such services and organisational structure as approved by Conference from time to time;
(e)   to provide and maintain benefits and services for members and dependants as approved by Conference from time to time;
(f)   to assist its members in learning, maintaining and improving standards of conduct;
(g)   to provide learning, training and development opportunities;
(h)   to spread knowledge and understanding in all aspects of a member's working environment;
(i)   to provide protection in relation to third-party claims where appropriate;
(j)   to provide a death benefit;
(k)   to secure full trade union rights and equality of opportunity for its members;
(l)   to secure facilities agreement with all employers where the association actively recruits full members;
(m) to achieve full staffing levels in all establishments where POA members are employed.

These objectives have changed a little in 90 years (and the language has become more technical) – years that, at times, have seen enormous industrial unrest in the Prison Service. While the demand cited in 1916 to prevent 'outsiders' becoming warders or holding more senior posts is missing, this can be compared to the opposition held by the POA today to direct entry to governor grades. One 'new' objective – the need to support members in legal claims and proceedings – reflects the increasing use and influence of such procedures in all occupations.

During the 1920s, the *Prison Officers' Magazine* was taken over by 'E. R. Ramsay' (in reality Hubert Witchard, a former prison officer and contributor to the magazine). Thomas (1972) makes strong claims for the influence of Ramsay:

Ramsay became a folk hero to an earlier generation of English prison officers. His influence on them, and ultimately on the prison system, was enormous. His early articles were highly critical ... He became the mouthpiece of staff discontent, and built their grievances into a staff culture. He set the tone of the *Prison Officers' Magazine* for all time. (Thomas 1972: 146)

Thomas links the tone of the *Magazine* at that time to the creation of an emergent prison officer culture. If 'culture' is defined as a sense of common identity, there is some truth in his statement – it is possible to understand how a central media can shape as well as represent the views of officers. But the term 'creation' implies that this culture emerged from nowhere. In truth, prison officers already felt discontented with their treatment and continued to feel so during the late 1920s and 1930s.

In 1939, prison officers were finally granted a union of their own, the Prison Officers' Association. The previously unofficial *Magazine* became the POA's official publication. Thomas treats the word of the POA from 1939 onwards as representing the feelings of most prison officers ('the officers thought ...'). There are interesting questions to be asked about how far this is in fact the case, some of which are raised by the publication of a POA paper in 1963.

'The Role of the Modern Prison Officer'

The article 'The Role of the Modern Prison Officer' (POA 1963) demonstrates the apparent disjuncture between the statements of the union and the feelings of individual officers. 'The Role of the Modern Prison Officer' was a plea from the POA to involve prison officers in the wider welfare aims of imprisonment (the very reformative move that the POA saw as responsible for the increasing problems in the control of prisoners, as we suggested in our introduction), at a time when they appeared to be increasingly sidelined.

The post-war period saw an increasing influx of specialists into prisons, charged with introducing 'reform'. Watching prisoners gain more privileges and becoming harder to discipline and feeling that their own needs were being studiously ignored, prison officers chose to act pragmatically. Unable to reconcile the contradictions they perceived as inherent in these twin goals, officers chose to do the bare minimum required of them. Yet at the same time, some officers wanted to be involved in the moves to reform prisoners. The article claims that officers were feeling uninvolved and bereft of an important role; the modern officer was no better than the 'turnkey' of old. It complains of the remoteness and impersonality of the central administration, the difficulties of having a non-uniformed governor staff, the paucity of training, the 'dull, repetitive and uninteresting' work, the poor promotion prospects, the ease with which officers become 'institutionalised', and the difficulties of reconciling the contradictions between the 'reform' ethos and the strict Code of Discipline for officers that forbade 'any undue familiarity' with prisoners (POA 1963: 331–2).

According to the article, it was the prison officer who was best suited to help with the rehabilitative task:

> Those engaged in rehabilitation should be people who are always there and who thoroughly understand the prisoner; people who understand his background outside and his behaviour inside; people who can talk the same language. In the prison world the person who is best fitted to do all these things is the prison officer ... It is the prison officer who because of this personal and constant contact, knows the man better than the governor, better even that the welfare officers. (POA 1963)

The article has some contradictions within it: officers are wary of befriending prisoners because of the Code of Discipline, yet they still have personal and constant contact with the prisoner; the officer is no more than a 'turnkey', yet is able to engage with and help prisoners; the distinction between uniformed and non-uniformed staff is problematic, but more officers should be promoted out of uniform; and so on. It is a confusing read – perhaps the confusion in the mind of officers about their role is reflected in the mind of the writer. The proposal of the article, that there be five different types of officer, produced no great reaction among official organisations – nor, it seems, among officers themselves.

When describing the 'Role of the Modern Prison Officer' article, Thomas again confuses 'the POA' with 'the officer', citing the document as 'an account of the officer's position as he saw it' (Thomas 1972: 207), rather than as 'an account of the officer's position as the POA saw it'. Interest by prison officers in the proposal might be demonstrated by the letters pages of the *Prison Officers' Magazine* ('the voice of staff culture') over the next few issues. While Hugh Klare of the Howard League praised the article as a 'milestone', letters from officers were concerned with the pragmatics of their pay position, schedules of attendance, the five-day week, and so on; no officer wrote in to comment on the article.

The POA article represented an attempt to make the relationships between officers and prisoners something beyond the maintenance of secure custody. Thomas calls the article a 'wild blow at the forces whose encroachment was lowering the status of the officer' (Thomas 1972: 208).[10] In effect, the article called for a dual role for the prison officer – the 'traditional' custody and control role, plus the relatively new task of providing welfare to prisoners.

Recent developments

Poor industrial relations continued throughout the 1970s and 1980s, culminating in a series of major disturbances in 1986 that were directly linked to national industrial action falling short of a strike, involving an overtime ban, the withdrawal of the POA from meetings and a refusal to supply information to management (HMCIP 1987). Fresh Start eliminated management dependence on overtime by prison officers and put relationships on a new footing. But limited industrial action continued. By the early 1990s the then Conservative government decided it was time to tackle the POA via private sector competition and tighter legislation. In the 1994 Criminal Justice and Public Order Act, the position was clarified (following a test case decided by Justice May in 1993, *Home Office* v. *Evans*) that prison officers had no right to instruct their members to take industrial action (section 127). They would be in breach of the Prison Act 1952, which states that prison officers have the same powers as police constables (section 8). Agreement to these conditions was negotiated in return for recognition of the POA as an independent trades union. New procedures were introduced to determine the pay and conditions of officers (the Pay Review Body (PRB)). From 1994 then, the objectives of the Association and its influence related mainly to management practices and employment conditions. With the right to take industrial action formally denied to the POA and the organisation of the Association on local lines, this occurred principally in the context of individual establishments. Private sector competition and the threat of market testing led to a new degree of cooperation between local POA branches and management attempts to reshape working practices. Local POAs generally cooperated with 'performance improvement' plans in their own establishments, which inevitably led to cost efficiencies.

In this atmosphere of improved relationships, the Labour government made a pre-election commitment to revoke section 127 and to replace it with a Voluntary Agreement or compensatory mechanism. Labour's election in 1997 meant that by 2001, following extensive negotiations, a new industrial relations procedure was agreed by both the POA and the Prison Service, involving an independent and binding arbitration process enforceable by the courts. Some disagreements persisted over what matters were included in the process, but overall this contractual arrangement was used, in return for which the POA gave an undertaking that they would not resort to industrial action. The Pay Review Body's first pay award to prison officers (in 2002) was 6 per cent. Thereafter, the Labour government consistently met the PRB's pay recommendations, which tended to fall between the POA's claims and the government's offers.

From 2004 this Voluntary Agreement became the Joint Industrial Relations Procedural Agreement (JIRPA). The government dis-applied section 127 for prison officers in England and Wales (but not for those working in Northern Ireland and not for private sector custody officers). An apparent slowdown in the use of market testing from 2006 (the 'Sheppey decision') and a reluctance by the private sector to take on dilapidated and struggling prisons (such as Brixton) led to a loss of some of the POA's initial fears about competition. The POA nationally made several legal challenges to the Prison Service's interpretation of the legislation on industrial action during this period, and in the light of decreasing pay awards towards the end of Labour's third term, increased its pressure throughout 2007 and 2008 to restore full trade union rights (including the right to take industrial action) to its members. On 8 May 2007, the POA gave notice of its intention to withdraw from JIRPA, effective from 8 May 2008. Talks facilitated by the TUC began. On 29 August 2007, the POA called for national strike action for the first time in its history. Several branches took such action, remaining outside their establishments for the entire day. The consequences in those establishments were serious – court appearances were cancelled, transfers could not take place, prisoners were held in police cells, and in one young offender institution (Lancaster Farms), a major disturbance occurred, taking three days to bring under control. All establishments were short of staff.

At this point, relationships deteriorated further. The government took a decision in January 2008 to make an amendment to the Criminal Justice and Immigration Bill making it possible to suspend or revive section 127 in order to avoid leaving the POA with a window of opportunity for further industrial action, effectively ending any pretence that a voluntary agreement was sufficient. The new legislation clearly prohibited the 'inducement of a prison officer to withhold his services as an officer' or 'to commit a breach of discipline' or to 'take any industrial action' (section 127 as amended in the Criminal Justice and Immigration Act 2008, section 138). This obligation is 'a duty owed to the secretary of State', contravention of which leading to 'loss or damage' is actionable. 'Industrial action' includes 'any action that would be likely to put at risk the safety of any person (whether a prisoner, a person working at or visiting a prison, a person working with prisoners or a member of the public'.[11]

On 1 May 2008 local action was taken at three Yorkshire prisons following a disciplinary procedure against a member of staff. One of the establishments involved (Lindholme Immigration Removal Centre (IRC)) had a disturbance as a result of the lack of staff and internal security provision.

Meanwhile, the Prison Service was attempting to introduce a 'second Fresh Start': Workforce Modernisation. This was 'the key' to future negotiations. A package amounting to £50 million (allowing for a multi-year pay deal) was made available by the Treasury to help 'secure the right deal' for prison officers and the National Offender Management Service (NOMS). Relationships at the time were tense (Jack Straw referred to 'profound differences between us' in his speech to the POA Annual Conference in 2008), but considerable energy was being expended to work towards agreement on new working practices, management-proposed change processes and constructive disputes procedures. A new Prison Service Order (8525) accompanied by a joint statement by the Prison Service and the POA encouraging constructive methods of engagement at local level was published in November 2008. An Employee Relations Committee consisting of three members of the POA Committee and three members of the NOMS Board has been established to make decisions and advise on how to resolve disputes in the future.

These developments (which are ongoing) serve as an important reminder that officer unrest poses a major risk to the safety of staff and prisoners and to the stability of establishments and that a clear government strategy on the role of unions, and especially of strikes, in essential public services is needed. They also raise questions about the proper role of the Prison Officers' Association in a climate of severe financial restraint, population growth, prison expansion, the restructuring of prison officer working practices and private sector competition. None of these questions have easy answers. What should the modern role of the Prison Officers' Association be? Most commentators have an aspirational vision of shared and constructive working between the Prison Service and the Association. In a true partnership, each should be prepared to tackle issues and problems without rancour and with the objectives of the National Offender Management Service in mind. Whether this vision of shared working can be achieved via PSO 8525 remains to be seen. There are inevitable conflicting views between the POA and others, but also within the Prison Service about appropriate levels of pay, the length and content of training courses and staffing levels. Questions about what the *economic value* of prison officers' work is are related to visions of *who* the prison officer is: a professional, or a 'turnkey'? In turn, these matters are related to our vision of the prison and its function.

Derek Lewis simply said that the POA should become a 'more representative and effective body' (Lewis 1997: 142). The 1997 Prison Service Review accepted that the POA had experienced substantial problems during the 1990s and recognised that recent changes made effective officer representation more important, but did not explain in any detail how this might occur:

The contracting-out of services, the involvement of the private sector in running whole prisons, Quantum, and the POA's loss, through legislation, of the right to take industrial action, have made good industrial relations harder to achieve – and yet, at the same time, all the more necessary. At a time of enormous pressure, turbulence and change, it is all the more essential to work hard and effectively to promote a spirit of openness, dialogue and a readiness to listen to and act on expressed concerns. (Prison Service 1997: 128)

The then Chief Inspector of Prisons felt that the POA had the potential to effect both a helpful as well as malign influence upon modern prisons:

The POA claims to be responsible and constructive in its approach, and we have found this to be true in a number of prisons ... But it has been completely the opposite in too many for me to be able to support its claim without qualification. Our reports (on some prisons) illustrate what I would expect a responsible and constructive staff association to distance itself from ... Not to repudiate such behaviour, and attitude to authority, gives the impression that it is in favour of it, which I am sure that it does not want to do. (HMCIP 2000: 39)

He recognised that blaming the culture of a difficult prison on the POA is too simplistic:

> But there is far more to the cultural problem than parts of the POA. The culture of (some prisons) had been ingrained in too many staff for too many years. It was based on a totally unacceptable attitude to the treatment of and conditions for prisoners, that has no place in any civilised society, let alone a modern Prison Service. This has to be eliminated. (HMCIP 2000: 39)

There is a clear view in these accounts of what the POA should not be and how it should not act. What is less evident is the role it should adopt in a changed industrial relations era. Jacobs argues that prison officer unions could make it easier to introduce penal reform under the right circumstances, and when unions embody 'rational self-interest':

> The diffuse emotional opposition to new programs that sometimes surfaces among the guards presents greater obstacles to reform than the more rational opposition of a centralised union leadership open to negotiation and compromise. (Jacobs and Crotty 1978: 43–4)

These sentiments were echoed at the 2008 POA Conference in a speech by Jack Straw:

> It is very striking, when you cut through the issues which divide us and actually sit down with Prison Officers or your representatives nationally, we actually start to talk about how we make for a better service the things we can change. All of us always come away not only better informed about what's going on in the Prison Service but with a list of things that we want to take action on. We are going to continue to co-operate with you to improve your working conditions. We are well aware that the environment in which you operate can be dangerous. Violence towards Prison Officers and other staff cannot, and will not be tolerated, and that's why I have personally very strongly backed your campaign of zero tolerance and made sure that the Prison Service as a whole backs it. I have spoken to the Attorney General and the Home Secretary to ensure that the Police and the Crown Prosecution Service take a more vigorous approach to prosecuting assaults on staff. It is not acceptable that Prison

Officers should have to work under the spectre of violence and we are going to work with you and your members to give you greater protection. (Straw 2008: 4)

One of the expressed and legitimate roles of the POA is to generate recognition for the officer:

Prison officers are not going to come and say, 'I've just stopped a £200 million riot', but they have and nobody recognises it. You just do it and get on because you haven't got the time to spend telling your senior officer what you have done. (Brian Caton, General Secretary of the POA, interviewed in the *Prison Service Journal*, March 2001)

Local POA branches exist in every establishment, with the chair (and occasionally the secretary) often being granted a number of hours per week to conduct relevant work. This includes casework and welfare support, recruitment, meetings with senior managers, negotiating re-profiling exercises and attendance at the Annual Conference. Individual officers often say that their membership of the local POA branch is mainly 'for legal protection'. The mood and tone of local POA branches varies widely, another interesting dimension of the officer union-culture framework deserving of further attention.

Conclusions

Prison staff cultures can be healthy and unhealthy, or simply a reflection of current 'biographical' developments in an establishment at a particular time. Managers are aware that they have to engage with the culture of staff in each prison and this is sometimes influenced by the character of the local POA or of the local POA officials. This engagement with local culture is illustrated in the work of Sparks *et al.* (1996). At the time of their research, Albany was a tightly controlled prison but had experienced a riot a few years before. The incoming governor arrived just after this riot:

Looking around I saw fear and anxiety in people's eyes and real twitchiness and I thought 'I must start from where we are, make something of what they've got and what they believe in, and then build upon that' ... They were shell-shocked and physically fearful. (Sparks *et al.* 1996: 136)

The Long Lartin governor also had to work with the grain of the staff culture to effect change:

> Many of them knew that in many areas things were totally unacceptable. I felt that the main element there when I came was fear. Fear of individual cons collectively, fear of a riot, fear of losing the roof. (Sparks *et al*. 1996: 136)

Sometimes cultures are unhealthy and have to be changed. In these circumstances senior managers cannot work 'with the grain' of an establishment's culture and set about deliberately to improve it. This can be one of the most difficult management tasks prison governors attempt to achieve.

Commentators on the prison do not have the equivalent knowledge about prison staff culture that exists in policing. There are often several 'subcultures' in a prison (there may be distinct cultures in segregation units for example) and they are likely to be different in the late-modern prison, perhaps less imbued with masculinity and power than they once were. But these are empirical questions deserving of further research attention. Prison staff cultures provide a framework within which daily practices take place. Staff can be more or less fearful, distrusting of change, pessimistic and unsupported – or they can be enthusiastic, open, loyal and confident. The shape of this culture is related to history, current conditions and management style. Sometimes individual officers feel frustrated by their own establishment's culture but feel powerless to change it.

Overall, we can argue from our review of several studies that prison officers are:

- generally committed to their work and to achieving high standards;
- often cynical – yet at the same time optimistic that some of their work will have a positive effect;
- aware of the (sometimes traumatic) effects of prison work – yet they enjoy the social contact and experience of working closely with others; and
- strongly influenced by the need to know that other officers will support them in moments of danger.

Officers respect strong and involved leadership. In particular, they are encouraged when senior managers understand the demands of their role, and the skills used to achieve the apparently quiet day.

Officers feel they are 'at their best' when 'they are led, not driven'. Their resistance to change can be understood and counteracted, but changing penal cultures seems to be a delicate and difficult task.

Finally, we turn to the question of management.

Notes

1 Alison Liebling and Ben Crewe have conducted an observational and interview-based study of senior managers in public and private corrections as part of their ESRC-funded study, *Values, Practices and Outcomes in Public and Private Sector Corrections*. They are due to report in 2010.

2 With the exception of groups such as the 'Prison? Me? No Way!' project, much of the widespread charitable work done by prisoners and prison officers, and specific offending behaviour programmes, tend to go unreported and unnoticed.

3 It is also worthwhile considering the words of social theorist Zygmunt Bauman. In *Modernity and the Holocaust* (1989), Bauman examines the role of bureaucracy in making the Holocaust possible. This is not limited to the organisational possibilities of bureaucracy, but also the way in which it facilitates the abdication of moral responsibility by employees who can claim that they are just 'doing their job'. See also Milgram (1974) and Haney *et al.* (1973), referred to in Chapter 5.

4 Studies of officers often find that individuals do not completely subscribe to the 'subultural norms' but fear stepping out of line – Toch and Klofas (1982) and Cheek and Miller (1983), for example. Future work might consider relating this fact and other aspects of prison life and culture to 'masculinity' (see Jefferson and Carlen 1996 and Sim 1994, for example).

5 This recalls Fleisher's remark about the 'positive social benefits of getting involved in violence ... Staffers who hadn't said anything to me before this ... now began to pay attention to me ... I felt a sense of belonging to the group.'

6 That is, manning the cell blocks of 60 prisoners with one other officer.

7 Continuity of staff, predictability of shift attendance and assurance of staffing levels being met also contributed to the positive working ethos of the Unit.

8 A suicide prevention initiative intended to improve the experience of prisoners on entry into custody in particular. See further Arnold *et al.* (2007) and Liebling *et al.* (2005).

9 Two senior managers have completed Masters theses on the role of the POA (Calvert 2000; James 2000). A PhD student, Claire Lea, has recently started a study of the role of the POA under the supervision of Alison Liebling.

10 This account illustrates the difficulties in making assumptions about the officer without systematically exploring their views first. The POA could be judged guilty of the same lack of consultation with its membership of which it so often accuses Prison Service management.

11 A Human Rights Joint Committee intervention led to the specification that this meant action likely to put safety at risk. The POA are challenging this provision in Europe.

Chapter 8

The prison officer in a modern bureaucracy

I don't believe there is any such thing as a bad prison or bad staff. I think it's just a case of how you run it, basically. (Governor grade, cited in Liebling *et al.* 1997)

Job satisfaction and/or organisational commitment have been shown ... to be related to productivity, attendance at work, turnover, retirement, participation, labour militancy, sympathy for unions, and psychological withdrawal from work. (Camp 1994: 280)

Introduction

One of the major tensions of prison life is the tension between tradition-based experience and future-oriented organisational development. We have shown that due to the complex and sometimes risk-laden nature of their work, prison officers inevitably tend to have short time horizons. Getting to the end of the day peacefully is a major priority and a major skill, grounded in experience. Senior managers and senior headquarters managers have longer time horizons, strategic visions and aspirational corporate agendas. Some of the resistance officers express to constant change is related to real tensions between 'what seems to work', 'what external agencies say is right' and 'what might be better'. This chapter looks briefly at how officers regard their governors and at some of the pressures their governors might be under from those above them. What does the world above officers look like, how has it changed and what are the implications of the modern management agenda for the prison officer?

There have been substantial and far-reaching internal changes to prison management and organisation in the last 20 years, with a much needed 'improvement' agenda driving the Prison Service out of its former crisis-laden state (Cavadino and Dignan 1997). Prison officers often find this change process difficult and frustrating, despite some clear relief about improvements to conditions, delivery and leadership. Power has shifted upwards, despite devolution, so that greater central control and direction is exerted over how establishments 'perform'. From Fresh Start in 1987 through to Agency status in 1993, the introduction and spread of prison privatisation and the growing influence of managerialism (in the form of Key Performance Targets (KPTs) and the Business Planning process, for example), and with Workforce Modernisation (or its equivalent) around the corner, the Prison Service has for 20 years been in a state of constant administrative change.

The structure of the Prison Service in 2010

The regional structure of the Prison Service and the National Offender Management Service (NOMS) to which it belongs 'is beginning to bed down following the review which saw the creation of Directors of Offender Management: newly powerful regional posts at the heart of delivery and commissioning decisions' (Wheatley 2010: personal communication). Further structural change is imminent following the election of a Conservative-Liberal Democrat coalition in May 2010 and the announcement of severe public spending cuts. The fact that prison staff work in a rapidly and profoundly changing organisation is, in itself, significant. In addition to this uncertainty about key organisational arrangements, the Prison Service has faced unprecedented population pressure (requiring new capacity) and stringent financial restraint.

In 2010 ('a challenging time for the Prison Service'), the managerial and organisational structure of the Prison Service was as follows: the Prison Service is part of the National Offender Management Service, which is an Agency of the Ministry of Justice (established in 2007). The purpose of the NOMS organisation is to 'drive forward the management of offenders, focus resources on front-line delivery and further improve efficiency' (letter to the Service, 29 January 2008):

At the heart of its work will be the twin aims of protecting the public and reducing re-offending, by giving offenders the support and challenge they need to turn away from crime and to live useful lives. (Jack Straw's Foreword to the National Offender Management Service Agency Framework Document 2008 – see NOMS 2008).

The Agency is required 'to show early and clear evidence that it can deliver more efficient and effective offender management service, both in custody and the community' (p. 5). The clear emphasis is on working within a challenging financial climate to deliver improved and effective services.

The outgoing Director General of NOMS, Phil Wheatley, retired after 40 years' service in June 2010. He was replaced by his Deputy, Michael Spurr, who became the Agency's Chief Executive Officer. Michael Spurr is accountable, through the Prisons and Probation Minister, to the Secretary of State for Justice. The Framework Document outlines the responsibilities of NOMS. As part of the review of the Agency's structure the governance arrangements within the Agency were reviewed. As a result a monthly NOMS Agency Board (NAB) meeting focusing on strategic Agency priorities including change, performance, risk and investment was established with a weekly NOMS Executive Management Committee (NEMC) meeting to support the Director General in the day-to-day running of the Agency. Supporting both, a comprehensive range of subcommittees reporting to the Board and Executive Management Committee have been introduced.

The NAB is responsible for the 'delivery of offender management', including regional management (via Directors of Offender Management) and commissioning of offender management services from public and private sector prisons, the delivery of a prison building programme and the establishment of probation trusts. Colleagues from the Agency's parent Department sit on the NAB to ensure the overall direction of the Agency is consistent with its strategic priorities as agreed with Ministers and to support the Agency's contribution to the corporate issues of the Department.

The NAB has eight executive members, five ex-officio members (the Secretary to the Board, the Head of the Agency's Communication function, a Race Equality Adviser, the Head of Audit and Assurance and the Director General's Private Secretary) and is chaired by the Director General. The executive members are the Chief Operating Officer (who has responsibility for all operational matters), the

Director of Human Resources, the Director of Commissioning and Operational Policy, the Director of the Capacity Programme (responsible for building and provision), the Director of Finance and Performance, the Director of Information and Communication Technology, the Department's Director General of Justice Policy and the Department's Director General of Finance and Commercial. Three Non-Executive Directors also attend.

The NEMC is also chaired by the Director General. The three Non-Executive Directors and representatives from the Ministry of Justice do not attend nor does the Head of Audit and Assurance. Otherwise membership is the same as for the NAB except that the Director of Offender Health, the Director of High Security, a Legal Adviser and a Departmental Press Officer attend.

The NAB is responsible for 136 public and private sector prisons. These are grouped into nine regions and Wales. Additionally, the high security prisons are managed functionally. Each region and Wales has its own Director of Offender Management (DOM) based in the region and reporting directly to the Chief Operating Officer. This role was introduced in April 2009. The role of the Director of Offender Management, together with the Regional Custodial Manager, is to establish with the governor of each prison a 'service delivery agreement' which defines in detail the function and activities of the establishment and the resources to enable these to take place. The role of the Director of Offender Management is increasingly concerned with managing resources as well as performance. How this role is performed varies according to the individuals involved but tends to be diverse, involving various skills and approaches. Directors of Offender Management are more likely to be 'commissioners' or purchasers of services.

At the establishment level, life is also fundamentally set to change. At the time of writing, the governing governor is supported by various other operational senior managers and administrative heads of department. In a large prison, there can be as many as three layers of managers above the uniformed grades of senior and prison officer. Principal officers, who were traditionally in charge of one wing or discrete function (such as security), have recently been replaced by 'developing managers' – an out-of-uniform role. Senior officers now 'run wings' with prison officers below them. Not including the governing governor, the number of management layers has been reduced to three in smaller prisons and four in some large establishments.

Management change in the Prison Service

Since the 1980s there has been a 'new managerialist' influence on the way the Prison Service operates at a senior management level, with increasing emphasis on setting objectives, measuring achievements in relation to these objectives, raising standards, stringent financial control, and componentiality (discrete functional responsibilities and policies).[1] Critics of new managerialism are cynical about these developments, seeing them as systems-driven and overly concerned with presentation and control; others view these changes as necessary in an organisation trying to introduce improvements and a more rigorous and performance-driven management style. The recent changes to the NOMS structure have introduced greater integration between services, stronger central prescription and a sharper focus on performance and resources. This may be felt as eroding the independence of governors and other criminal justice professionals. Some 'robust' and sometimes harsh decisions have been made about improving those prisons perceived as 'failing' by headquarters senior management (including time limited chances to improve and threats of subsequent market testing without an in-house bid). Some staff, individual governors and external commentators are critical of these changes, feeling that the pace is too fast, the style too insensitive and the goals somewhat narrow. The pace of change is set to increase, with stringent budget cuts and increasing expectations of joint working, the delivery of services and reducing reoffending targets around the corner.

Despite a certain nervousness about the pace and scope of change, there has clearly also been a marked improvement in the management of the Prison Service, more visible leadership and a greater willingness by Prison Service senior managers to tackle 'big issues' (such as racism, violence, under-performance, inefficiency and so on). While the pressure from above is intense, efforts have been made to support establishments, and to be seen by and to listen to staff (for example, the staff consultation exercises which over several years have involved director-led one-day meetings on unlimited subject matter with about 3,000 different staff). There is a clear understanding that failure on performance at an individual and institutional level is no longer tolerated – a sea change in a traditional public sector organisation. The greater emphasis on accountability is related to the government's establishment of public service agreements (PSAs) with each ministry. PSAs are defined in terms of output delivery and resources and are reinforced at the highest level by bilateral meetings the Prime Minister holds with each Secretary of State. 'New managerialism' is arguably more than bureaucracy in a new guise: there has been substantial investment in regime developments since 1999, representing a transformation in the public and Ministerial perception of imprisonment (that is a faith that it can be constructive). But such investment has come with high expectations. Much rides on the successful delivery of constructive regimes and the outcomes of a new 'What Works' agenda.

The move to modernisation and managerialism

The current emphasis on modernising the Prison Service has its origins in the early 1980s, the period following the publication of the May Report (Home Office 1979). The pressures towards modernisation were both internal and external and related primarily to practical problems of budget management, but there were related philosophical issues concerning the proper role of prisons (and therefore of prison officers) also to be resolved. Within the then Prison Department, concerns about the ineffectiveness of management systems which did not facilitate the control of resources were being expressed throughout the 1970s – a period of deteriorating industrial relations and prisoner unrest. Overtime was out of control. As a result, prison costs (which are substantially staff costs) were escalating, and pressure was brought to bear on governors to be more accountable for prison officer time.

The problem of poor management was practical and ideological. As 'manpower' issues were discussed, questions arose about the role of prison officers. Their deployment was largely based on a nineteenth-century paramilitary model of a prison which was no longer relevant to contemporary regimes. Increasingly, psychologists and other specialists had been recruited to work in prisons, without ever being formally integrated into staffing or management structures. Uniformed prison officers broadly worked to chief officers, particularly in relation to their shift systems, leave provision, overtime and sickness cover, while non-uniformed specialists and assistant governors worked to governors. Governors were not managing their staff directly or effectively, although assistant governors managed aspects of regime delivery involving staff deployment such as group work and personal officer schemes. There was an identifiable management malaise about these arrangements, which ultimately led to the unification of officer and governor ranks and the abolition of overtime in new working arrangements introduced in 1987 which became known as Fresh Start.

At the same time, ideas of efficiency and greater management control within the public sector were beginning to spread throughout the civil service, driven by the severe recession of the late 1970s and the emerging 'new right' philosophies of the incoming Conservative government of 1979. In 1982, Chris Train was appointed Director General of the Prison Service, with a clear brief to see through a process of management modernisation. One of his major reforms was the introduction of 'contracts' for prisons in 1984, based on a new statement of purpose (see Maguire *et al.* 1985: 184–6). Once this idea had been introduced, the next step was to create a coherent management framework within establishments capable of delivering agreed objectives. Each member of staff within a prison was to be brought within one managerial structure. Fresh Start was an attempt to achieve this.

The aim of Fresh Start, then, was to produce an efficient system of line management, with clear demarcation of responsibilities and accountability, from the prison officer upwards through their functional manager, to establishment governor, the former regional director rank, the Director General and, ultimately, the Home Secretary. Fresh Start saw the abolition of paid overtime in exchange for a significantly enhanced basic salary, the abolition of the chief officer rank (merged with the governor grades) and the introduction of 'group' working. The latter two reforms were, and some might argue, still are, the most contentious.[2] The concept of 'group' working was that instead of being centrally deployed, effectively by the chief officer, officers were to work as teams within certain functions (residential, visits, security and operations) and were to be deployed and managed by the principal and senior officers in charge of their group who, in turn, reported to their line managers in the governor grades.

The implementation of Fresh Start was not smooth and caused considerable resentment – particularly the financial losses for those who did considerable overtime and the abolition of the chief officer rank. Many officers felt that they no longer had a leader or someone who could champion their cause within the management structure. Additionally, governor grades were not adept at managing the new arrangements which required a change in their role as well as that of officers. Fresh Start weakened the power of the POA, which hitherto could exercise considerable influence by getting officers not to work overtime, on which establishments had grown to depend. However, group working was diluted by the retention (or reintroduction) of central detailing, the problems several establishments experienced with cross-deployment of officers from one group to another, and a reduction in officers' weekly hours from a high of about 56 each week before overtime was abolished to 39 within six years of Fresh Start being introduced and the efficiency savings this required. The arrangements under which Fresh Start was introduced are documented in 'Bulletin 8' (Home Office Prison Service 1987). There are still differing views among managers as to whether it represents a constraint on managerial effectiveness or a workable set of arrangements within which managers have the scope to manage effectively and efficiently.

What Fresh Start did not address, but what the 1989 'Review of the Prison Service above establishment level' attempted to examine, was the organisational rift between the 'centre' and the 'field' on the one hand, and 'operations' and 'policy' on the other. By 1990 the four regional directors, nominally answerable for all that went on in establishments but more practically concerned with managing the prisoner population, industrial relations, budgets and operational crises, were regarded as the four 'robber barons' of the Prison Board – remote from it and yet with an effective veto on what occurred in establishments, when it occurred and how.

Regional directors were abolished and a new area manager structure was introduced in September 1990 following a report from external consultants (the first time an outside company had reported on the organisation of the Prison Service). Area managers were required to manage the governors under them more effectively and to ensure the delivery of national policies within each establishment.[3] To complement this change, an operational and a policy function were brought under three operational directors to bridge this persistent gap between administration (policymaking) and management (delivery). The location of area managers' bases in London symbolised further the bringing together of the Service and the development of a more 'corporate' and centralised organisation, but this arrangement did not last long and area managers were soon relocated in areas, with weekly trips to London for meetings with headquarters personnel and monthly bi-laterals with the (now) Chief Operating Officer. The co-location of policy and operational responsibilities physically and structurally did not resolve the tensions between the two, although it did improve matters. What exposed the enduring tension in and complexity of the relationship between policy and operations, or between headquarters and 'the field', were the Whitemoor and Parkhurst escapes (1994 and 1995 respectively) and the sentence calculation debacle in 1996 which resulted in 542 prisoners being released without warning. Area managers based in headquarters bring an operational dimension to the policymaking process, while area managers in areas can ensure firmer adherence to policy in practice. Both functions are necessary. The move to make DOMs responsible for the performance of establishments may risk losing some of the operational and 'eye-witness' expertise developed over the intervening period. 'Management-at-a distance' has become one of the hallmarks of the modern, lean organisation. It is worthwhile continuing to describe the evolution of these intermediary management arrangements further, as well as outlining the arguments used to justify them.

The Lygo report and Next Steps

In 1991, the Lygo report – commissioned to further examine the management of the Prison Service – included the view that:

> The Prison Service is the most complex organisation I have encountered and its problems some of the most intractable. (Lygo 1991: 2)

In Lygo's view, the Prison Service needed 'visible leadership', autonomy, a clear purpose and more compliance with the instructions of headquarters. Lygo believed that making the Prison Service a Next Steps Agency (making it a separate entity within the then Home Office) would bring these benefits – but that the Home Secretary would only grant it if there was 'confidence in the management structure and reassurance that the organisation is managing itself properly and in accordance with the objectives set out in the Framework Document (the document launching Agency status)' (Lygo 1991: 10–11).

Agency status was granted in April 1993. It marked a new phase in the development of managerialism in the culture of the Prison Service. Corporate and Business Plans were now regularly published, outlining objectives related to improving quality of service and increasing value for money. The Prison Service was from that point onwards clearly focused on performance. To emphasise this further the government market tested Manchester prison following its reconstruction after the Strangeways and other disturbances of April 1990. The fact that the government accepted that the private sector could be contracted to carry out this grave state function was a severe jolt to a Service isolated from private sector management influence. In a major break with the past, a Director General from outside the public sector was appointed (Derek Lewis, formerly head of Granada Television). Whatever the arguments for and against private sector involvement in managing prisons, market testing, followed by directly contracting out the design, construction, management and financing (DCMF) of new prisons to the private sector, provided a spur to change within the public sector Prison Service (the 'cross-fertilisation' argument; see Harding 1997). The original cost difference between comparable private and public sector prisons was as high as 15 per cent but a drive for greater efficiency in the public sector saw this reduced by about 2.5 per cent each year for the first five years, until the cost differences were negligible.

The drive for efficiency raises key issues of measurement. How are 'inefficient' or poor performing prisons identified? Savings have been demanded from every prison, no matter how they perform. It is clear that in practice some establishments were already leaner than others. Geographical and design features influence the cost of running a prison. Work has been ongoing in this area of performance and cost measurement and comparison (see Woodbridge 1999; Liebling, assisted by Arnold 2004).

The private sector has also spurred the development and use of new technology. Proposals for two to three new large, lean, 'Titan' prisons (housing up to 2,500 prisoners each) were accepted by the Labour government in 2007 but their planned size was reduced to 1,500 following debate. Whether there are limits to efficiencies remains to be seen.

The Prison Service has been required, then, since the early 1990s to publish objectives and targets for each three-year period. Initially, these targets were quite loose. In the first year of Agency status, there were six KPIs relating to escapes, assaults, purposeful activity, visits, cost per place and prison conditions. By 2000, there were 15 KPIs. By 2008, the number had reduced to 12. Figure 8.1 details the NOMS vision statement which identifies its broader aim, vision and values. These aims signal the Prison Service's integral relationship to the wider criminal justice system.

Though KPTs have become increasingly important within the Prison Service, their introduction did not mark the end of (or only manifestation of) organisational change. Further significant moves have occurred that warrant discussion: changes following the Prison Service Review of 1997, and the changing demands on prisons following the Carter Review of 2007.

OUR STATEMENT OF PURPOSE
Protecting the public and reducing reoffending by delivering the punishment of the courts and reforming offenders.

OUR VISION
As part of a world-class justice system we aim to be an internationally recognised leader in public protection and reducing reoffending.

OUR VALUES
We will:
Treat offenders lawfully and with decency;
Value individuals and treat each other with respect; be open, honest and transparent and incorporate equality and diversity in all we do;
Use public resources to achieve best value;
Empower and support each other to work collaboratively within the Ministry of Justice and across the Agency;
Reach out to work with other organisations on joint agendas;
Embrace change and innovation to achieve our purpose and vision.

HOW WE WORK
We manage a mixed economy of providers. Decisions on what work is to be done and who it is to be done by will be based on evidence and driven by best value. Working with partners and providers we will manage offenders in the community and in custody in an integrated and effective manner.

Figure 8.1 NOMS Vision and Values 2008

The 1997 Prison Service Review was established by the then Director General, Richard Tilt, the first Director General who had been a prison governor. Looking back at previous work, the Review considered 14 previous organisational reviews, six of which (not including itself) had occurred between 1994 and 1997. The Review concluded that the Prison Service suffered from a lack of clarity and leadership at top management level, and that significant investment was required in senior management recruitment, training and development. In common with many previous reviews and reports on the Prison Service, it found poor relations throughout: between Ministers and headquarters, between headquarters and prisons, and between management and staff within prisons. One major concern of staff in prisons was the apparent remoteness of those working in headquarters (many of them were generalist administrative grades with policy responsibilities), leading to operational staff implementing new policies often perceived as unrealistic, demanding or inappropriate. Low levels of compliance with central instructions was therefore unsurprising and common.[4] The Review prompted changes which focused on attempting to implement a rigorous and robust line management of establishments, which Laming recognised (Home Office 2000). The changes can be seen as part of a drive to make 'managerialism' and the delivery of constructive regimes more effective.

Officers' thinking about management

Each of these changes over the last 20 years has had an influence on the way prisons are managed and therefore on the way officers are required to perform their role. The role of the prison officer in essence has not changed, but the organisation of their role and work has. The introduction of a composite Operational Support Grade (OSG)[5] in 1996 has resulted in the withdrawal of officers from many tasks which do not involve contact with prisoners and the contracting out of escort services has seen their withdrawal from some that do. These developments have been contentious but have helped to reduce the cost of increasing prison use and to refocus the officer's role on work which involves the range of interpersonal and peacekeeping skills we have examined in this book. Further such changes under the Workforce Modernisation programme raise (but do not resolve) many fundamental questions about what it is that prison officers do, how they should be managed to best effect, and the 'economic value' of different aspects of their work, as indicated in the previous chapter. These questions remain highly significant and will need revisiting in future analyses of the role of the prison officer.

The various organisational changes introduced over the last 20 years raise the questions of what officers think of managers and of modern styles of management.

> You work well for a good governor, no matter what job you're in. (Officer)

Prisons differ considerably in staff–management relationships. A strong and well-liked management team can transform a prison and provide the kind of leadership staff respond to well. During the various pieces of our own research, the same requirements prisoners have of officers have been voiced by officers about management.

For 'willing compliance' to be encouraged, prison officers need legitimate 'authority' or good practical and interpersonal treatment. They complain of insufficient management attention and contact, of a 'them and us' state between management and staff, with prisoners often coming first, and of resource problems, particularly staffing shortages and the need for extended duties at short notice. There is sometimes a feeling that senior managers are 'running a business' rather than 'providing leadership'. Staff sometimes comment that they are 'closer' to prisoners and have more in common with them than with management. The same stereotypes staff and prisoners use about each other can be heard when staff speak of management, with the same basic lack of trust. At one of our establishments (Whitemoor), staff commented that management were 'a lot better than they used to be', that they were 'approachable and supportive', and most of the staff singled out two or three individuals who they had most contact with for high praise. At other establishments (Holme House and Bullingdon), officers were unusually positive about their senior managers, feeling that they, as staff, were trusted, supported and highly valued. There is a general preference for 'strong' leadership and 'no yes-men'. Officers use the word 'straight', meaning honest and fair. Staff draw important links between their views of management and their relationships with prisoners:

> If we have got confidence in management, we can then be confident to prisoners. (Officer)

Staff (and some prisoners) feel that management give 'shape' to their work. Much of this comes from the relationships management have with staff and with prisoners:

> If they [management] become authoritarian with us, then it goes straight down the line. If I've been told to make sure that this happens and that it will happen by a certain time, then I will make sure it will happen, because I do not want to be answering to him. (Officer)

The governor 'sets the tone' of an establishment and models relationships by dealing with prisoners and staff in full view of others. Staff need to know that senior managers can resort to 'winning games' with prisoners. At the end of the day, it is the responsibility of senior managers to set the boundaries and determine what 'right relationships' are. If they do not, officers and prisoners will define those boundaries, with the inevitable lack of consistency that this entails.

The standard officer response to a question about management is to complain (with increasing fervour as they look upwards through the management chain) – managers do not take sufficient notice of the views of officers, do not appreciate the work officers put in, are more anxious to please prisoners than please staff and are not prepared to support staff on all issues. Officers like strong managers who are prepared to support them in the face of prisoner protest or at adjudications, and they seem primarily concerned with having account taken of their views and needs. There is an assumption that senior managers in headquarters design policy and 'send that policy down', but little feeling that policies are effectively designed (that is designed with staff in mind).

One of the occasions when officers, prisoners and managers meet together is in the adjudication room. Adjudications are an important formal stage on which all participants can be carefully observed by each other. They are a testing-ground on which each party present learns much about the others. Governors (and now private prison directors) use them to discover the capabilities of their officers and to learn about the prisoner in front of them; officers find out if the governor is prepared to support them. Prisoners demand the highest standards of fairness from governors, and want to see their side of the incident sufficiently explored – prisoners do not necessarily expect a favourable verdict, but they do expect a fair hearing. Different personalities are evident in the ways that different governors take charge in the adjudication room, though most adhere to the laid-down procedure.

We cannot address 'the role of the governor' in detail here (see, however, Bryans and Wilson, 2000; Liebling, assisted by Arnold 2004: ch. 8; and Gadd in progress). However, we have noted the significant influence of committed and charismatic individuals in leading or motivating their staff to provide the conditions in which any regime innovation may be successful. The 'quality and commitment' of the individual governors in well-performing establishments should not be underestimated (e.g. HMCIP 1993b: 2). Effective wings seem to be led by committed wing managers, and so on. Careful consideration should be given to the contributions of these individuals, around whom best practice seems to percolate. It would be valuable to try to identify what these characteristics are and whether they can be replicated or encouraged to develop via training and other forms of support, and in general what features of organisational management influence the performance and satisfaction of staff (see further Camp 1994).[6]

Thinking theoretically about managerialism

Clearly, the organisation of the Prison Service has undergone substantial change in the last two decades, and increasingly over the last few years. Traditional administrative public sector management has (largely) given way to a new form of 'new public managerialism' reflected in the use of information technology, a greater emphasis on performance monitoring and improvement (at lower cost), flatter management structures and a culture imported from the private sector of 'service delivery to customers' (Hood 1991; Ferlie *et al.* 1996). The growth of managerialism has been linked to four 'administrative mega-trends': attempts to slow down or reverse government growth; a shift towards privatisation; automation (IT); and the development of a more international economy. There have been different phases or styles of managerialism prevalent at different stages over the last 20 years (Quinn 1985; Pollitt 1993). Ferlie *et al.* describe four identifiable such phases: the efficiency drive (e.g. emphasising greater attention to financial control and value for money); downsizing and decentralisation (for example, growth in the use of external contracts); in search of excellence (for example, the ascendancy of 'the learning organisation'); and the public service orientation (a fusion of public and private sector ideas – with a return of some traditionally public sector tasks and values within the new efficient, performance-led framework), each with different core features (Ferlie *et al.* 1996).

What are the implications of managerialism for the prison officer?

The preceding analysis shows that the Prison Service has moved significantly towards a managerialist mode of operation, particularly in the creation of objectives, targets and standards, with the introduction of a general performance culture and some centralisation of procedural aspects of performance. The remaining part of this chapter considers some of the effects of these management changes on the role of prison officers. There are a number of issues, in particular the influence of targets on prison officers' work and the meaning of the term 'professionalism'.

Managerialism in its earliest phase tended to concern itself with goals and results rather than process. It encouraged the development of professional skills through the devolvement of power and the flattening of the prison hierarchy. Many aspects of prison work – from counselling a prisoner in distress to persuading 60 prisoners to disappear willingly behind a locked door each night – remain unchanged and are arguably difficult aspects of the job to quantify. How appropriate is the use of targets and goals to the work of the prison officer? An escape is relatively easy to quantify; an assault is more problematic, but it is possible to follow rules about what constitutes a 'serious assault', as the Prison Service defines them. Quantifying how long prisoners spend in purposeful activity raises problems, as prisoners sometimes watch videos in workshop areas to 'make the figures up', but is still measurable in some form or another. Relationships, however – central to the running of prisons – are another matter. Creating a 'target' for good or right relationships is more difficult. The Measuring the Quality of Prison Life Survey (MQPL) is a serious attempt to do this – see further Liebling, assisted by Arnold (2004). In addition to the natural tendency in any form of work to concentrate on such aspects of work that produce concrete results, as King and McDermott state (1995), the appearance of so many key performance targets (KPTs)[7] brings additional incentives to concentrate on those aspects of work that are both quantifiable and that are Prison Service priorities: as the adage says, 'you tend to do what is inspected not what is expected'. Morgan (1997) argues that while the current targets and objectives can measure (and improve) the delivery of services to prisoners, they do not address the basic question, what are prisons for? While managerialism has undoubtedly helped to address the 'material' crisis experienced by prisons throughout the 1980s, there remain some lingering uncertainties about the 'moral' crisis – that is, the primary purpose of imprisonment. It is difficult to measure the delivery of important and publicly expressed penal values (humanity, justice, respect and so on), especially when these values are ill-defined. Can these values remain at the heart of prison work if they are not part of what is measured?

It has not traditionally been part of a prison officer's training to consider what the aims of imprisonment are. Yet it is clear that ideas about punishment and its purpose (in particular the purpose of imprisonment, which we should separate from the aims of sentencing), and ideas about penal values, influence practice (Dunbar 1985; Bottoms 1989). Having a shared understanding of the overall purpose of imprisonment in general, and the purpose and 'ethos' of any single establishment in particular, is a difficult but important task for the Service to achieve. Lack of clarity about some of these issues has contributed to some of the Prison Service's major difficulties as well as to many of its minor ones. Lord Justice Woolf argued that insufficient clarity about the role of the Prison Service contributed to the Manchester and other disturbances, as well as to problems in the handling of these disturbances (Home Office 1991: para. 10.1). On the other hand, those establishments identified as exceptional tend to have clear value statements, often communicated by individual governors with a moral 'sense of direction'.

The prison does much more than 'protect the public' and 'reduce reoffending'. In some ways, these are its most difficult and technical, and some would argue contested, tasks. There are arguably more reliable social mechanisms which are better placed for achieving these tasks (Garland 1990: 289). The prison is a social institution, which embodies and expresses public sentiment, serves to 'enforce the law, regulate populations, realise political authority ... enhance solidarities, emphasise divisions and convey cultural meanings' (Garland 1990: 284). Garland argues that part of the function of the prison is 'the pursuit of values such as justice, tolerance, decency, humanity and civility' and that these things should be 'intrinsic and constitutive aspects of its role' rather than a diversion from its 'real' goals or an inhibition on its capacity to be 'effective' (Garland 1990: 292). In other words, the role of the prison, embodied in the role of the prison officer, is a moral and symbolic one. In a recent statement to the House of Commons, Jack Straw, Secretary of State, argued that the key functions of the prison include 'punishment' and 'reform'. The re-emergence of 'punishment' in official statements of its aims may have serious implications for life inside prisons and for perceptions of what acceptable standards look like.

Concentration on 'systemic' or bureaucratic measurement alone runs the risk of undermining the traditionally individualised, person-centred and 'normative' approach to criminal justice characteristic of a different historical period (for example, Borstal training, social work, rehabilitation and personal development). Bottoms argues that this 'consumerist' approach to criminal justice embodies a particular concept of personhood, reflected in the actuarial and apparently value-free language of KPIs which is used in place of the moral language of justice and fairness (Feeley and Simon 1992; Bottoms 1995). This is not an argument against measurement or monitoring, but an argument about the choices of regime features measured and their operationalisation, and the dangers of the model of the person on which they are based. This critique is important in so far as it articulates a sense expressed by staff at all grades that they have reservations and uncertainties about the precise purpose and nature of KPIs and that they fail to capture the 'essence of their work'. Staff respond negatively to any sense that they are not being treated as individuals or 'moral agents' but as tools for the achievement of predicted outcomes. Some staff derive great satisfaction from and can identify with the type of direction and clarity the KPI culture can bring. Others feel their work requires recognition in supplementary and more 'appreciative' ways.

The issues of discretion and officers' wish to participate in decision-making raise important questions about the role of the modern prison officer, the training officers receive and the management of officers in their work (see Stohr *et al.* 1994). The 'professionalisation' of prison officer work and the more demanding nature of modern prison regimes require, on the one hand, a move away from rigid organisational control, yet on the other, carefully managed systems of guidance and accountability. Hands-on leadership is essential in such a complex working environment.

At the time of writing, a major management revolution, including a reconceptualisation of the role and structure of employment of the prison officer, was about to be implemented. The effects of these changes remain to be seen.

Notes

1 This structure achieves clearer accountability within each function.
2 The abolition of the chief, which officers mention often (even those not old enough to remember chief officers), is used to symbolise something for which officers yearn. Whether or not these attributes were ever embodied in chief officers, their mention has come to represent a feeling of being 'known' over long periods of time, of the world being more certain and predictable, and of clear standards, straight answers, visibility and discipline. Despite recounting countless stories of 'getting a bollocking from the chief', officers like to have superiors 'you feel like standing up for, and calling "Sir"'. Their 'role model' governors often combine this type of authority with a more modern unified management style.
3 The 1997 Prison Service Review found this arrangement to be much more effective than the regional structure it replaced.
4 Learmont (Home Office 1995) famously recorded the amount of paper received by prisons from headquarters over one year as amounting to a pile higher than Ben Nevis. Laming (2000) found one category C

establishment receiving 981 communications from headquarters during one year, containing over 1,700 requests for action.

5   A composite uniformed grade of those who support the basic security and routine operation of the establishment (including the former 'auxiliaries', night patrols, gatekeepers, storekeepers, those who escort lorries, sort mail, operate in a communications room, and work in a canteen). They are not expected to have sustained contact with prisoners.

6   Vicky Gadd, a PhD student at the Cambridge Institute of Criminology, is conducting research on this question.

7   Key performance targets are subordinate performance indicators, representing a narrower and more sharply focused band of performance areas, but supporting the KPIs. They are tailored to establishment type and weighted accordingly.

Chapter 9

Conclusions

The role of the prison officer is arguably the most important in a prison. The precise nature of that role and, more importantly, how it is performed on a daily basis have been neglected in most studies of the prison, until recently. There has been a gap in the literature, in research and the Prison Service's own recognition of what it is that makes the prison officer's job so highly skilled. This book originally set out to fill that gap, and to stimulate further research and reflection on the work of prison officers. It also aimed to introduce an appreciative perspective into what has been a blunt tradition in which prison officers have been stereotyped and labelled negatively. The book arose from interest shown in the findings of several key pieces of research undertaken for the Prison Service and others by the Cambridge Institute of Criminology over several years, which we were asked to bring together and reflect upon, in a single accessible volume. Central to these research projects was the use of 'appreciative inquiry', which critically and, we hope, respectfully engaged prison officers, other staff and prisoners in discussing the nature of the prison officer's role. Since the first edition of the book was published in 2001, there have been several important new studies – on the emotional lives of prison officers (Crawley 2004), on the effects of prison work (Arnold 2005) and the qualities of high-performing prison officers (Arnold 2008), on culture (Liebling 2008a; Arnold *et al.* 2007), on care (Tait 2008a, 2008b), on public-private sector comparisons (McLean and Liebling 2008) and on the use of power (Liebling 2008b; Crewe 2009) – which have together provided greater understanding of the complexities and demands of prison work. Further studies are underway (see, for example, the collection by Liebling (ed.), in progress). We can confidently argue that prison officers are finally receiving the research attention they deserve.

We have argued that prison officers play an important 'peacekeeping' role. They use considerable discretion, and paradoxically they perform 'at their best' when they underuse their power, in the right kind of way. There is a difference between laxity or carelessness about the use of power, and the judicious use of the right amount for the right reasons. The prison officer's role is complex and cannot be taken for granted. Prison work involves more than common sense, although because of the experience-laden nature of the best of their work, officers often mistake a highly skilled performance for common sense. Part of the reason their work is regarded in these terms is because the work of the prison officer is 'low-visibility' work. We try in this book to identify the 'very hard work' involved in establishing and re-establishing order, in defusing tension, in keeping communication flowing to keep the peace. Being a good prison officer involves being good at *not* using force but still getting things done, and being *prepared* to use the various power bases officers can draw on when necessary. It means being capable of using legitimate authority and being in control without resorting to the full extent of the officer's powers. It means establishing 'right' relationships and investing those relationships with real aspects of one's personality. These are aspects of the officer's work which officers value highly in themselves and in their colleagues. These skills are not often explicitly noted or rewarded.

Most officers describe 'life at its best' for them as officers as 'the absence of trouble' – a day without tension and confrontation, when there is a feeling of teamwork, of taking part and being involved. It means feeling supported, mainly by immediate colleagues but also by their managers. This 'absence of trouble' is not a negative concept implying contentment with doing little or dealing with routine administration. Getting to the end of the day involves a variety of actions requiring skill, foresight, diplomacy and humour. Officers are highly motivated to and derive considerable satisfaction from 'getting relationships right'. They are proud when they manage to 'create a pleasant atmosphere on the wing'. Relationship building establishes credit which officers expect to (and often successfully) draw on at difficult or testing times. We hope we have managed to describe these best aspects of prison officer work.

Conclusion: the prison officer in the twenty-first century

The move away from traditional person-centred social work[1] towards a more managerially driven and focused form of 'tackling offending behaviour' which challenges the offender, is research-based and has a centrally prescribed format has been one of the key reasons for a partial resolution of the historic conflict between 'custody' and 'care' identified by Thomas (1972) and others in the past (see Chapter 1). We suggest that the gap between 'custody' and 'care' has been narrowed in some respects, with a less liberal model of 'care', and controversial but corresponding changes to the work of the Probation Service, bringing the traditionally distant correctional services – the custodians and those who 'advise, assist and befriend' – more closely together (operationally if not ideologically; see McAllister *et al.* 1992; Scott 1999). It could be argued that care for prisoners now takes place within a victim-oriented and public protection framework rather than an offender-based framework (see, for example, Christie 2000). This shift has some dangers (limits to care and increasing punitiveness are two),[2] but also has the potential to place the prison officer nearer the centre in prison-based offence-related work. This kind of work may require more training than is currently offered. This form of work is laden with power, however, with implications for prisoners (for example, relating to progress and release) that may be underestimated.

The rise of new public managerialism in its 'purest' (undiluted) form in the Prison Service continued up to the time of the escapes of category A prisoners from two maximum security prisons in 1994 and 1995 and the subsequent dismissal by the then Home Secretary, Michael Howard, of the then Director General, Derek Lewis in 1995, who had been recruited from the private sector. Some detected a change in the nature of managerialism in the Prison Service after that, with a return to some of the traditional public sector values (for example, of decency, care, humanity and community) apparently neglected by a purely managerialist ethos. This is consistent with recent developments in political and economic theory which call for more sensitive concepts of rationality, value for money and service to be used than those typically employed in 'the new penology' (Feeley and Simon 1992). In the year 2010, the Prison Service is more professionally organised, more successful (in terms of most of its own targets) and more vociferous about standards of fairness and decency than it once was (see, for example, the 'practical humanity' framework[3]). But there are dangers in the current context of rising prison populations, stringent budget cuts, lack of public tolerance for offenders and high public and Ministerial expectations of a return to punishment. The prison is a unique and moral place, requiring some generally desired and some unique skills among prison officers. The officer's role in this new climate could be a highly skilled one. But it can always revert to a narrow and dangerous preoccupation with 'security and discipline'. Where prison officers come to stand is shaped to a significant degree by the moral leadership offered by individual governors.

Since the first edition of this book was published, certain key aspects of the prison officer's role and context remain the same. The landing remains a landing, and the core task is getting peacefully through the day with as little disruption as possible. Most prison officers want to do meaningful work; they express how important it is to feel valued by those above them and by the public; the personal officer role is still underdeveloped in practice. Most important, the words of a prison officer can make a difference between a prisoner surviving and not surviving prison life (see Liebling and Tait 2006).

There are several significant areas where life seems to have changed which may be worthy of further exploration. Officers' relationship with the Prison Service organisation is less tight (due to local recruitment and routes into the job, the impact of the private sector and changing employment patterns: 'They come into the job a bit more casually these days', Principal officer). Management grip from a distance, on the other hand, has tightened: there are better and more numerous sources of information, and expectations of performance have increased. This poses a challenge which staff talk about with mixed emotions:

There's no cancelling the gym now – it's all gone in the other direction. (Officer)

We were all plodding – we've had a shake and if I am honest, that's been good. (Officer)

Rather like prisoners felt post-1995, prison staff are feeling the effects of a tightly managed Prison Service following more of its own instructions:

We had a culture where nothing was done for years. Then we suddenly get robustly managed ... It sometimes seems like no bugger above us trusts us. (Officer)

Training has reduced. The officially stated purpose of the prison (protecting the public and reducing reoffending) has changed in emphasis, away from 'a last resort for the violent' to a place of punishment, re-education and reform, of a certain narrowly prescribed kind. Relationships with prisoners are in places closer and more supportive, but also more intrusive (for example, in relation to the role of safer custody officers, Audit and Corporate Assurance (ACA) work, offender management roles, risk assessment, and so on). They still sometimes 'go wrong' (see, for example, Tait 2008a). The role of the POA is in transition. Their power to 'resist' declined during the 1990s, but has resurged in 2007–10 as a troublesome feature of life in prison – 'you felt you had somewhere to go where someone would listen if the job was getting to you' (Officer). A strike in August 2007 shocked and disappointed some governors, who thought they had built sufficient trust with their staff at establishment level to weather national pay deal storms.

The size and composition of the prison population has changed considerably. Prisoners' sentences are more complex, as the problem of progression (or recall) looms large for many. There are new forms of uncertainty (a growing Muslim population, the policing of language/talk/banter, and some recent threats to order). Staff said in group discussions as this edition was under preparation that they were 'losing confidence' in some areas of their work. Staff, and their senior managers, are somewhat less certain than they once were about what is 'virtuous and humane' (Smith 1759, reissue 2006). Meanwhile, the relative pay of prison officers has declined relative to the police, alongside increased concern about the shortening length of the initial training officers receive in practice. There is more research available, and more research interest in the role of prison officers, in the UK and elsewhere. A House of Commons Justice Committee report on the *Role of the Prison Officer* (2009) usefully brought together a growing body of evidence on the complexity and significance of the role.

What can we conclude about the role of the prison officer in the late modern prison? In our view, formed over thirty 'person-years' and a total of 21 research projects, prison officers are the human face of the Prison Service. As human beings, they are both special and fallible. The power they hold has the potential to corrupt, and the world they work in can be dangerous, difficult and always a challenge. Prison officers are able to challenge and help prisoners with their offending behaviour. Some officers are outstanding at this kind of work. Prisoners have written letters to us following lively group discussions, because they 'didn't feel able to say this in the group, but officers have gone out of their way to help me on several occasions'. There are myths and passions about who prison officers are. This book constitutes a first general attempt to consider the evidence, and stimulate further work in this area.

Notes

1 With all its flaws, including a lack of focus, a weak research base and little evidence of effectiveness, as well as some significant strengths.
2 Other dangers include a lack of diversity of approaches to offending behaviour as agencies merge, ideologically and in their working and training practices.
3 Interview with Martin Narey conducted by Liebling and Sparks (October 2000) during which he outlined the difference between 'high-level, aspirational' aims, and those which can be translated into behaviour. Humanity is a term which has 'a very practical application'. See further Liebling, assisted by Arnold (2004).

Appendix

The Prison Staff Quality of Life Survey[1]

Note

1   This survey was developed collaboratively by Alison Liebling, Sarah Tait, Clare McLean, Vicky Gadd, Guy Shefer and Helen Arnold. It was refined over the course of several research projects on aspects of prison officer work and prisoner quality of life conducted by members of the Cambridge University Prisons Research Centre (PRC): see Liebling, assisted by Arnold (2004), Arnold *et al.* (2007), Gadd and Shefer, with Liebling *et al.* (2007) and Tait (2008c). It has been used on an ad hoc basis by the Prison Service since 2006 and continues to be used and developed by members of the PRC team.

SQL staff questionnaire dimensions and items

Final version January 2006

Reliabilities (α) are reported for n = 742
Reliabilities marked with * are reported for n = 371

α	Dimension	Q	Item	Recoded
0.93	Treatment by senior management	35	I feel respected by senior managers.	y
		24	I am valued as a member of staff by senior management.	y
		18	I am trusted by senior managers in this prison.	y
		49	I have a good relationship with senior managers.	y
		57	Senior managers are approachable when I need to discuss an issue with them.	y
		39	I am treated fairly by senior managers.	y
		28	I feel supported in my work by senior management.	y
0.89	Attitudes towards senior management	11	I trust the senior managers in this prison.	y
		30	I feel a sense of loyalty to the Governor of this prison.	y
		61	The SMT in this prison are competent.	y
		63	I have confidence in the SMT in this prison.	y
		113	The Governor is concerned about the well-being of staff in this prison.	y
		60	This prison has the right kind of Governor for current needs.	y
		68	I try not to get too involved in the Governor's agenda in this prison.	n
		64	I often see senior managers around this prison.	y
		93	There are times where Governors in here fail to support staff in dealing with prisoners.	n

Appendix continues over

Appendix continued

α	Dimension	Q	Item	Recoded
0.85	Perception of Prison Service	23	I am valued as a member of staff by the Prison Service.	y
		16	I am trusted by the Prison Service.	y
		13	I trust the Prison Service.	y
		40	I am treated fairly by the Prison Service.	y
		92	I feel a sense of identity with the goals and objectives of the Prison Service.	y
0.87	Relationship with peers	29	I feel supported in my work by officers/colleagues.	y
		31	I feel a sense of loyalty to colleagues in the prison.	y
		14	I trust colleagues in this prison.	y
		17	I am trusted by colleagues in this prison.	y
		22	I am valued as a member of staff by colleagues.	y
		34	I feel respected by colleagues in this prison.	y
		38	I am treated fairly by colleagues in this prison.	y
		79	There is good communication among my colleagues.	y
		50	I have a good relationship with colleagues.	y
0.91	Relationship with line management	37	I feel respected by line management in this prison.	y
		12	I trust my line managers in this prison.	y
		19	I am trusted by line management in this prison.	y
		48	I have a good relationship with line management.	y
		56	My line manager is approachable when I need to discuss an issue with him/her.	
		27	I feel supported in my work by my line manager.	y

212

0.90	Treatment by SOs and POs	24	I am valued as a member of staff by Senior Officers.	y
		25	I am valued as a member of staff by Principal Officers.	y
		41	I am treated fairly by Senior Officers.	y
		42	I am treated fairly by Principal Officers.	y
0.89	Commitment	32	I feel a sense of loyalty to the Prison Service.	y
		33	I feel a sense of loyalty to this prison.	y
		54	I feel a sense of commitment to this prison.	y
		55	I feel a sense of commitment to the Prison Service.	y
0.79	Safety/control/ security	86	The general atmosphere in this prison is tense.	n
		102	This prison is poor at delivering good order and discipline.	n
		106	This is a well-controlled prison.	y
		7	Security in this prison is good.	y
		69	Assaults by prisoners on staff are rare in this prison.	y
		99	I feel safe in my working environment.	y
0.86*	Recognition and personal efficacy	1	The success that I achieve in my working day in this prison is recognised and rewarded.	y
		98	Praise for my work and achievements is rarely given to me.	n
		2	This prison is good at encouraging staff to use their initiative in this job.	y
		89	Staff morale is good in this prison.	y
		9	I am satisfied with the amount of training I receive in this prison.	y
		90	I am given opportunities to use my initiative in my job.	y
		3	I am given the right amount of responsibility in my job in this prison.	y
		104	I have the appropriate level of authority to do my job properly.	y
		97	I feel dissatisfied with my career development opportunities in this prison.	n

Appendix continues over

Appendix continued

α	Dimension	Q	Item	Recoded
0.78	Involvement in prison	96	The management style in this prison is progressive.	y
		70	This prison is well organised.	y
		72	My experience of communication between staff and management is good in this prison.	y
		83	I rarely feel involved in the decision-making processes in this prison.	n
		80	I am kept well informed of what is going on around the prison.	y
		85	I do not feel part of the bigger picture in this prison.	n
0.88	Involvement in work	5	I don't feel motivated to do more than the minimum required in my work.	n
		58	It is not worth putting in extra effort in this prison as it would go unrecognised.	n
		87	I am willing to work hard to get things done to meet goals and targets.	y
		88	I feel that my job is meaningful.	y
		105	My working day passes slowly in this prison.	n
		107	I look forward to coming to work in this prison.	y
		109	I feel proud of the job I do in this prison.	y
		6	I get a lot of enjoyment from my work in this prison.	y
		118	Overall quality of working life (scale of 1–5, recoded 1–5).	y*
0.79*	Stress	84	The stress levels in my job cause me concern.	n
		73	Working in this prison is highly emotionally demanding.	n
		94	Many of the stressful aspects of this work stay with me when I am at home.	n
		119	Current level of work-related stress (scale 1–10, recoded 1–5).	y*

Prisoner-related dimensions, including professional orientation

0.79	Relationships with prisoners	36	I feel respected by prisoners in this prison.	y
		20	I am trusted by prisoners.	y
		51	I have a good relationship with prisoners in this prison.	y
0.78*	Professional support	76	Sometimes you should be an advocate for a prisoner.	y
		77	It is important to take an interest in prisoners and their problems.	y
		74	I feel unsure of how to support prisoners and so avoid this type of work.	n
		8	Supporting prisoners is an important part of my job.	y
		103	I enjoy helping prisoners to reach goals and targets.	y
		4	Officers should be involved in rehabilitation programmes.	y
0.79*	Social distance	75	You get to like most prisoners in here over time.	y
		78	Most prisoners are decent people.	y
		95	I am prepared to do more because I care about prisoners.	y
		100	Most prisoners can be rehabilitated.	y
		65	I try to build trust with prisoners.	y
		67	It's important to have compassion for prisoners.	y
		81	The most satisfying jobs involve prisoner contact.	y
		117	Prisoners tend to come to me with their problems because they know I will sort them out.	y
0.74*	Authority maintenance	46	The best way to deal with prisoners is to be firm and distant.	n
		52	I tend to keep conversations with prisoners short and businesslike.	n
		53	Friendly relationships with prisoners undermine your authority.	n

Appendix continues over

Appendix continued

α	Dimension	Q	Item	Recoded
0.84*	View on punishment and control	15	I trust the prisoners in this prison.	y
		108	Prisoners who attempt suicide are attention-seeking and trying to manipulate staff.	n
		82	This prison is too comfortable for prisoners.	n
		110	Prisoners spend too much time out of cell in this prison.	n
		101	The adjudication system in this prison does not teach prisoners anything.	n
		112	If a prisoner lies to me I don't make an effort to help them.	n
		59	Prisoners take advantage of you if you are lenient.	n
		91	Prisoners should be under strict discipline.	n
		47	The level of power that prisoners have in this prison is too high.	n

Stand-alone items, grouped conceptually

Staff support

α	Dimension	Q	Item	Recoded
		111	Some staff get away with 'coasting' in this prison.	n
		10	Staff on long-term sick are closely monitored.	y
		26	The facilities available for staff in this prison are inadequate.	n
		71	It is hard to get leave in this prison at the times I require it.	n
		114	Staff need more training and support in dealing with the effects on them of suicide and self-harm.	n
		115	Dealing with suicide and self-harm by prisoners is extremely stressful.	n
		62	I have confidence in the system of performance measurement used in this prison.	y

Power distribution

43   The level of power and responsibility that Prison Officers have is too low.   n
44   The level of power and responsibility that Senior Officers have is too low.   n
45   The level of power and responsibility that Principal Officers have is too low.   n

Reactions to race relations policy

66   Dealing with concerns about race relations prevents staff from getting on with real prison work.   n
116   Race relations training is a public relations exercise.   n

References

* Denotes recommended further reading.

Advisory Council on the Penal System (ACPS) (1968) *The Regime for Long-Term Prisoners in Conditions of Maximum Security*, The Radzinowicz Report. London: HMSO.

Ahmad, S. (1996) *Fairness in Prisons*. PhD thesis, University of Cambridge.

Annual Survey of Hours and Earnings (ASHE) (2005) See website: http://www.statistics.gov.uk/statbase/product.asp?vlnk=13101.

Arnold, H. (2005) 'The effects of prison work', in A. Liebling and S. Maruna (eds), *The Effects of Imprisonment*. Cullompton: Willan, pp. 391–420.

Arnold, H. (2008) 'The experience of prison officer training', in J. Bennett, B. Crewe and A. Wahidin (eds), *Understanding Prison Staff*. Cullompton: Willan, pp. 399–418.

*Arnold, H., Liebling, A. and Tait, S. (2007) 'Prison officers and prison culture', in Y. Jewkes (ed.), *Handbook on Prisons*. Cullompton: Willan, pp. 471–95.

Ayres, I. and Braithwaite, J. (1992) *Responsive Regulation – Transcending the Deregulation Debate*. Oxford: Oxford University Press.

Baldwin, R., Scott, C. and Hood, C. (1998) *A Reader on Regulation*. Oxford: Oxford University Press.

Banton, M. (1964) *The Policeman in the Community*. London: Tavistock.

Barry, A., Osborne, T. and Rose, N. (1996) *Foucault and Political Reason*. London: UCL Press.

Bauman, Z. (1989) *Modernity and the Holocaust*. Cambridge: Polity Press.

Ben-David, S. (1992) 'Staff-to-inmate relations in a total institution: a model of five modes of association', *International Journal of Offender Therapy and Comparative Criminology*, 36 (3): 209–21.

Ben-David, S. and Silfen, P. (1994) 'In quest of a lost father? Inmates' preferences of staff relation in a psychiatric prison ward', *International Journal of Offender Therapy and Comparative Criminology*, 38 (2): 131–9.

*Bennett, J., Crewe, B. and Wahidin, A. (eds) (2007) *Understanding Prison Staff*. Cullompton: Willan.

Biggam, F. H. and Power, K. G. (1997) 'Social support and psychological distress in a group of incarcerated young offenders', *International Journal of Offender Therapy*, 41 (3): 213–30.

Bittner, E. (1967) 'The police on skid row: a study of peacekeeping', *American Sociological Review*, 32 (5): 699–715.

Bottomley, A. K. (1994) *CRC Special Units: A General Assessment*. London: Home Office.

Bottomley, A. K., James, A., Clare, E. and Liebling, A. (1997) *An Evaluation of Wolds Remand Prison*, Research Findings No. 32. Home Office: London.

*Bottoms, A. E. (1989) 'The aims of imprisonment', in D. Garland (ed.), *Justice, Guilt, and Forgiveness in the Penal System*, Centre for Theology and Public Issues Occasional Paper No. 18. Edinburgh: University of Edinburgh, pp. 3–33.

Bottoms, A. E. (1995) 'The philosophy and politics of punishment and sentencing', in R. Morgan and C. M. V. Clarkson (eds), *The Politics of Sentencing Reform*. Oxford: Clarendon Press, pp. 17–49.

Bottoms, A. E. (1998) 'Five puzzles in von Hirsch's theory of punishment', in A. Ashworth and M. Wasik (eds), *Fundamentals of Sentencing Theory: Essays in Honour of Andrew von Hirsch*. Oxford: Clarendon Press, pp. 53–100.

Bottoms, A. E. (1999) 'Interpersonal violence and social order in prisons', in M. Tonry and J. Petersilia (eds), *'Prisons', Crime and Justice: A Review of Research*, Vol. XXVI. Chicago: University of Chicago Press, pp. 205–82.

Bottoms, A. E. (2000) 'Evaluation of a policy initiative', in A. E. Bottoms *Restorative Justice in Sociological Perspective*. Paper delivered at Restorative Justice Symposium: Cambridge, 7–8 October 2008.

Bottoms, A. E. and Light, R. (1987) *Problems of Long-Term Imprisonment*. Aldershot: Gower.

Bottoms, A. E., Hay, W. and Sparks, R. (1990) 'Situational and social approaches to the prevention of disorder in long-term prisons', *Prison Journal*, 70: 83–95.

Bryans, S. (2007) *Prison Governors: Managing Prisons in a Time of Change*. Cullompton: Willan.

Bryans, S. and Wilson, D. (2000) *The Prison Governor: Theory and Practice*. Aylesbury: Prison Service Journal.

Calvert, D. (2000) *The Role of the Prison Officers' Association*. MSt thesis, University of Cambridge.

Camp, S. D. (1994) 'Assessing the effects of organizational commitment and job satisfaction on turnover: an event history approach', *Prison Journal*, 74 (3): 279–305.

Camp, S. D. (1999) 'Do inmate survey data reflect prison conditions? Using surveys to assess prison conditions of confinement', *Prison Journal*, 79 (2): 250–68.

Carter, P. (2003) *Managing Offenders, Reducing Crime: A new approach*. http://webarchive. nationalarchives.gov.uk/+/http://www.cabinetoffice.gov.uk/strategy/downloads/files/managingoffenders.pdf

Caton, B. (2001) General Secretary of the POA, interviewed in *Prison Service Journal*, March.

Cavadino, M. and Dignan, J. (1997) *The Penal System: An Introduction*. London: Sage.

Chan, J. (1996) 'Changing police culture', *British Journal of Criminology*, 36: 109–34.

Chan, J. (1997) *Changing Police Culture: Policing in a Multicultural Society*. Cambridge: Cambridge University Press.

Cheek, F. E. and Miller, M. D. (1983) 'The experience of stress for corrections officers: a double-blind theory of correctional stress', *Journal of Criminal Justice*, 11: 105–20.

Cheliotis, L. K. and Liebling, A. (2006) 'Race matters in British prisons: towards a research agenda', *British Journal of Criminology*, 46: 286–317.

Christie, N. (2000) *Crime Control as Industry: Towards Gulags, Western Style*. London: Routledge.

Clare, E. and Bottomley, A. K. (2001) *An Evaluation of Close Supervision Centres*, Home Office Research Study No. 219. London: HMSO.

Cohen, S. and Taylor, I. (1972) *Psychological Survival: The Experience of Long-Term Imprisonment*. London: Penguin.

Colvin, E. (1977) *Prison Officers: A Sociological Portrait of the Uniformed Staff of an English Prison*. PhD thesis, University of Cambridge.

Cooke, D. J. (1989) 'Containing violent prisoners: an analysis of the Barlinnie Special Unit', *British Journal of Criminology*, 29 (2): 129–43.

Cooke, D. J. (1991) 'Violence in prisons: the influence of regime factors', *Howard Journal of Criminal Justice*, 30: 95–109.

Cox, T., Griffiths, A. and Thomson, L. (1997) *The Assessment and Management of Work-Related Stress in Prison Staff*. Nottingham: Centre for Organisational Health and Development.

Crawley, E. (2001) *The Social World of the English Prison Officer: A Study in Occupational Culture*. PhD thesis, Keele University.

Crawley, E. (2004) *Doing Prison Work*. Cullompton: Willan.

Crewe, B. (2006) 'Male prisoners' orientations towards female officers in an English prison', *Punishment and Society*, 8 (4): 395–421.

Crewe, B. (2009) *The Prisoner Society*. Oxford: Oxford University Press.

Crouch, B. and Alpert, G. (1982) 'Sex and occupational socialisation among prison guards: a longitudinal study', *Criminal Justice and Behavior*, 9 (2): 159–76.

Davies, W. and Burgess, P. W. (1988) 'Prison officers' experience as a predictor of risk of attack', *Medicine, Science and the Law*, 28 (2): 135–8.

Deighton, G. and Launay, G. (1993) 'The Blantyre House Experience'. Unpublished report to the Area Manager.

Department of Justice (1997) *Census of State and Federal Correctional Facilities, 1995*. Washington, DC: US Department of Justice.

Ditchfield, J. (1990) *Control in Prisons*. London: HMSO.

Ditchfield, J. (1997) 'Assaults on Staff in Male Closed Establishments: A Statistical Study'. Unpublished report, Prison Service.

Dixon, D. (1997) *Law in Policing: Legal Regulations and Policing Practices*. Oxford: Clarendon Press.

Downes, D. (1988) *Contrasts in Tolerance*. Oxford: Clarendon Press.

Drake, D. (2008) 'Staff and order in prisons', in J. Bennett, B. Crewe and A. Wahidin (eds), *Understanding Prison Staff*. Cullompton: Willan, pp. 153–67.

Driscoll, W. (1997) From Bill Driscoll: *Prison Britain III – Fresh Start*, BBC Radio 4, 5 August.

Dunbar, I. (1985) *A Sense of Direction*. London: Home Office.

Dworkin, R. (1977) *Taking Rights Seriously*. Cambridge, MA: Harvard University Press.

Elliott, C. (1999) *Locating the Energy for Change: A Practitioner's Guide to Appreciative Inquiry*. Winnipeg: International Institute for Sustainable Development.

*Elliott, C., Liebling, A. and Arnold, H. (2001) 'Locating the energy for change: appreciative inquiry in two local prisons', *Prison Service Journal*, 135: 3–10.

Emery, F. (1970) *Freedom and Justice within Walls: The Bristol Prison Experiment*. London: Tavistock.

Enterkin, J. (1996) *Female Prison Officers in Men's Prisons*. PhD thesis, University of Cambridge.

Evershed, S. and Fry, C. (1991) 'Parkhurst Special Unit: the first two years', in R. Walmsley (ed.), *Managing Difficult Prisoners: The Parkhurst Special Unit*. London: Home Office.

Farkas, M. A. (1999) 'Correctional officer attitudes toward inmates and working with inmates in a "get tough" era', *Journal of Criminal Justice*, 27 (6): 495–506.

Farnworth, L. (1992) 'Women doing a man's job: female prison officers working in a male prison', *Australian and New Zealand Journal of Criminology*, 25 (3): 278–96.

Federal Bureau of Prisons website: http://www.bop.gov.

Feeley, M. and Simon, J. (1992) 'The new penology', *Criminology*, 30 (4): 449–74.

Ferlie, E., Pettigrew, A., Ashburner, L. and Fitzgerald, L. (1996) *The New Public Management in Action*. Oxford: Oxford University Press.

Fleisher, M. (1989) *Warehousing Violence*. London: Sage.

Gadd, V. (in progress) 'Effective Senior Management Teams in Public Sector Prisons'. PhD thesis.

Gadd, V. and Shefer, G. with the assistance of Liebling, A., Tait, S. and McLean, C. (2007) 'Measuring the Quality of Prison Life: Staff Survey'. Unpublished report to the Prison Service – Institute of Criminology, Cambridge University.

Galligan, D. (1986) *Discretionary Powers*. Oxford: Clarendon Press.

*Garland, D. (1990) *Punishment and Modern Society*. Oxford: Clarendon Press.

Garland, D. and Sparks, R. (2000) 'Criminology, social theory and the challenge of our times', *British Journal of Criminology*, 40 (2): 189–204.

Genders, E. and Player, E. (1995) *Grendon: A Study of a Therapeutic Prison*. Oxford: Clarendon Press.

Giddens, A. (1984) *The Constitution of Society*. Cambridge: Polity Press.

Giddens, A. (1990) *The Consequences of Modernity*. Cambridge: Polity Press.

*Gilbert, M. J. (1997) 'The illusion of structure: a critique of the classical model of organisation and the discretionary power of correctional officers', *Criminal Justice Review*, 22 (1): 49–64.

Gilligan, C. (1986) *In a Different Voice: Psychological Theory and Women's Development*. Cambridge, MA: Harvard University Press.

Goffman, E. (1961) *Asylums: Essays on the Social Situation of Mental Patients and Other Inmates*. Harmondsworth: Penguin.

Goffman, E. (1968) 'On the characteristics of total institutions: staff–inmate relations', in D. Cressey (ed.), *The Prison: Studies in Institutional Organisation and Change*. New York: Holt, Rinehart & Winston.

Goodin, R. E. (1986) 'Welfare, rights, and discretion', *Oxford Journal of Legal Studies*, 6 (3): 232–61.

Grounds, A., Howes, M. and Gelsthorpe, L. (2003) 'Discretion in access to forensic psychiatric units', in L. Gelsthorpe and N. Padfield (eds), *Exercising Discretion: Decision-making in the Criminal Justice System and Beyond*. Cullompton: Willan, pp. 125–38.

Haney, C., Banks, C. and Zimbardo, P. (1973) 'Interpersonal dynamics in a simulated prison', *International Journal of Criminology*, 1: 69–97.

Harding, R. (1997) *Private Prisons and Public Accountability*. Buckingham: Open University Press.

Harrison, R. (1992) 'The equality of mercy', in H. Gross and R. Harrison (eds), *Jurisprudence: Cambridge Essays*. Oxford: Clarendon Press.

Hart, H. L. A. (1958) 'Dias and Hughes on Jurisprudence', *Society of Public Teachers of Law*, 4: 144–5.

Harvey, J. (2007) *Young Men in Prison: Surviving and Adapting to Life Inside*. Cullompton: Willan.

Hawkins, G. (1976) *The Prison: Policy and Practice*. Chicago: University of Chicago.

Hawkins, K. (1984) *Environment and Enforcement*. Oxford: Clarendon Press.

Hawkins, K. (1992) *The Uses of Discretion*. Oxford: Clarendon Press.

*Hay, W. and Sparks, R. (1991) 'What is a prison officer?', *Prison Service Journal*, Spring, pp. 2–7.

Hemmens, C. and Stohr, M. K. (2000) *RSAT in Idaho: A Comparison of Inmate and Staff Perceptions of the Programme*. Paper presented at the American Society of Criminology Conference, San Francisco.

Hepburn, J. R. (1985) 'The exercise of power in coercive organisations: a study of prison guards', *Criminology*, 23 (1): 145–64.

Hepburn, J. R. (1987) 'The prison control structure and its effects on work attitudes: the perceptions and attitudes of prison guards', *Journal of Criminal Justice*, 15: 49–64.

HMCIP (1987) *Report of an Inquiry by Her Majesty's Chief Inspector of Prisons for England and Wales into the Disturbances in Prison Service Establishments in England between 29 April–2 May 1986*. London: HMSO.

HMCIP (1993a) *Doing Time or Using Time*. London: Home Office.

HMCIP (1993b) *Inspection of HM Prison Blantyre House*. London: Home Office.

HMCIP (1993c) *Unannounced Inspection of HM Prison Grendon*. London: Home Office.

HMCIP (2000) *Annual Report 1998–1999*. London: Home Office.

HMP Risley (2000) *The Personal Officer*. Booklet produced by HMP Risley.

Hofling, K. C., Brotzman, E., Dalrymple, S., Graves, N. and Pierce, C. M. (1966) 'An experimental study in the nurse–physician relationship', *Journal of Nervous and Mental Disorders*, 143: 171–80.

Holloway, K. (2000) *Mental-Health Review Tribunals*. PhD thesis, University of Cambridge.

Home Office (1979) *Committee of Inquiry into the United Kingdom Prison Service*, The May Inquiry, Cmnd 7673. London: HMSO.

Home Office (1984) *Managing the Long-term Prison System: The Report of the Control Review Committee*. London: Home Office.

Home Office (1987) *Special Units for Long-Term Prisoners: Regimes, Management and Research*. London: HMSO.

Home Office (1991) *Prison Disturbances 1990*, The Woolf Report. London: HMSO.

Home Office (1994) *The Escape from Whitemoor Prison on Friday, 9th September 1994*, The Woodcock Report, Cmnd 2741. London: HMSO.

Home Office (1995) *Review of Prison Service Security in England and Wales*, The Learmont Report, Cmnd 3020. London: HMSO.

Home Office (1997) Prison Disciplinary Statistics.

Home Office (2000) *Modernising the Management of the Prison Service: An Independent Report by the Targeted Performance Initiative Working Group*, The Laming Report. London: Home Office.

Home Office Prison Service (1987) *Fresh Start – The New Improvements*, Bulletin 8. London: HM Prison Service.

Hood, C. (1991) 'A public management for all seasons', *Public Administration*, 69 (1): 3–19.

House of Commons (2003–4) HC Deb (2003–2004) 422, written answers, col. 1170W–1171W.

House of Commons Justice Committee (2009) *Report on the Role of the Prison Officer*. Online at: http://www.publications.parliament.uk/pa/cm200809/cmselect/cmjust/361/36102.htm.

Huckabee, R. G. (1992) 'Stress in corrections: an overview of the issues', *Journal of Criminal Justice*, 20: 479–86.

Jacobs, J. B. (1977) *Stateville: The Penitentiary in Mass Society*. Chicago: Chicago University Press.

Jacobs, J. B. (1978) 'What prison guards think: a profile of the Illinois Force', *Crime and Delinquency*, April, pp. 185–96.

Jacobs, J. B. and Crotty, N. M. (1978) *Guard Unions and the Future of Prisons*. New York: Institute of Public Employment Monograph.

James, A. L., Bottomley, A. K., Liebling, A. and Clare, E. (1997) *Privatising Prisons: Rhetoric and Reality*. London: Sage.

James, C. (2000) *Meeting Each Other's Needs: An Explanation of the Interrelationship Between Local and National Industrial Relations*. MSt thesis, University of Cambridge.

Jefferson, T. and Carlen, P. (1996) 'Masculinities, social relations, and crime', *British Journal of Criminology*, Special Edition.

Jefferson, T. and Grimshaw, R. (1984) *Controlling the Constable: Police Accountability in England and Wales*. London: Sage.

Johnson, R. (1977) 'Ameliorating prison stress: some helping roles for custodial personnel', *International Journal of Criminology and Penology*, 5: 263–73.

Johnson, R. and Price, S. (1981) 'The complete correctional officer: human service and the human environment in prison', *Criminal Justice and Behaviour*, 8: 343–73.

Joint Industrial Relations Procedural Agreement (2004) Voluntary Agreement (JIRPA).

Jones, K. and Fowles, A. J. (1984) *Ideas on Institutions: Analysing the Literature on Long-Term Care and Custody*. London: Routledge & Kegan Paul.

Jurik, N. (1985) 'Individual and organizational determinants of correctional officers' attitudes towards inmates', *Criminology*, 23: 523–39.

Kauffman, K. (1988) *Prison Officers and Their World*. Cambridge, MA: Harvard University Press.

King, R. D. and McDermott, K. (1995) *The State of Our Prisons*. Oxford: Oxford University Press.

King, R. D. and Morgan, R. (1979) *The Future of the Prison System*. Farnborough: Gower.

Klofas, J. (1986) 'Discretion among correctional officers: the influence of urbanization, age and race', *International Journal of Offender Therapy and Comparative Criminology*, 30: 11–124.

Klofas, J. and Toch, H. (1982) 'Alienation and desire for job enrichment among correction officers', *Federal Probation*, 46 (1): 35–47.

Kriminalforsorgens Uddannelsescenter (1994) *Indstilling Om Konfliktforebyggelse Og-Losning*. Copenhagen: Kriminalforsorgens Uddannelsescenter.

Laming, Lord (2000) *Modernising the Management of the Prison Service*. London: Home Office.

Lasky, G. L., Gordon, B. C. and Srebalus, D. J. (1986) 'Occupational stressors among federal correctional officers working in different security levels', *Criminal Justice and Behaviour*, 13 (3): 317–27.

Lewis, D. (1997) *Hidden Agendas*. London: Hamish Hamilton.

Liebling, A. (1992) *Suicides in Prison*. London: Routledge.

Liebling, A. (1995) 'Vulnerability and prison suicide', *British Journal of Criminology*, 35 (2): 173–87.

Liebling, A. (1999) 'Doing prison research: breaking the silence?', *Theoretical Criminology*, 3 (2): 147–73.

*Liebling, A. (2000) 'Prison officers, policing, and the use of discretion', *Theoretical Criminology*, 4 (3): 333–57.

Liebling, A. (2008a) 'Why prison staff culture matters', in J. M. Byrne, D. Hummer and F. S. Taxman (eds), *The Culture of Prison Violence*. New York: Pearson, pp. 105–22.

Liebling, A. (2008b) 'Incentives and earned privileges revisited: fairness, discretion, and the quality of prison life', *Journal of Scandinavian Studies in Criminology and Crime Prevention*, 9: 25–41.

Liebling, A. (ed.) (in progress) *Prison Officers, Relationships and Prison Culture*.

Liebling, A. and Krarup, H. (1993) *Suicide Attempts and Self-Injury in Male Prisons*. London: Home Office Research and Planning Unit.

Liebling, A. and Price, D. (1999) *An Exploration of Staff–Prisoner Relationships at HMP Whitemoor*, Prison Service Research Report No. 6. London: Prison Service.

Liebling, A. and Sparks, R. (2000) Interview with Martin Narey.

Liebling, A. and Tait, S. (2006) 'Improving staff–prisoner relationships', in G. E. Dear (ed.), *Preventing Suicide and Other Self-Harm in Prison*. London: Palgrave-Macmillan, pp. 103–17.

Liebling, A., Tait, S., Stiles, A., Durie, L. and Harvey, J.; assisted by Rose, G. (2005) *An Evaluation of the Safer Locals Programme*, Report submitted to the Home Office, pp. 215.

*Liebling, A., assisted by Arnold, H. (2004) *Prisons and Their Moral Performance: A Study of Values, Quality and Prison Life*. Oxford: Oxford University Press.

Liebling, A., Elliott, C. and Arnold, H. (2001) 'Transforming the prison: romantic optimism or appreciative realism?', *Criminal Justice*, 1 (2): 161–80.

Liebling, A., Price, D. and Elliott, C. (1999) 'Appreciative inquiry and relationships in prison', *Punishment and Society*, 1 (1): 71–98.

Liebling, A., Muir, G., Rose, G. and Bottoms, A. (1997) *An Evaluation of Incentives and Earned Privileges: Final Report to the Prison Service*. Cambridge: Institute of Criminology.

Livingstone, S. and Owen, T. (1998) *Prison Law*. Oxford: Oxford University Press.

Lombardo, L. (1981) *Guards Imprisoned: Correctional Officers at Work*. New York: Elsevier.

Long, N., Shouksmith, G., Voges, K. E. and Roache, S. (1986) 'Stress in prison staff: an occupational study', *Criminology*, 24 (2): 331–45.

Loucks, N. (2000) *Prison Rules: A Working Guide*. London: Prison Reform Trust.

Lucas, J. R. (1980) *On Justice*. Oxford: Clarendon Press.

Lygo, R. (1991) *The Management of the Prison Service*. London: Home Office.

McAllister, D., Bottomley, A. K. and Liebling, A. (1992) *From Custody to Community: Throughcare for Young Offenders*. Aldershot: Avebury.

McDermott, K. and King, R. (1988) 'Mind games – where the action is in prisons', *British Journal of Criminology*, 28: 357–77.

McDermott, K. and King, R. (1989) 'A Fresh Start: the enhancement of prison regimes', *Howard Journal*, 28 (3): 161–76.

McKenzie, I. K. and Gallagher, G. P. (1989) *Behind the Uniform: Policing in Britain and America*. New York: St. Martin's Press.

McLean, C. and Liebling, A. (2008) 'Prison staff in the public and private sector', in J. Bennett, B. Crewe and A. Wahidin (eds), *Understanding Prison Staff*. Cullompton: Willan, pp. 92–114.

Maguire, M., Vagg, J. and Morgan, R. (1985) *Accountability and Prisons: Opening Up a Closed World*. London: Tavistock.

Mandaraka-Sheppard, A. (1986) *The Dynamics of Aggression in Women's Prisons in England*. Aldershot: Gower.

Marquart, J. W. (1986) 'Prison guards and the use of physical coercion as a mechanism of prisoner control', *Criminology*, 24 (2): 347–66.

Marsh, A., Dobbs, J. and Monk, J. (1985) *Staff Attitudes in the Prison Service*. London: Office of Population Censuses and Surveys.

Martin, J. P. (1991) 'Parkhurst Special Unit: some aspects of management', in R. Walmsley (ed.), *Managing Difficult Prisoners: The Parkhurst Special Unit*. London: Home Office.

Milgram, S. (1974) *Obedience to Authority*. London: Tavistock.

Morgan, R. (1997) 'Imprisonment since World War II', in M. Maguire, R. Morgan and R. Reiner (eds), *The Oxford Handbook of Criminology*. Oxford: Oxford University Press.

Morris, T. and Morris, P. (1963) *Pentonville*. London: Routledge & Kegan Paul.

Muir, W. K. (1977) *Police: Streetcorner Politicians*. Chicago: Chicago University Press.

National Offender Management Service (NOMS) (2008) Foreword by Jack Straw to the Agency Framework Document: http://webarchive.nationalarchives (full document available at: http://www.justice.gov.uk/news/announcement170708a.htm).

Needs, A. (1993) *Hull Special Unit: A Descriptive Report Covering the Third and Fourth Years of Operation*. Unpublished report submitted to the Home Office.

Office for National Statistics (1990) *New Earnings Survey 1990*. London: Office for National Statistics.

Office for National Statistics (1996–9) *New Earnings Survey 1996, 1997, 1998, 1999*. London: Office for National Statistics.

Office for National Statistics (2005) *Annual Survey of Hours and Earnings 2005*. London: Office for National Statistics.

Padfield, N. and Liebling, A., with Arnold, H. (2001) *An Exploration of Decision-Making at Discretionary Lifer Panels*, Home Office Research Study No. 213. London: Home Office.

Personnel Directorate (1997) *Equal Opportunities in the Prison Service*. London: Prison Service.

Pilling, J. (1992) 'Back to Basics: Relationships in the Prison Service', Eve Saville Memorial Lecture, ISTD; reprinted in Revd A. R. Duce (ed.), *Relationships in Prison* (transcript of a Conference held 18–25 April 1993 at Bishop Grossteste College, Lincoln). Lincoln: Bishop of Lincoln.

Pogrebin, M. and Poole, E. (1997) 'The sexualised work environment: a look at women jail officers', *Prison Journal*, 77 (1): 41–57.

Pollitt, C. (1993) *Managerialism and the Public Services*. Oxford: Blackwell Business.

Pratt, J. (2000) 'The return of the wheelbarrow men; or the arrival of postmodern penality?', *British Journal of Criminology*, 40 (1): 127–45.

Price, D. and Liebling, A. (1998) 'Staff–Prisoner Relationships: A Review of the Literature'. Unpublished manuscript submitted to the Prison Service.

Prison Governors' Association (2001) *The Key* (magazine of the PGA), January.

Prison Officers' Association (POA) (1963) 'Memorandum on the role of the modern prison officer', *Prison Officers' Magazine*, November, pp. 1–3.

Prison Service (1990) *Report on the Work of the Prison Service 1989–1990*. London: HMSO.

Prison Service (1994) *Prison Service Briefing 74 – Staff Survey*. London: Prison Service.

Prison Service (1997) *Prison Service Review*. London: Prison Service.

Prison Service (2000a) 'Prison Service Staff Survey'. Unpublished report.

Prison Service (2000b) *Prison Service Business Plan 2000–2001*. London: Prison Service.

Prison Service (2000c) *Prison Service Annual Report 1999–2000*. London: Prison Service.

Prison Service (2006) *Prison Service Annual Report 2005–2006*. London: Prison Service.

Prison Service Pay Review Body (2001) see online at: http://www.ome.uk.com/Prison_Service_Pay_Review_Body.aspx

Prison Service Pay Review Body (2005) *Privately Managed Custodial Services*. Liverpool: MCG Consulting.

Prison Service Pay Review Body (2006) *Fifth Report on England and Wales*. Norwich: HMSO.

Prisons Ombudsman (2000) *Annual Report*. London: Home Office.

Punch, M. (1983) 'Officers and men: occupational culture, inter-rank antagonism and the investigation of corruption', in M. Punch (ed.), *Control in the Police Organisation*. Cambridge MA: MIT Press.

Quinn, P. M. (1985) 'Prison management and prison discipline: a case study of change', in M. Maguire, J. Vagg and R. Morgan (eds), *Accountability and Prisons: Opening Up a Closed World*. London: Tavistock.

Quinn, P. M. (1995) 'Reflexivity run riot: the survival of the prison catch-all', *Howard Journal*, 34 (4): 354–62.

Rasmussen, K. and Levander, S. (1996) 'Individual rather than situational characteristics predict violence in a maximum security hospital', *Journal of Interpersonal Violence*, 11 (3): 376–90.

Reiner, R. (1992) 'Police research in the United Kingdom: a critical review', in N. Morris and M. Tonry (eds), *Modern Policing*, Chicago: Chicago University Press.

Reiner, R. (1997) 'Policing and the police', in M. Maguire, R. Morgan and R. Reiner (eds), *The Oxford Handbook of Criminology*. Oxford: Oxford University Press, pp. 997–1050.

Relationships Foundation (1995) *Relational Prison Audits: Methodology and Results of a Pilot Audit – Greenock Prison, November/December 1994*. Cambridge: Relationships Foundation.

Rorty, R. (1989) *Contingency, Irony and Solidarity*. Cambridge: Cambridge University Press.

Rose, N. and Miller, P. (1992) 'Political power beyond the state: problematics of government', *British Journal of Sociology*, 43: 173–205.

Rowan, J. R. (1996) 'Who is safer in maximum security prisons?', *Corrections Today: Journal of the American Correctional Association (ACA)*, 58, April.

Rutherford, A. (1993) *Criminal Justice and the Pursuit of Decency*. Winchester: Waterside Press.

Rynne, J. (2007) Personal communication.

Saylor, W. G. (1984) *Surveying Prison Environments*. Washington, DC: Federal Bureau of Prisons.

Saylor, W. G. and Wright, K. N. (1992) 'Status, longevity, and perceptions of the work environment among federal prison employees', *Journal of Offender Rehabilitation*, 17 (3/4): 133–60.

Scott, A. (1999) 'The Role of the Probation Service in a Local Prison'. MSt thesis, Cambridge University.

Shapira, R. and Navon, D. (1985) 'Staff–inmate co-operation in Israeli prisons: towards a non-functionalist theory of total institutions', *International Review of Modern Sociology*, 15: 131–46.

Shefer, G. and Liebling, A. (2008) 'Prison privatisation: in search of a business-like atmosphere?', *Criminology and Criminal Justice*, 8 (3): 261–78.

Sim, J. (1994) 'Tougher than the rest? Men in prison', in T. Newburn and E. Stanko (eds), *Just Boys Doing Business: Men, Masculinities and Crime*. London: Routledge, pp. 100–17.

Skolnick, J. H. (1966) *Justice Without Trial*. New York: Wiley.

Smith, A. (1759, reissued 2006) *The Theory of Moral Sentiments*, Dover Philosophical Classics Series.

Smith, D. (1986) 'The framework of law and policing practice', in J. Benyon and C. Bourne (eds), *The Police: Powers, Procedures, and Proprieties*. Oxford: Pergamon.

*Sparks, R., Bottoms, A. E. and Hay, W. (1996) *Prisons and the Problem of Order*. Oxford: Clarendon Press.

Stern, V. (1987) *Bricks of Shame*. London: Penguin.

Stern, V. (1993) *Bricks of Shame*, 2nd edn. London: Penguin.

Stohr, M. K., Lovrich, N. P. and Wilson, G. L. (1994) 'Staff stress in contemporary jails: assessing problem severity and the payoff of progressive personnel practices', *Journal of Criminal Justice*, 22 (4): 313–27.

Stohr, M. K., Lovrish, N. P. and Wood, M. J. (1996) 'Service versus security concerns in contemporary jails: testing gender differences in training topic assessments', *Journal of Criminal Justice*, 24 (5): 437–48.

Straw, J. (2008) Foreword to the National Offender Management Service Agency Framework Document 2008 – see NOMS (2008) online at: http://webarchive.nationalarchives.

*Sykes, G. (1958) *The Society of Captives*. Princeton, NJ: Princeton University Press.

Sykes, G. and Brent, E. (1983) *Policing: A Social Behaviourist Perspective*. New Brunswick, NJ: Rutgers University Press.

Tait, S. (2008a) 'Prison officers and gender', in J. Bennett, B. Crewe and A. Wahidin (eds), *Understanding Prison Staff*. Cullompton: Willan.

*Tait, S. (2008b) 'Care and the prison officer: beyond "turnkeys" and "carebears"', *Prison Service Journal*, 180: 3–11.

Tait, S. (2008c) *Prison Officer Care for Prisoners in One Men's and One Women's Prison*. PhD thesis, Institute of Criminology, University of Cambridge.

Tait, S., Gadd, V., Shefer, G., Liebling, A. and McLean, C. (in progress) 'Measuring Staff Quality of Life: Implications for Research on Prison Culture'.

Taylor, I. (1999) *Crime in Context: A Critical Criminology of Market Societies*. Oxford: Polity Press.

Thomas, J. E. (1972) *The English Prison Officer since 1850*. London: Routledge & Kegan Paul.

Thornton, D., Curran, L., Grayson, D. and Holloway, V. (1984) *Tougher Regimes in Detention Centres: Report of an Evaluation of the Young Offender Psychology Unit*. London: HMSO.

Toch, H. and Klofas, J. (1982) 'Alienation and desire for job enrichment among correction officers', *Federal Probation*, 46 (1): 35–47.

Triplett, R., Mullings, J. L. and Scarborough, K. E. (1996) 'Work-related stress and coping among correctional officers: implications from organisational literature', *Journal of Criminal Justice*, 24 (4): 291–308.

Twining, W. and Miers, D. (1991) *How to Do Things With Rules*. London: Butterworths.

Tyler, T. R. (1990) *Why People Obey the Law*. London: Yale University Press.

Waddington, P. A. J. (1999) 'Police (canteen) sub-culture: an appreciation', *British Journal of Criminology*, 39 (2): 287–309.

Wheatley, P. (2010) Personal communication.

White, S. and Howard, L. (1994) *Survey of Prison Service Staff 1994*. London: Home Office.

White, S., Howard, L. and Walmsley, R. (1991) *The National Prison Survey 1991: Main Findings*. London: HMSO.

Whitehead, J. T., Linquist, C. and Klofas, J. (1987) 'Correctional officer professional orientation: a replication of the Klofas-Toch Measure', *Criminal Justice and Behavior*, 14 (4): 468–86.

Willett, T. (1983) 'Prison guards in private', *Canadian Journal of Criminology*, 25 (1): 1–18.

Williams, M. (1999) Personal communication.

Williams, M. and Longley, D. (1987) 'Identifying control problem prisoners in long-term dispersal prisons', in A. E. Bottoms and R. Light (eds), *Problems of Long-Term Imprisonment*. Aldershot: Gower.

Williams, T. A. (1983) 'Custody and conflict: an organisational study of prison officers' roles and attitudes', *Australian and New Zealand Journal of Criminology*, 16: 44–55.

Williams, T. A. and Soutar, G. N. (1984) 'Levels of custody and attitude differences among prison officers: a comparative study', *Australian and New Zealand Journal of Criminology*, 17: 87–94.

Wilson, P. (2000) 'Experiences of Staff Working in Close Supervision Centres'. Unpublished MSt thesis, Cambridge University.

Woodbridge, J. (1999) *Review of Comparative Costs and Performance of Privately and Publicly Operated Prisons 1996–97*. London: Prison Service.

Wright, K. N. and Saylor, W. G. (1991) 'Male and female employees' perceptions of prison work: is there a difference?', *Justice Quarterly*, 8 (4): 505–24.

Wright, K.N., Saylor, W. G., Gilman, E. and Camp, S. (1997) 'Job control and occupational outcomes among prison workers', *Justice Quarterly*, 14 (3): 525–46.

Zimbardo, P. (2007) *The Lucifer Effect: How Good People Turn Evil*. London: Random House Group/Rider & Co.

Index

Added to a page number 'f' denotes
  a figure, 't' denotes a table and 'n'
  denotes notes.

abilities 49–50t, 52
absence of trouble 6–7, 205
Abu Ghraib 119
abusive behaviour 116
accommodation(s) 102, 131, 133, 134, 135
accountability 189
action and beliefs, gap between 157
adjudications 57–60, 62n, 73, 151n, 198
administrative mega-trends 199
administrative staff 16t, 17f
afternoon work 46–7
age 19–20, 29, 69
age/experience 69, 72
ageing process 19
agency 56, 111
Agency status 186, 193, 194
aiding escape 112
aiding fellow officers 161
alienation 3, 4, 97
ambiguous rules, need for discretion
  125
Annual Survey of Hours and Earnings
  (2005) 23–4, 26
antagonism 133
anxiety 119
appeasement 135
appreciative inquiry 6–12, 204

area managers 192, 193
Askham Grange 31f, 33f
assaults 67–72, 73, 194
associate professional and technical
  occupations 24f, 25–6, 25f
asymmetric deference norm 141
attitudes 153, 169, 211
Australia 77, 81–2n
authority
  elements of 128–9
  enforcement 140–1
  knowledge and wise use of 103
  legitimate 8, 129, 205
  maintenance 215
  police culture 157
  resistance to 114–15, 122, 129
autonomy 67, 193
avoiders 53, 55t

Back to Basics: Relationships in the Prison
  Service 91–2
banter 139, 208
basic-level privileges 122
Beck's Hopelessness Scale 119
'best' form, of prison work 131–2, 147
best practice 6, 168
'bigger picture' 61, 111, 143, 149, 150
Blantyre House 165
bonding 165
Bottoms, A.E. 147–8, 148–9
boundaried use, of discretion 147–50

boundaries
  and communication 47
  communication of 56
  female officers' awareness of 76
  importance of 10
  maintenance of 52, 56
  male officers' concerns 75
  possible corruption 111–14
  prisoner concern for 90
  rule bending 145
  of staff power 93–4
Bristol prison 87–8
brutality 117
'bullshit detector' skills 11
bullying 34
bureaucracy 137

calming effect, female staff 73
camaraderie 158, 161, 165, 169
Cambridge Institute of Criminology 122
Cardiff Prison 32f
care 4, 10, 37f, 39, 55 64, 92, 96–7, 206
category B and C prisons, staffing 30
centralisation 192
Chan, J. 154, 155, 158
change
  managerial 189–90
  resistance to constant 185
chaplaincy 16t
chief officers 12n
Chief Operating Officer 192
Circular Instructions 138
civility 201
classification, of prisoners 151n
Close Supervision Centres 91
closeness, staff-prisoner 55, 86, 90
Code of Discipline 175
coercive power 126, 128, 130, 134, 135,
  136
Colvin, E. 39, 154, 161, 165
comfort of prisons, views on 38–9
commitment 67, 91, 185, 198, 213
common sense 8, 103, 140, 205
communication 34, 46–7, 80, 90
complaints 158, 198
compliance 126, 129, 135, 136, 151n, 195
concern, for fellow officers 164
conditioning 47, 84
confidence 76, 78, 86, 168, 208
conflict resolution 88

conflicted officers 96, 97
consent, of prisoners 132, 136, 137, 142
consistency 10, 90, 107, 108, 147, 150, 168
consultative/conciliatory approach 57
consumerist approach, to justice 201
continuity 47, 90, 91
contracted supplementary hours (CSH)
  22, 27–8, 30
contracts 191
control
  care conflated with 96
  informal 137
  need for balance between care and 10
  over performance 186
  over work process 67
  preference for 4
  prisoner ambivalence towards 94–5
  security and 46, 64, 83, 98, 213
  staff-prisoner relationships 147
  therapeutic regime and maintenance
    of 89
  views on 216
control and restraint 76, 130
Control Review Committee (CRC) 91
Corporate and Business Plans 193
correctional role 64, 78
corruption(s) 111–14, 127, 131, 132, 133,
  150n
counselling 37f, 38, 66
courage 52
courts, intervention in prison life 138
criminal justice 201
Criminal Justice and Immigration Act
  (2008) 178
Criminal Justice and Immigration Bill
  177
Criminal Justice and Public Order Act
  (1994) 150n, 176
critical incident debriefs 66
criticising fellow officers, norm against
  163
cultures
  reluctance to use staff care services
    66
  staff-prisoner relationships 111
  see also organisational culture;
    performance culture; police,
    culture; prison officer culture;
    prisoner culture; rights-based
    culture

custody and care, conflict between 4, 64, 206
cynicism 10, 156, 157, 164

damaged officers 96–7
danger 157, 166
decency 201, 206
decision-making 34, 50, 67, 100, 102, 144, 149, 202
decisiveness 76
Denmark 77
dependency 73, 117, 118
depression 65, 117, 118, 119
desensitisation 160
design features, and costs 194
developing managers 188
dialogue 110, 115, 149
Director General of NOMS 188
Directors of Offender Management (DOMs) 186, 187, 188, 193
discipline 89, 166–7
discretion 3, 121–52
    boundaried use of 147–50
    IEP policy 121–2
    inevitability of 121, 124–6
    organisational benefits of greater 67
    police use of 136–7, 156
    positive and successful use of 147
    and power see power
    prison officer use of 56, 140–5
    role of modern officer 202
    rule enforcement 123
    staff–prisoner relationships 87, 100
    value-based ends 124
discrimination 34
dismissals 20
dispersal prisons 62n, 90
dispositional hypothesis 117
distance, staff–prisoner 5, 37f, 86, 90, 93, 122, 133, 134, 215
distributive power 105, 106
diversity of circumstances, discretion and 125
Doncaster Prison 165
downsizing 199
Driscoll, Bill 169–70
drug smuggling/trafficking 112, 161–2
dynamic security 61, 64

'earning' respect 111
East Sutton Park 32f
economic value, prison work 179
educational qualifications 33, 73
'effects of punishment on learning' 116
efficiency 186, 191, 194, 199
Emery, F. 88
emotional entanglement 132–3
empathy 52
Employee Relations Committee 178
employment conditions 22–9
enforcers 53, 54–5t
engagement, with prisoner distress 37f, 38
The English Prison Officer since 1850 3
entry level salary 22, 23
equality 152n
equality of treatment 107, 147
escape(s) 13n, 64, 92, 112, 192, 194
ethnic origin, prison officers 18–19
ethos, prison establishments 200
European Convention on Human Rights 138–9
exchange power 134, 135
exclusion 74
expectations, relationships 93
experience 8, 69, 72, 146
expert power 134, 135, 136
extra-institutional pressures 133

failing prison 13n
failures, prison officers 155
fairness 19, 92, 101, 105–8, 115, 147, 198, 201, 206
family relationships 78, 85
fear 109, 122, 133
fellow officers, officer's code 161, 162, 163, 164
Feltham YOI 31f, 33f
female officers 16–18
    hours or work 26, 27f
    length of service 21, 22f
    pay 23–4, 25f
    proportion of, establishment type 31, 32f, 33f
    role in male prisons 72–6
female prisoners 76
female prisons 31f, 33f, 68f, 69t, 70t, 71t
fictional representations 14, 39, 154–5
fitness requirement 33

Fleisher, M. 72
flexibility 50, 76, 86, 90, 108, 147, 148, 149
flexible consistency 150
force, use of 167
formal sanctions/procedures 5, 122
Framework Document (NOMS) 187
Fresh Start 19, 33, 69, 128, 186, 191–2
frustration(s) 37, 48, 104
Full Sutton 165

'gangster' notion, of respect 109
Garth Prison 31f, 33f
gatekeepers 106
Genders, E. 88, 89, 160
geographical features, and costs 194
Giddens, A. 103
Gilbert, M.J. 52–3
Gladstone Committee 4
good relationships 111, 122–3, 200
governmentality 125
governors 15, 16t, 188, 189, 190, 191, 197, 198
grasses 114
Grendon Prison 88–90, 165
group solidarity 156
group working 191
Guantanamo Bay 119

Haney experiment 116–18
harassment 34, 74
Harrison, R. 148, 149–50
Hay, W. 8, 90
headquarters staff, remoteness of 195
helplessness 117, 118
Hemmens, C. 78
Holloway 31f, 33f
Holme House 165, 197
honesty 10, 52
hopelessness 119
Hospital Anxiety and Depression Scale 119
hours of work 26–9, 33, 192
Howard League 175
Howard, Michael 206
Huckabee, R.G. 64
Hull Special Unit 91
human relations skills 52
Human Rights Act (1998) 138–9
human services orientation 45, 64

humanity 109, 111, 201, 206
humour 55, 57, 76

ideal officers 48, 49–50t
ill health 65
impartiality 152n
imprisonment 190, 200
improvement agenda 186
incentives
    Hollesley Bay regime 91
    increased use of 131
Incentives and Earned Privileges (IEP) 5, 121–2, 126, 135
individuality 56, 89, 92, 109–10
industrial action 150n, 151n, 176, 178
industrial relations 176
informal sanctions/procedures 122, 137
informing on colleagues, norm against 162–3
injustices 84, 104, 115
institutional racism 153
Instructions to Governors 138
instrumental reasons, importance of staff–prisoner relationships 99
integral sanitation 72
interaction, staff–prisoner 46–7, 83, 121
interpersonal skills 73, 74
involvement 90, 214
isolation 65, 66
Israeli prisons 133

job dissatisfaction 65
job satisfaction 34, 35, 38, 39, 45, 67, 157, 185
job security 33
Joint Industrial Relations Procedural Agreement (JIRPA) 177
judgement 8, 146, 148, 149
junior officers, employment conditions 23
justice 100, 101, 115, 152n, 201

Kauffman, K. 158–9, 166–8
key performance indicators 71, 92, 194, 201, 202
key performance targets 200, 203n
knowledge, of prisoners 64, 100, 102

Lancaster Farms 165, 177
late modernity 12n

233

late-modern prison officer 3–4, 128–31
leadership 52, 189, 193, 197, 202, 207
legitimacy
    authority 8, 129, 205
    force 127, 137
    power 128, 134, 135, 136
    prison 129, 131, 132
    relationships as instruments of
        115
length of service 20–1, 22f
Lewis, Derek 170–1, 179, 194, 206
liberal optimism 135
limited carers 96
Lindholme Immigration Removal Centre
    178
line management, staff survey 34, 35,
    36f, 212
Liverpool Prison 31f, 33f
locks, bolts and bars (LBB) tasks 46
Lompoc 72
Long Lartin 31f, 33f, 182
long-term prisoners 77, 135
'losing' respect 111
Loucks, N. 137–8
loyalty, to other officers 161
*The Lucifer Effect: How Good People Turn
    Evil* 119
lugging, norm against 161–2
Lygo Report 193–6

machismo 157
major incidents, impact of 95
male officers
    educational qualifications 73
    and female staff 73, 74–5
    hours of work 26f
    length of service 22f
    pay 24f, 28f
male prisons 30, 31f, 33f, 68f, 69t, 70t,
    71t, 72–6
management
    change 189–90
    lack of recognition from 65
    officer views about 196–8
management-at-a-distance 193, 207
managerialism 186, 189, 206
    implications for officers 199–202
    modernisation and 190–3
    staff views 38
    theoretical thinking about 199

managers
    female 17, 18
    numbers 15, 16t, 17f
    stress 67
    see also area managers; senior
        managers; wing managers
Manchester Prison 161, 193, 201
manifest disaster criterion 13n
market testing 66–7, 128, 176, 177, 193
masculine subculture 72
May Report (1979) 190
media portrayal 14, 39, 154–5
medical staff 16t, 17f
mental capacity, ideal officers 49t
mercy 147, 148
Milgram experiments 115, 116
mind games 93, 128
mistrust 98, 111, 164
modern prison officer 3, 78–81, 174–6,
    202
    see also late-modern prison officer
modernisation 190–3
moral courage 52, 110–11
moral crisis 200
moral leadership 207
morale 91
morality, internalised 129
Mountbatten Report 4
mutual dependence 133

National Offender Management Service
    (NOMS) 178, 179
    Agency Board (NAB) 187–8
    Executive Management Committee
        (NEMC) 187, 188
    Framework Document 187
    purpose 186–7
    vision and values (2008) 195f
National Staff Survey 34
negative cultural attitudes 169
negative image, of officers 39, 154–5, 170
negative police conduct 141
negotiation 135
New Jersey State Prison 126, 128
new managerialism; *see* managerialism
'new right' philosophies 191
Next Steps Agency 193–6
non-compliance 126
non-law-enforcement 137
non-unified staff 16t, 17f

normative reasons, importance of staff–prisoner relationships 100
Norway 72, 77
Norwich Experiment 87–8

obedience studies 116
obligation, to aid fellow officers 161
occupational culture; *see* prison officer culture
offence-related work 57, 206
Office of Population and Surveys 32–3
officer grades 15, 16t, 17f
'old school' officers 96
operational directors 192
operational problems, and stress 66
Operational Staffing Requirement (OSR) 30
Operational Support Grade (OSG) 16t, 17f, 23, 196
order 8, 100, 101f, 126, 127, 136, 142
organisational aims, discretion and 125
organisational commitment 185
organisational culture 153, 156
organisational problems, and stress 64–5
over-policing 137
overtime 27, 28, 33, 69–72, 190, 191

parents, officer similarity to 145
Parkhurst 90, 92, 192
passivity 117, 118
paternalistic-therapeutic orientation 55
patience 52, 55, 76
pay and conditions 22–9, 208
Pay Review Body 20, 21, 23, 28, 30, 34, 176, 177
peacekeeping 2, 7, 8, 47, 131, 137, 146–7, 205
peer group allegiance 157
peer relationships 36f, 92, 212
penal values 200
performance culture 37, 67, 193
performance measurement 37–8
permissiveness 89
personal boundaries 113
personal efficacy 213
personal identity 117
personal officers 77–8, 90
personal power 135, 136
personal security 96

personality 9, 10, 44, 48, 60, 154, 157, 198
pessimism, police culture 156
physical coercion 126, 130
Pilling, Joe 91–2
Player, E. 88, 89, 160
police
    culture 155–8
    discretion 136–7, 156
    enforcement of authority 140–1
    pay 24–5, 27
policing 136, 137
power
    late modern prison and return to 128
    of prison officers 134–6, 150n
        defects of total 126–7
        forces undermining 128–9
        SQL survey 217
    respect as 109
    staff–prisoner relationships 85, 93–4, 100, 103
    upward shift in 186
    use of 2, 52–3, 56
        over-use 115–19
        un-exercise of 127, 131–4
'power of presence' 128
practical consciousness 103, 104, 148–9
pragmatic culture 96, 157
principal officers
    female 16, 17f
    length of service 21
    numbers 15, 16t, 17f
    replacement by developing managers 188
    treatment by 213
Prison Act (1952) 138, 150n, 176
prison costs 190, 194
prison life, court interventions 138
prison officer code 161–4
prison officer culture(s) 153–69
    effects of prison work 158–60
    non uniformity of 39
    prison officer code 161–4
    three types of 'working' 154
    unhealthy 119
    value of prison work 165–9
    see also subcultures
prison officers
    age 19–20, 29, 69
    alienation 3, 4

assaults on 67–72
discretion; *see* discretion
employment conditions 22–9
ethnic origin 18–19
failures 155
good 8–9
good days 9–10
as 'invisible ghosts' of penality 4
length of service 20–1, 22f
managerialism, implications of 199–202
media portrayal 14, 39, 154–5
numbers 15, 16t, 17f, 20
personal 77–8, 90
prison rules 137–40
recruitment 20, 195
relationships; *see* relationships
right place for 140f
role 2
    camaraderie as central to 158
    conflict between security and rehabilitation 3
    diversity of 61, 76–7
    importance 204
    perceptions 38, 61
    questioning of 190
    see also prison work
role model 48–57
skills 11, 43f, 52, 102
staffing levels 29–32
stress 63–7
suicide 66
turnover rates 20, 21, 67
typologies 52–3, 96–7
versatility and flexibility 48
views
    about management 196–8
    about prison work 32–9
    on fairness 106–7
working styles 52–3, 54–5t, 132, 166
see also female officers; male officers; modern prison officer
Prison Officers Association (POA) 170, 171–4, 176, 177, 178, 179, 180, 181, 191, 208
Prison Officers' Federation 172
Prison Officers' Magazine 172, 173, 174, 175
prison population 18, 208

Prison Rules 138
    see also rules
Prison Service
    crisis-controlling structure 3
    England (1877–1965) 4
    improvement agenda 186
    Lygo Report 193–6
    management *see* management; managerialism
    official purposes, and discretion 125
    organisational culture 153
    Pay Review Body 20, 21, 23, 28, 30, 34, 176, 177
    perceptions of 36f, 212
    staff surveys 33–9
    structure (2010) 186–8
Prison Service Journal 8
Prison Service Orders (PSOs) 138, 178
Prison Service Review (1997) 179, 195–6, 202n
Prison Service Standards 151n
prison warders 172
prison work 2
    complex and challenging nature 42–3
    discretion in *see* discretion
    economic value 179
    involvement in 214
    job description 43f
    lack of literature/information on 8, 14, 44
    life at its best 6–7, 79–80, 205
    loss of confidence in 208
    as low visibility work 2, 45, 205
    as peacemaking 146–7
    prison officer culture 158–60
    professionalisation 202
    rewards 44
    routine 9, 78–9, 147
    specialist 3
    targets and objectives 199, 200
    typical day 46–8
    value of 165–9
prisoner : officer ratio 30–2
prisoner behaviour 60, 91, 114, 127, 131
prisoner distress 37f, 38, 119
prisoners
    classification of 151n
    knowledge of 64, 100, 102
    perceptions of legitimacy of prison regime 131

positive attitude to female staff 74
risk of suicide 64
turnover 48
see also staff prisoner distance;
  staff–prisoner interactions;
  staff–prisoner relationships
prisons
  brutality of 117
  role and functions 201
Prisons Ombudsman 138, 151n
Prisons and Their Moral Performance 115
private sector
  employment conditions 23
  length of service 21
  management 67, 193–4
  salaries 22, 23t
  staffing levels 29–30
privatisation 33, 66, 128, 186, 199
privileges 130–1
  see also Incentives and Earned
    Privileges
problem-solving 51, 88, 141
professional power 134, 135
professional support 215
professionalism 8, 52, 60, 199, 202
progressive work 3–4
protectiveness (male) 73
psychological distress 119
psychologists 16t, 17f, 190
public image 39, 154–5, 170
public service agreements (PSAs) 189–90
public service orientation 199
punishment(s) 116, 130, 131, 142, 201,
  216
punitiveness 37f, 39, 206

qualities, ideal officers 48, 49–50t, 52
quality of life surveys 34–9, 169, 200,
  210–17
quiet power 136

race relations policy 19, 157, 217
Ramsay, E.R. 173–4
reason, trained application of 147–50
reciprocators 53, 54t
recognition 65, 80, 213
recruitment 20, 195
reformative goals 3
regional directors 192
rehabilitation 3, 38, 175

relationships
  social practices 85
  terminology 84–5
  see also peer relationships; staff–
    management relationships;
    staff–prisoner relationships
Relationships Foundation 119–20n
resignations 20
resistance, to authority 114–15, 122, 129
'resort to basic' privileges 122
respect 10, 57, 92, 101, 108–11, 115
retaliatory violence 163
Review of the Prison Service (1989) 192
reward power 134, 135
'right place', for prison officers 140f
right relationships 8–9, 84, 87–95, 111,
  119, 197, 200, 205
right-based culture 170
rights, rewards perceived as 130–1
role conflict 64
role model officers 48–51, 51–7, 80
Role of the Modern Prison Officer 174–6
Role of the Prison Officer (2009) 208
routine work 9, 78–9, 147
rule 111, 123, 126, 141, 145
rule enforcement 86, 101, 106, 110, 123,
  139, 143
  see also under-enforcement
rules
  differential application of 148
  officers and 137–40
  of POA 173
  wording of, and discretion 124–5
  see also Prison Rules

sadistic prison officer 155
safety 34, 39, 75, 100, 213
sanctions, use of formal/informal 5, 122,
  137
savings 194
schooling, of new officers 134
security 3, 46, 60–1, 64, 83, 96, 98, 107,
  213
self-control 115
senior management
  need for investment in 195
  staff survey 34, 36f, 211
senior managers
  concerns about rule enforcement/
    non-enforcement 144–5

impact on quality of life 37
improvement of staff culture 182
lack of trust towards 36
views about 197
senior officers
female 16, 17–18
length of service 21
numbers 15, 16t, 17f
pay 22
treatment by 213
vision 143
sense of duty 129
sense of purpose 156, 157, 168
sensitivity 8, 146
serious assaults 68, 69t, 70t, 71t
Sex Offender Treatment Programme
(SOTP) 55
sexist behaviour 74
shared working 179
shift work 47
Significant Others Scale (SOS) 119
situational factors, assaults 68
skills 11, 43f, 52, 102
Slovenia 77, 81n
'smooth flow of the prison' 9, 134, 136
social factors, assaults 68
social forces, power 116–17
social institutions 116, 129, 201
social practices, relationships 85
social support 119
solidarity 156, 163, 164
Sparks, R. 8, 90, 182
Special Security Unit, Whitemoor 62n,
151n, 168
special units (CRC) 91
Spurr, Michael 187
Staff Care and Welfare Service (SCWS)
66
Staff Quality of Life Survey (SQL) 34–5,
120n, 169, 200, 210–17
staff support 216
staff–management relationships 92, 195,
196, 212
staff–prisoner relationships 5, 37f, 46–7,
83–120, 121, 208
audit work 119–20
boundaries and possible corruption
111–14
building 11, 205
centrality of 48, 84

control 147
dynamics of 113f
fairness 105–8, 115
female staff 73, 75–6
impact of major incidents on 95
importance of 83, 99–103
involvement cycle 86
limits to 114–15
officer and prisoner views of each
other 95–9
over-use of power 115–19
perceptions of 37f, 38
power 85, 93–4, 100, 103
prisoners views 104–5
respect 108–11, 115
shift work and structure of 47
smooth flow of the prison 136
staff survey 215
successful officers 44
use of formal/informal sanctions 5
Whitemoor 55–7
see also good relationships; right
relationships
staffing levels 29–30
statement of purpose 77
status-enhancing effects, punishments
130
'stepping out of role', respect by 109
stereotypical representations 14, 109,
154–5
Stern, Vivien 15
Stohr, M.K. 78
Straw, Jack 150n, 178, 180, 201
stress 35, 36, 37, 63–7, 119, 214
structural change 186
subcultures 72, 182
Sudbury Prison 30, 31f, 33f
suicide 64, 66, 73
support 6, 37f, 38, 76, 119, 161, 215, 216
supportive role 37f, 38
suspiciousness 156
Sykes, Gresham 126, 127, 128–31, 133–4
symbolic role, of fairness 107

Tait, Sarah 96–7
targets, prison work 199, 200
teamwork 6, 168
technology, use of new 194
therapeutic regime, Grendon 88–90
therapeutic relationships, desire for 119

Thomas, J.E. 3, 4, 13n
Tilt, Richard 195
time off in lieu (TOIL) 28
Titan prisons 194
tolerance 89, 201
trafficking 112
Train, Chris 191
'trained application of reason' 147–50
training 3, 77, 91, 134, 168, 195, 200
true carers 96
trust 36, 38, 86, 89, 98, 111, 115, 132,
   165
Tumim J 84, 88
turnover rates, prison officers 20, 21, 67

unconditional positive regard 10
under-enforcement 84, 139, 141, 146
unfair outcomes, equality of treatment
   107
unionisation 169–81
United States 19, 72, 77, 81n

value for money 193, 206
values 124, 200, 201, 206
verbal skills 52
vigilance 64
violence 73, 163, 165
   see also assaults
visible leadership 189, 193
vocation, sense of 165
Voluntary Agreement 177
voluntary early retirement and severance
   (VERSE) programme 19
vulnerability, to corruption 112, 133
vulnerable prisoners 119

Waddington, P.A.J. 156, 157, 158
Walpole Prison 161, 162, 163, 164
wariness 98–9, 109
welfare 38, 77, 79, 174
Whatton 31f, 33f
Whitemoor
   escapes (1994) 192
   liberal optimism 135
   officers
      protection 166
      role model 51–7
      views on management 197
      views of prisoners 97–8
      vulnerability to corruption 112
   positive culture 165
   prisoner : officer ratio 30, 31f
   Special Security Unit 62n, 151n, 168
   staff–prisoner relationships 92–5
   wing differences and adjudications
      57–60
willingness 166, 167, 168
wing differences, adjudications,
   Whitemoor 57–61
wing managers 198
Woodhill Prison 165
Woolf Report 129, 135, 200–1
work relationships 85
workforce modernisation 178, 196
working personalities 154, 157
working styles 52–3, 54–5t, 132, 166

Young Offender Institution Rules 138
young offender institutions 30, 31f, 33f,
   68f, 69t
young prisoners/offenders 77, 78, 119